Colette Bréger, *Ecriture* (Writing)

# POST-GIBRAN
Anthology of New Arab-American Writing

# POST-GIBRAN
*Anthology of New Arab American Writing*

## Edited by Munir Akash & Khaled Mattawa

A Jusoor Book, 1999
Distributed by
Syracuse University Press

3 1450 00402 4972

# JUSOOR 11/12

**editor/publisher**
A. Munir Akash

**co-editor**
Amira El-Zein

**poetry editor**
Daniel Moore

**JUSOOR**
is published by Kitab, Inc.
P. O. Box 34163, W. Bethesda, Maryland 20827-0163 USA.
TEL: (301) 263 02 89, FAX: (301)263 02 55
Email: Jusoor@aol.com

**SUBSCRIPTIONS**
in the USA and Canada (4 issues):
individuals $45.00; institutions $100.00.
Subscribers outside of the USA add
$14.00 for Surface-mail, $35.00 for Air-mail.
Address subscriptions to :JUSOOR
P.O.Box 34163, Bethesda, Maryland 20817 USA.

**DISTRIBUTION**
Jusoor Books are available to bookstores through our primary distributor
Syracuse University Press, 621 Skytop Rd. Suite 110,
Syracuse, NY 13244-5290 USA, Tel (for order only): (800) 365-8929
Fax: (315) 433-5545, email:taliz@summon3.syr.edu / twalsh01@syr.edu

**JUSOOR** was founded in 1992 by **A. Munir Akash**

# Contents

Acknowledgment                                                                  ix

Introduction                                                                    xi

DIANA ABU-JABER .................................................................  1
The Way Back

NUAR ALSADIR ....................................................................  9
The Day
Aftermath
The Window's Oven

SAMUEL HAZO .....................................................................  13
Innocent Bystanders
The Origins of Western Love
The Egyptian Movie Star

ELMAZ ABI NADER ................................................................  19
Sixty Minutes
Daughter of Arabs

MUNIR AKASH .....................................................................  43
The Lower Organs of Beirut

KHALED MATTAWA .................................................................  49
Freeways and Rest Houses
Ode to Mejnoon
Gilgamesh

LISA SUHAIR MAJAJ ..............................................................  67
New Directions: Arab American Writing at Century's End
Poppies
Departure
Seabones

PATRICIA SARRAFIAN WARD ........................................................  83
The Bullet Collection

SHARIF S. ELMUSA ...............................................................  99
No Statues Were Built in the Camp
The Love Song of Ibrahim Abdelmadi
Juxtaposition
Soliloquy
Request

EVELYN ACCAD ....................................................................  107
From My Cancer Journal

Contents

NAOMI SHIHAB NYE ............................................................ 127
    Long Overdue

DAVID WILLIAMS ................................................................ 133
Between Words
Inheritance
We're History

NATHALIE HANDAL ............................................................. 139
    Poetry as Homeland
    A Butterfly Gaze
    Escape

ETEL ADNAN ......................................................................... 145
    Like a Christmas Tree

AMIRA EL-ZEIN ................................................................... 171
    Is This Devastation for me Alone?
    The Masks of The Crane

HALIM BARAKAT ................................................................. 191
    The Crane

KATHRYN ABDUL-BAKI ...................................................... 199
    Ghost Songs

DANIEL MOORE (ABDAL HAYY) ....................................... 213
    The Blind Beekeeper

EVELYN SHAKIR .................................................................. 221
    Remember Vaughn Monroe?

PAULINE KALDAS ................................................................ 237
    Fraudulent Acts
    From a Distance Born

PAULA HAYDAR .................................................................. 243
    Picture Us

HAYAN CHARARA .............................................................. 245
    Hamza Aweiwi: A Shoe Salesman in Hebron
    The Pregnancy
    Camp Dearborn

SEKEENA SHABEN ............................................................... 251
    Twentieth Ode
    April 5/97

# Contents

SALADIN AHMED ................................................................. 255
    Poem for Countee Cullen
    Umar: An Affirmation Two Hours Later
    Gravity

MOHJA KAHF ..................................................................... 261
    My Body is not Your Battleground
    More than One Way to Break Fast
    Read

WALID BITAR .................................................................... 267
    Perfect Gallows
    Saltimbanque
    The Menaced Ventriloquist

DUNYA MIKHAIL ............................................................... 273
    Five Minutes

HASAN NEWASH ................................................................. 277
    The Scream 98

PENNY JOHNSON ............................................................... 280
    The Lessons of Leila

SALAH EL-MONCEF ............................................................ 297
    A Tree With a Dream

JOE GEHA ......................................................................... 315
    *Back in the Black*

SUHEIR HAMMAD .............................................................. 327
    Heifers and Heroes
    October's Daughter

MECHELLE ZAROU ............................................................. 333
    There is no Love Here
    Every Poem a Prayer

NADIA BENABID ................................................................ 337
    Ode 124
    Gacela of the Terrifying Presence
    The Hunt
    Without Rhyme or Reason
    To a Lady
    Yazid to his Father Moawiah

SARA NADIA RASHAD ......................................................... 343
    The Zaire

Contents

HAKIM ARCHLETTA ............................................................ 346
    Like a Rain

HISHAM SHARABI ................................................................ 355
*Embers and Ashes*

### FRAGRANCE FROM THE GARDEN

MAHMOUD DARWISH: We will Choose Sophocles ............ 386
Translated by Patricia Khleif

TAWFIQ AL-HAKIM: The Song of Songs ............................ 393
Translated by Noel Abdulahad

YUSUF HABASHI AL-ASHQAR: The Shadow and the Echo 407
Translated by Paula & Adnan Haydar

ADNAN HAYDAR ................................................................ 425
*Mkhammas Mardûd* in Lebanese *Zajal*

TAHA HUSAIN'S FAILURE (by George Tarabishi) 439
Translated by Elie Chalala

SARAH ROGERS ................................................................ 447
In Mona's Garden

Cotributors' Notes.................................................................. 455

# Acknowledgment

Post-Gibran *could not have been published without some very important people, especially those who worked in the background and perhaps from their far places in other states. Any anthology of this sort requires the support, suggestions, and assistance of more people than can named here. Each of them knows who she or he is, and to each of them, many thanks. Special notes of gratitude are of course due to each of our brilliant extraordinary contributors. Appreciation is also expressed to Sharif S. Elmusa who provided me with editorial support and useful comments; Barbara Nimri Aziz and Aisha al-Saqqaf for their active encouragement and their help along the way; my wife Amira El-Zein who gave me the original idea, made very important suggestions, performed the difficult task of keeping me organized, and shared with me the reading of manuscripts thoroughly and intelligently. Very special thanks to Daniel Abdal-Hayy Moore, Jusoor's poetry editor, for his painstaking review and editorial expertise. A heartfelt expression of gratitude to Mary Selden Evans for her indefatigable care as Acquisition Editor.*

*I have to thank my dear friend Khaled Mattawa for honoring me and* Jusoor Books *by accepting my invitation to become visiting editor of this anthology. Khaled's drive and vision and unstinting editorial guidance turned a dream into realtiy.*

*I hope all the extraordinary contributors understand that their spirit lives within this anthology in the most positive way.*

*Finally I have to admit that all the great work in this issue exists thanks to these wonderful people who transform our hyphenatied existence into a creative paradise, and that every mistake in it is mine.*

***Munir Akash***

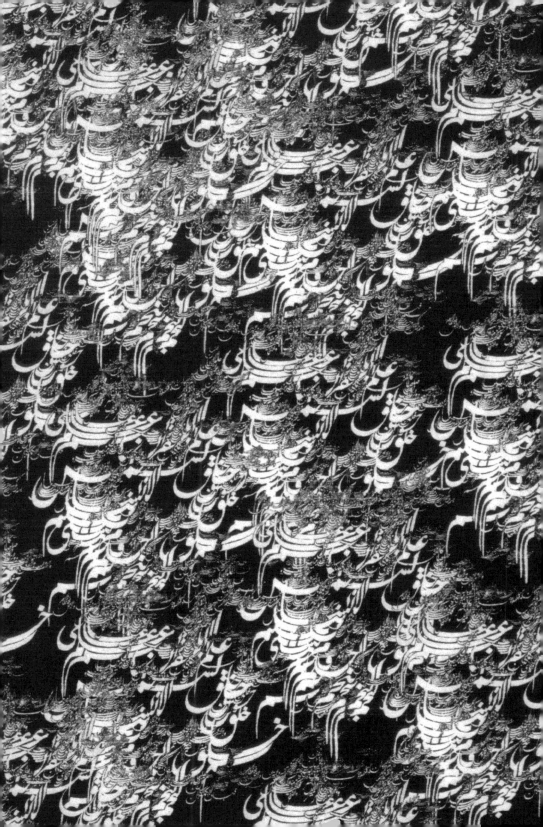

# Introduction

# POST-GIBRAN

*Reports of our demise have been greatly exaggerated.*
*-- Mark Twain*

In requesting contributions to this anthology, we wanted to re-examine the field of contemporary Arab writing in the United States and the manifold ways in which Arabness and its system of values, attitudes and manners define the "Arab-American" world.

This anthology bears witness to the enduring ordeal of our spirit of Arabness. If the image of us is truly being created by the American imagination, the time has come to invalidate that image and render it unrecognizable both to ourselves and to the world. That false image of ourselves has power over us only if we choose to accept an alien design for our destiny. However slow and painful the recovery, Arab-American destiny will continue to come under Arab-American control so long as the image of the Arab-American comes increasingly under the control of Arab-American writers. We have the means to reforge our civilized multicultural traditions, our Gelgamishian spirit, and to do this we have only to look to the rich heritage of our past. From Gilgamish to Mahmoud Darwish and from Innana to Nazik al-Mala'ika, we continue to carry the traditions of our civilization which forged the very humanness of our humanity.

We feel it is the duty of *Jusoor* to present to American readers not secondhand versions of their own works, but to expand aspects of the creativity that lies at the heart of our native Gelgamishian spirit in conformity with a world view which is our own. And our criteria of Arabness, it should be noted, is cultural, not restricted to an strictly racial/ethnic definition, as the inclusion of many of our contributors attests to. Among this bouquet of mixed flowers are Americans whose identity is not Arab at all, but who still project a flavor of what we are calling "Arabness." Besides, the definition of Arabness itself is open, as it always has been, since the core of our civilization has spawned countless variations over time and space from the earliest millenniums onward.

Khalil Gibran found his way to the American heart, not because he was a great poet, but because he strove to manifest positive aspects found in our traditional writing. The traditions he mined from are not always concerned with the liturgical, cultic, and esoteric elements of the Gelgamshian spirit, but are nevertheless created according to its norms and principles, according to the concept of *man* as a bridge between heaven and earth, the *anthropos*, the Promethean, or, in the Qur`anic sense, the vicegerent of God.

Since *Grape Leaves: A Century of Arab American Poetry*, no anthology of our literature, even partial, has come out. And no literary journal has yet to devote an issue to it. Rather than survey the field to select the best representative works, we wanted this anthology to infuse a new energy into this area of writing. We sought new and previously unpublished works, and were particularly interested in writing that confronted issues Arab-American writers have not tackled in the past.

As members of a demonized minority, Arab-American writers in the United States have, of necessity, tended to address communal concerns more than individual ones. We could not write without somehow addressing the influence of our mother culture and the subsequent tensions we encounter within the dominant American one. At this time, however, there is an upsurge of Arab presence in the United States, such as a growing presence of Arab-American writers, scholars, journalists, venerated celebrities, as well as producers and directors in the electronic and print media. The work of

Arab-Americans fills store shelves more and more. And it is for this reason that in this anthology we wanted to know what adjustments Arab-American writers are making, both in their own self-image and the understanding of their Americanness, now that their Arabness has become more visible and is gaining a seemingly lasting presence.

Within the Arab-American literary scene, there is much more poetry than fiction, a sizable quantity of memoir or biography but almost no dramatic works. In our emphasis on "new" works, we were particularly interested in any literary experiments Arab-American writers are engaged in, what they are doing with the language, and if they, as individual writers, have found a vocabulary that negotiates the Arabic language and Arab concerns.

We encouraged cross-genre experiments. We asked poets to send us their experiments in fiction, essayists their attempts at drama or a screenplay, and so on. Changes in form, we felt, are important signifiers of changes in both subject matter and tactics. We asked writers to send us the best of their most daring works. The present shift in the *mise-en-scene* demands it.

The response was better than our most fervent hopes. Arab-American writers as a whole turn out to be a highly versatile bunch, and they generously shared with us the best of their output. The proverbial image of the literary editor buried under piles of mediocre writing in search of a gem was far from our experience in editing this anthology. We received polished works of the highest quality, from known names as well as unknown ones. We read with joy works that moved us, and we kept as many as of them as we could use.

We hope your reading experience will reflect our delight in this assembly of some of the best of ourselves.

**--The Editors**

He put you between His kingdom and His realm
So you may learn your majestic rank among His creatures,
That your shell contains a hidden pearl.
Your uniqueness is like a sunrise --
It appears on the horizon but doesn't belong to the horizon.
          *--Ibn Ata'illah* (a 14th-century Egyptian  Sufi)

*Kalima* (which means
'*word*') in florid Kufic
style. From a14th-century
Qur`an. Topkapi
Museum, Istanbul.

# Diana Abu-Jaber

# THE WAY BACK
## an excerpt from *Memories of Birth*

Kalim, husband, your eyes are purple roses, your hair as black as thorns. Your fingers run along my shoulders like foam rolling the ocean. Your arms are full and bright as the moon; your sex cherry sweet and taut.

You come to me, your hands search me out in our bed, your fingers describe the shapes and shadows of me. You hold back for a while, let my mouth find the rise of your shoulder blade, the damp at the nape of your neck, my head *fills* with the scent of your skin, your damp armpits. Then when I say, oh now, please come into me please. Then you fill me, I expand with you. We ride our movement, my eyes shut. I ride on the waves. He is taking me somewhere, I think, I am going away, deep down into him, away.

Then the white hem, the clear brow of dawn in our arms, still entangled in sleep after desire. He gets up and washes and comes with a warm cloth for me. He sits pure and still in the chair beside our bed and *reads* the beautiful words:

"*Ha Mim*. Hereby the Book that brings light to bear. We have sent it down on a night that is blessed--for it has been Our wont to give warning--a blessed night in which everything is, by command of Ours, duly ordered in wisdom--for it has been Our wont to communicate to man--in act of mercy from your Lord who sees and knows all, Lord of the heavens and of the

1

earth and all they encompass, if only you knew it for certain."

When we first moved to the camp, my mother stopped praying. She said she had lost the habit of praying: she could no longer remember what it was good for. When Abdul-Baki wanted to start his school under the trees, where little boys and girls would study the Quran, my mother refused to let me go saying that she was no longer on speaking terms with God.

Listening to my husband read the sweet, pure words, the voice of the messenger of God, peace be upon him, was like hearing a letter from a distant acquaintance, speaking of events I'd never seen and people I'd never met. Just like listening to the priest recite scripture at Mam's church.

I wanted to believe for Kalim, for the terrible ache of love, but I'd developed no capacity for faith. I was cut off from history and memory, and even perhaps, from soul.

But ours was the beautiful love story, I remind myself, the one that people want to believe in. It happened to me with the first man I ever loved. I married him: he brought some of the world back to me.

On our wedding night, deep in our bed, in the silent, held-breath of the first night, I lay awake after Kalim had fallen asleep, our bodies still entwined. A vision of a person came to me, rising above our bed like a *malak* or *djinn*--good or evil, I couldn't discern. I meditated on this image a moment, on the mystery of its identity, until I saw the transparent eyes filling with smoke, the mouth darkening, curling over like petals. It was my mother, standing at the edge of the marketplace, watching the driver who would take me to the boat, a single hand lifting, her eyes turning to me, never exactly finding me. As the car begins to take me away, I see a shadow falling over her, the sound of the car's motor. We turn the corner....

She is standing, a moonbeam, her face white as bone, her fingertips egg shells she lifts toward the bed.

"*Yemmah*," I call her, "Mother!" I try to take her fingers

2

but cannot find them, they are traces of light moving, so my fingers fall through hers. I try to rise from the bed to move closer, toward a place where I know I will keep falling. "Where are you, Mother," I ask her. "What happened to you?"

She allows me to look into her face and I see tears like branches of water, the muscles of her face smooth as earth, her eyes dark as dates, her hair a fall, a cave, a valley shadow. Relief and sadness sweep over me: she has gone like a dart to the center of my heart.

"Alia," Kalim says, holding out his hand. "What are you doing? Come back to bed, it's okay now. Everything is okay."

I nestle into the rich touch of his breath, the hair on his chest and arms as he encircles me, and I whisper, "I'll never see her again, will I? My home is all gone, there's not another thing like it, is there?"

He doesn't answer. In the night, his face looks like a dream, a wish of skin and bone that turns to powder and I fall asleep.

"All right," Kalim said to me early the next morning. "I want to show you something."

He borrowed a car from Mam's brother Teddy, who charged us ten dollars, and we drove north up the parkway, past the cut-away faces of cliffs called the Palisades and into burgeoning hillsides and the pine forests of New York State. For a while I thought we were going back to the Adirondacks resort where Kalim and I first met, but the land opened into a bowl of rivers and dairy farms and the drive went on for hours.

Finally we turned off the highway and passed a sign that said, "Welcome to Spring Festival" and under that jags and slashes that looked like another language. We passed a giant sign that said CIGARETTES in ten-foot red letters, other smaller signs that said Handguns and Liquor, then structures that were familiar to me: shacks of half-wood, half-automobiles, corrugated metal and tar paper and broken

3

glass. There were toys, chickens, wire, undressed children.

Scorched faces, hands, eyes like brands, they turned in the fields to look at us, or up from the steps of the little stores. Not until I'd seen their faces did I understand: I was back again. In the camp. Our car had found some hidden passage back.

"No, no," I said. I pushed down the lock on the car door. "I won't get out here. You can't make me stay."

Kalim tried to calm me. "You don't understand. I just wanted to show you what was here."

Every woman there wore grief the size and shape of my mother's grief wrapped tightly about their faces, cutting into their skin like netting. I was back in Beit el Salaam refugee camp, my mother's face wavering behind the skin of the women there, turning again and again to look at me.

The wind came roving over the hillsides, blowing back the women's hair, combing the wild grass down. We drove out the other side of the town, into land where houses were farther apart, front yards heaped up with motorcycles and cars on blocks, clotheslines layered and floating like sails. The sky turned silky and I thought it was swirling with ghosts, the wind fine and flat as a knife. Ghosts poured out of the sky, drumming on the roof of the car, the air moving in the muscular shape of a sob, everything rushing up toward the gray palm of road until I covered my face with my hands and said, "Enough, my God, Kalim, what place is this?"

We were turning back on to the highway, out of this nightmare, nestled in the secret valley. We passed a highway sign: Onondaga Nation.

"I'm sorry, I thought it might comfort you to be reminded," he said. "I mean--that home isn't so far away."

Half-bedouin half-city dweller, he knew what I had lost. He had the ability to see over valleys and through mountains to a point where land continues without end. He'd seen the loss in my face and throat; perhaps that is why he came to me in the first place, like a *malak* descends to a site of suffering, drawn

4

by its whorl in the air. He thought the sight of old memories would drive my sadness away, the shadow that edged my words, that made my voice dense with tears, even in laughter.

❏

What is a refugee camp? A skin between you and the elements, a place of laying bare, exposing throat and eyes, sister to the concentration camp. Death is there. It is in the sunrise when we wake; it is in the sewers running down the street, the homes of metal strips. Dust fills the air and coats our tongues.

There are no beginnings to stories in refugee camps. Children are born there, but from the moment of their birth their eyes are as old as stone. Still, we cook, we thank-God and scoop up the rice in one quick fist, we dance threaded together, give release to our spirits.

My mother's family was from a small village outside of Bethlehem. My mother was of a line of women as tall as the wind and brilliant as Shahrazad. At 18 she married, but only a few years later, she told me, my father was killed by the White Eyes. I was four years old; a year later we were driven out of our village.

I was six in 1949, when we moved to the place called Beit el Salaam camp. It was hidden away, far from roads or markets. The White Eyes had not discovered it. We began with bare ground and tents, which eventually grew stone sides and cement floors. Families came fractured over the borders into our wilderness, some killed, some left behind. We made a fragment of a community in a barren field, scribbled over with briars. As a pilgrim writes of Mecca on the walls of his house, our destiny was written on our faces.

My mother tells me she recreated herself when we first crossed the border. She put away her veil at the threshold of her new, leafy door, her root-knotted floor.

"We had walked for miles," she tells me. She is washing dishes with a briar of steel wool. Her skin has been hammered by the winds. "There were thousands of us at first, then fewer as

5

some fell, exhausted, starving.

"When we came to the river, it was huge and foaming. Not like now. We followed it--"

"You and who else?" I try to ask questions, to help her remember.

"You were in my arms. At six you looked like a four-year-old. You weighed less than bones and ashes. I walked days not knowing if you were still breathing. Thanks to God, the trees fanned air into your lips and the sun cloaked you in light.

"There were five other women from our village who clung together and survived. We didn't know where we were. We had a stone for a compass and had forgotten the map of the stars. That black year, though, I re-learned the faces of the stars. I grew as familiar with them as with the faces of my own family and many nights I thought I saw my parents' faces watching us from up there.

"When we reached the river, we knew that we had run out of homeland. The other side was a strange country. We followed the river and at last we came to the place where the river breaks through the hillsides into an inky sea. Salt coated everything like moonlight and rubbed into our palms and the soles of our feet. Nothing moved. Nothing was alive. There was only the shape of life--birds, wings raised in mid-flight--that had petrified into rock salt. This was where I would leave my heart for safekeeping."

Years before my departure for America, my mother used to say, "The loss of land is the loss of the soul."

If Umm-Nabil was sitting on the ground, doing her embroidery with us, she would say, "Souls, souls! This and that. Talk to me about soup not souls."

My mother laid her hands flat on the carpet before me and said, "Do you see? The knuckles are the hills and the fingers are the valleys. And here, look closely, the grain of the skin is the grain of the dirt itself. Someday soon, we will return.

I know the way back by heart." And she would draw it for me, maps on the ground, on the leaves, on the air.

She never left me, not in body or spirit, because she knew the way back.

Eventually I emigrated to America. I even found love and security. I married a man and began a new family. But sometimes the only comfort I found was in the form of prayer, words from a religion I used to know. My husband would read to me, and I would almost remember a way back.

"By the sun and the midday glory and the moon that follows after; by the day telling its splendor and the night that envelops it; by the heaven and its rearing; by the earth and its shaping; by the soul and its fashioning...true well-being is theirs who purify their soul."

Photo: Arthur Jafa

# Nuar Alsadir

# THE WINDOW'S OVEN
## and other poems

THE DAY

Too marvelous for anything unholy,
I walk towards water, follow birds.

The sky is as much there as it is
inside me: I keep my head down,

turn left on Cemetery Road. Not lost
but gone before, I tell them *The day*

*is beautiful. I* tell them *The mind*
*pushes hard against skull.* Tugged

to detach by an undertow, a spider
hangs head down in his web. I am

the distance the sand climbs starward.
Three trees stand like three trees standing.

## THE STREETLIGHT

One night, window cracked, she spoke.
She, with hair tied into horn. *Without walls*

*the world is a lodging,* she said,
locks slipping to absorb the inane.

As opposed to house or forgotten? I asked,
considering how she came: through window,

through sleep. *Let us think of ourselves,*
*how we destroy ourselves everywhere.*


## AFTERMATH

Today I felt happy for a moment on the corner,
but the sky descended with too much ease.

Everyone was upside down and falling out like change.
Sometimes it seems there was never a time before.

The walls we build are meager: a truck pulls
in front of your crossing and there is no tomorrow;

your hat flies off and suddenly you're facing home,
the man rushing by who bumps you is your father,

his strange eyes saying you *don't belong here,*
but with a blink it is he who has gone.

## THE WINDOW'S OVEN

God cooks food outside the house,
my grandfather tells me when he comes

from the dead to see me off in a dream.
I am running with my bags, afraid

of missing a flight. They fall one
then the other, come undone. The floor

spreads to sky beneath me, stirring
the colors of my clothes into white:

the after image of solitude stoked
into hunger steam and all it ignites.

# Samuel Hazo

# THE ORIGINS OF WESTERN LOVE
## and other poems

INNOCENT BYSTANDERS ARE
NEITHER INNOCENT NOR BYSTANDERS

> Question: What is the most dangerous
> profession in the world
> today?
> Answer : Innocent bystander.

It's easy to talk when the creek's
  a trickle or just a meandering
  fuse of slime between dry rocks.
But what will you say when the creek's
  a stream, and the stream's in flood,
  and the flood's upon you?
                    What
  will you do?
            Angry brown
  water's as deaf as falling
  bombs or charging bulls.
If you are spared, you'll wonder
  why you happened to be standing
  in the way.
        Why you?

13

Why there?
But then why not?
Later
you'll do what most survivors do--
live recklessly, live all
you can, live till it hurts.
In time the hurt will be enough
to make you think.
You'll cultivate
an interest in biography.
You'll read
about those kings who, facing death,
insisted that their tea be brewed
henceforth from women's tears.
You'll learn how frail Sir Antony
dined morning, night and noon
on lobster tails until the last.
You'll be intrigued but unimpressed.
To feel much less alone
you'll travel to decountrify yourself,
confide in sympathetic strangers
and return to what's no longer
quite the same as home.
You'll turn
from one diversion to another,
and they'll never seem to end.
But somehow they will help you
in the way a mirror curved
behind a bar convinces solitary
drinkers that they have at least
and still and finally one friend.

THE ORIGINS OF WESTERN LOVE

The Arabs of Andalus bequeathed
   the troubadours a minstrelsy
   where love and passion sang.
Latins ignored the song.
Gaius Valerius Catullus
  and his tribe preferred coupling
  on impulse and praising it in couplets
afterward.
          The mix created
courtly love.

          From courtly love
came all the legends of romance,
and from romance the dream where love
of passion seemed more impassioned
than the passion of love.
              Still, we must
be fair.
      Though wiving and wenching
gave way to wiving or wenching,
a few still lived the passionate
    friendship that is marriage.
               But
most remained as permanently
parallel as railroad tracks
that never meet except
at the horizon.
         And even there
it's an illusion.
         No wonder
choosing one another every
day became a chore while coupling
on the sly assumed the guise

of ecstasy.
But why be righteous?
We're lovers all, and love
  without responsibility is every lover's
  dream of happiness.
Yet all
  that lasts is not what prompts
  but what survives the act.
If man's
  a wallet waiting to be spent,
  the question's never whether
  but with whom.
And why.
If woman
  is a purse whose body's mouths
  are drawstrung shut until
  she gives herself away,
  the question's never whether
  but with whom.
And why.
The Arabs
  thought the why unsayable and sang
  the beauties of the where and when.
Catullus settled for the how.
Both felt they sang the answer then
  to something unexplainable
  before.
Or since.
Or now.

THE EGYPTIAN MOVIE STAR

In Arabic her name meant splendor,
  and splendorously she walked in lavender
  from scarf to shoe.
                    Her lips
  relaxed into a practiced smile.
Her hips did all the talking
  as she strolled like Nefertiti
  to the Chardonnay and shrimp.
                          Standing
  she seemed to move.
                    Moving,
  she stood in motion.
                    She said
  her gate to paradise was Hollywood,
  not Mecca.
              Sharif the Lebanese
  had made it in disguise.
                          Why couldn't
  a bonefide Cairene?
                    Splendor
  and Brando on a shared marquee...
Splendor's each handprint
  in cement...
              Splendor encircled
  by photographers...
                    For emphasis
  she crossed her arms beneath
  her breasts to give them lift
  and forward outwardness.
                          Later
  she crossed them differently
  to give them outward forwardness.

And so she ripened like an orchid
   waiting to be picked, her lashes
   inked with kohl, her earrings
   shimmering like tiny chandeliers,
   her Cleopatra-bracelets by the dozen
   adding splendor on splendor to Splendor.

# Elmaz Abinader

# SIXTY MINUTES
## a poem and a journal

*for Diem Jones*

> *Living here is an act of submission*
> *to the worst*
> > *--Etel Adnan*

Don't be afraid of the picture
you see of the hezbollah, faces wrapped
when they talk to the camera, so they won't
be recognized. Don't be afraid of the m-16's, strapped
like a quiver to their shoulders packed with ammo
instead of feathers that can end your life
or mine. Don't be afraid of their fast language
and its passion or its fear, the thing that keeps
them moving or hidden, praying and giving up one
more thing, one more day, one more night smoking
in the dark.

You remembered that I am an Arab when you saw them
on T.V., when you saw their chests heave. Their eyes
waver, their foreheads crease, their mouths roared--hands thrown
into the air. But the equation didn't balance. The land was dry

and dusty, their black boots almost gray from the stone.
I was born in Pennsylvania with fertile blue grass, and uncharred
trees. The camera roamed across a village to a mother
clutching her child to her skirt, to young men, not fighters
shaking their fists westward. The sky hissed from rocket launchers.


You looked for me in this landscape, wondered if I
had a suicide pact with someone, a battle plan, wondered
if the dark eyes you have stared into were an illusion,
if I had something behind my back, hidden beneath my clothes.
Or if I were a widow weeping into my apron, a mother holding
out the bloody child to the camera shouting, *show the world
what they have done.*


Or am I among the civilians killed that week hidden
in the bunker behind the school drinking water from plastic jugs
remembering I once had lamps that could shine all night,
a television blaring in the living room, was getting into health
foods and old jazz c.d's. You watch the bodies, limbs dangling
from the litters as they are put on trucks with sliding racks
like a bakery van. Do you see me on the second shelf?


The flight attendant on your last trip was Lebanese,
your accountant, a Jordanian. You notice the woman
taking your clothes at the dry cleaner has a name tag
that reads Samira. You go to the middle east grocer,
not to buy food but to look at the faces you superimpose
onto mine and mine onto theirs. You are vigilant, watchful
for their safety, stand at the window until the daughter
places her hand around her father's finger and crosses the street carefully.

21

I take this as an act of love. Your eyes searching the crowds
for me, watching the backs of people you don't know or ever
cared about. You have forgotten how my nights are filled
with silence, how I sit with one constant light, the one
you extinguished before you touched me. You have forgotten
my small hands can grip nothing bigger than a pen
or a needle, that my eyes wander; do not focus and aim.


But remember I am an Arab, too, looking for a home
of my own, unoccupied, without siege. I need my fires quiet,
my pockets empty; my water bottles full and cool.
At night I watch the moon that passed across Lebanon
before it came to this sky. The stars are your thousand eyes
watching the hezbollah move in the dark. And their glitter
is the name in my eyes that rises quickly and dies.

## DAUGHTER OF ARABS

Golf courses in the desert look like outposts on the moon--all sand, packed and slightly hilly. The little flags flutter in the light wind in Dahran, Saudi Arabia and the golfers roll their carts down a paved pathway. Some of the men are wearing thobes, long white gowns down to their ankles. On their heads is the checkered cloth called gutras in Saudi, kaffiyas in other countries. Other men, some westerners, have donned their plaid Jack Nicklaus golfwear. They walk in groups, talking and lining up for each hole. They play as if there is no airport just beyond them, no line of jets ready to take off for Iraq. They swing into the air, launching their balls high and watching them land less than a quarter of a mile from the airbase.

In the American compounds in Saudi Arabia, I accepted the illusions too--that golf courses can be made of sand, that women can drive cars, wear slacks, have jobs, that everyone speaks English, and the café serves hamburgers. Hussein shows me all this, as I sit in the back of his Fleetwood looking out at the streets named Willowbrook and Pine.

Inside his house are ancient artifacts of the desert: large clay urns, silver coins, woven pillow covers. He hands me a slab of metal that was sitting beside an inlaid box on his coffee table. It is shiny copper with a turquoise tinge, rough along the edges.

"Do you think it's pretty?" he asks.

I weigh it in my hands. "What is it?"

He takes it back and places it on the glass tabletop. "A piece of a scud missile. "

Jordan

Home: Leaving/Going to
4 January 1993

The woman in the window seat tells me all about her

23

company, how she got to Amsterdam, and how tough the music business is. She started producing with her boyfriend, except they broke up and well, she always ran the whole show anyway, so who needed him? Her lipstick is drawn to overstate her mouth which doesn't stop moving. I am still clutching my ticket—the thick multi-paged document the United States Information Agency sent me a month ago. My memory scans my luggage to assure myself that I have everything listed in the guide sheets for USIA speakers. I have been reading international temperature columns for a few weeks. Amman Jordan hovered around the mid-forties, Riyadh, Saudi Arabia never exceeded sixty, but Sanaa, Yemen's temperature hadn't appeared in the dailies. I brought sweaters, jackets, boots, hose, and nothing but skirts. Will my rain coat be enough to protect me as I stand on the rocks on the edge of the Red Sea?

I flip through my ticket book then stuff it into the outside pocket of my bag.

"Where are you going?" she stares down at my satchel.

"Oh, to the Middle East. "

"Really? I was in Jerusalem once. Where are you going to be?"

"Jordan, first. Amman." I don't want to explain my trip. My whole itinerary put together by faxes and teletypes.

"Oh, you must be going home." She runs her hands through her bleached blond hair.

I look at her and beyond her to the white outside. Home? She thinks I am a Jordanian, an Arab. I finger one of my gold hoops and think how to answer her. How to answer all the questions about who I am. My tickets were issued by the government of the United States, six embassies had requested my appearance, and yet my companion saw me as an Arab woman returning to her family.

"No, my home is San Jose." And has been a number of other places I can imagine as I cross country to get to Kennedy Airport. The Rockies of my western Colorado life weighs under

24

the heaviest snowfall in years. The farmland of Nebraska fades gray under the slate sky. My Lebanese mother and father sit in their western Pennsylvania house with the drapes drawn against the sleet beating against their windows. On our approach into Kennedy Airport, we tilt toward my home of fifteen years and its dusky skyline and the white strip of light on the horizon. All these homes, way stations to where?

Women: old and new
5 January 1993

Maha points to a low sandy colored building. "I used to teach there, but I quit." We are in her old beat up Subaru rolling into Salt, Jordan, an old village not far from Amman. Maha has offered me this tour in return for my sending any book of poetry I think she will like. She took me earlier that day to a bookshop where she bought an art magazine that was banned from the country. I watched her surface chatter with the old man behind the counter while he pulled out the magazine and slid it into a brown bag. "He didn't have the one I wanted, but this will do." I hadn't thought about censorship the night before I had sat with Palestinian poets at the Phoenix Gallery. They read about the children of stones and the intifada--a roomful of exiles, living away from their land and writing about it. I am taken aback at their ease with their anger--it is not a misplaced or exaggerated thing--it is natural.

Maha is smoking as we pull into the crowded streets of the center of Salt. Everyone smokes in Jordan. The streets of Salt are crowded with shoppers and school children. Women are draped in the long dresses and abayas; men wear thobes and kaffiyas. A group of school boys in blue shorts and matching jerseys run by chanting.

"What happend at the school that made you quit?" We are watching two men wind the twine around a hurry-burly in a corner shop. Maha greets them by calling them uncle. "It was a power struggle, pure and simple. The rector of the school didn't want us to support the students when they were protesting the changes in the program." She greets a bread maker who's leaning on the ledge of a stone window. Inside an open brick oven growls with flames and young men with long handled paddles slide the bread in and out.

"I was surprised you weren't at the embassy program last night."

"1 was not invited. I am never invited." She holds a bag full of warm bread and offers me some.

When I had arrived at the embassy the night before my trip to Salt and walked through its neo-Roman archway, I was greeted by Mrs. Harrison, the ambassador's wife. She had the look I associated with a Women's College administrator in her gray suit and neatly cropped hair. The women who gathered in the plush salon around the fireplace were in the Association of University Graduates. One was praised for being the oldest female Ph.D. in the country. The new graduates craned their necks to see the tiny gray haired lady sitting in the armed chair in the center of the room. She was not self-conscious like the women there in their high fashion. She reminded me of my Uncle Elias, Reverend Uncle, we called him since he was the pastor of the only Maronite Catholic Church in southwestern Pennsylvania. Sundays after Mass, we sisters sat in the living room in our dresses, vasolined patent leather shoes with matching handbag and hat, and waited for the adults to emerge from the study. A dish of jelly mints shaped like spearmint leaves lay in a dish on the mosaic coffee table. We weren't allowed any and we didn't take them. Our talk would disturb the adults so we sat knees together across from Uncle's three-dimensional holy picture. Leaning one way, the picture showed the Holy Family, leaning the other way, showed the Madonna and child, and from the direct center view, we saw a bluish Christ the King. We slowly swayed back and forth seeing if we could catch the movement when one picture would blur into the next. When the adults joined us, Uncle sat with us. He often took my hand into his big one. "How do you feel Uncle?" He clasped one hand over the other, "With my hands." He caught me with this little joke every week. Uncle was rarely instructive, even in his sermons. His dry humor and his comfort with the world made us and the parishioners smile.

The oldest female Ph.D. radiated the same softness. She possessed a secret that made nothing too dramatic; yet we all knew that her accomplishment must have been a struggle. She smiled at me as I adjusted the angle of my chair before I read.

"It was funny." I tell Maha of the night before. " A new Ph.D. was being congratulated by the group and one woman asks. 'Are you teaching now?' Another woman answers for her, 'NO, she got married.' Everyone beamed. That was so much better they thought. "

Maha points to the houses built in the side of the mountain. They remind me of the cliff dwellings in New Mexico, stacked on top of one another, looking precarious. I wonder how people get to their front doors which seem to be suspended in space.

"Now you know why," Maha tells me. "Why I am never invited to those things. These Americans just deal with the old guard. They do not include new ideas." We stop for a goatherder and his flock to pass. "They are not inclusive of people from the occupied territories. No matter what happens everyone wants to know where I am from. It doesn't make a difference that I spent ten years in the Midwest. I feel like I am becoming the woman Israel is creating--a resident of somewhere else."

Every shop and stand has its merchandise hanging on display. I pass sheep carcasses on a hook, cages of live chickens, piles of melons and oranges. From behind the low dusty buildings rise the slender minarets. I am attentive today to the call for prayer. I want to hear the voices echo through the sky. Last night awake from a rising fever, I walked onto the balcony around five when the call for prayer began. The voices seemed to sing out at once and ricochet throughout the sky. The city sat in the gray mist of the pre-dawn with minarets poking through the low clouds. I listened to the muezzins. Like the million bells of Rome, they rang out--a symphony in the gray dawn.

We return to the car and head up into the mountain. Maha and I discuss her life in Chicago and she tells me about an exhibit she had in New York. "I would love to see your work. "

She puffs on her cigarette. "They are all put away. I don't unwrap them. I show them to no one." The sky is hazy. A man walks with a hand plough across his rocky fields. We follow a tiny dirt road to an old village where the buildings are limestone bricks laid one atop the other. Maha takes me to a spot where we should be able to see the West Bank, but the sky is too obscure.

"Was it difficult for you to leave the U.S.? What brought you back?"

"The war, I think. There were certain things I kept saying that would never happen that happened." We pass a group of soldiers stopping cars on the road. They nab speeders and charge them a fine which has to be paid at the moment. Maha checks her purse for her papers.

When we return to the Jordan Intercon, the crowd in the lobby is thicker as is the smoke. Amman seems like a constructed city that is being developed in stops and starts. Maha points out elaborate houses that people don't live in because of the maintenance costs. She lives in Amman too, in her father's office since she is not comfortable at home. There, her brothers and father exercise their male power even to the point of choosing her clothes. She sleeps on her father's couch and leaves before office hours start. This is the woman the Israelis don't want her to be—one who still needs a home. This country of exiles looks out to the West Bank frustrated and homesick.

Saudi Arabia

Bad Girls
6 January 1993

I kept my seat, didn't go under a transformation like the others. We all sat there for most of the flight, our collars open, our shoes slipped off. We touched up our hair every now and then, slid a finger nail on the edge of the magazine, rubbed our feet. Each one reminded me of a cousin, could have been a sister: a Nadia, a Yasmin, or Souad. But then the procession started. First the woman with the long wavy hair in front of me left, then the short woman in the slacks and see-through blouse, and others, one by one, marched back to the lavatories. When the descent to Jeddah was announced the women emerged. The first who passed looked like she was the shadow of the second one--covered from head to toe in black with her hands gloved. The next was the same and the third identical to her. I could not connect these figures draped in black with the fashionable women who had been sitting around me. Finally the long black hair in front of me was replaced with a black veil. Before the final touch down, the women were totally concealed. Some men were wrapped in white terry cloth. I sat among them feeling foreign and western.

One customs line consists of pilgrims. Jeddah is the port of call for Mecca and Medina. Another is for Saudi residents and the last is for visitors. Saudi Arabia has no tourist trade--your business had to be approved and registered. You must be expected and escorted. In my pocket lies the list of contacts for the embassy in the three Saudi cities I am visiting.

The customs officer addresses me in Arabic. "I'm sorry I don't understand," I say. He flips through my passport and waves at me. "Go sit over there." He indicates a desk with a number 32 on it. Two soldiers sit behind it. I hoist my carry-on and my computer and walk to the spot. The desk is completely

29

empty.

The other passengers have nearly cleared the room and yet I sit. No one speaks to me and no other passengers are sent over. I rise and stand before a small uniformed man with very prominent crooked teeth. "What is happening? Why am I waiting?"

He yells across to another soldier who flaps his hands forward. The buck-toothed soldier gestures to me to follow him. We cross the customs room and stop at a dirty brown door. The soldier ushers me in then locks the door behind me. When I turn, I know something is wrong. The room has chairs along the wall with six or seven Filipino women lying or sitting in them. Nothing else. Clearly these women have been here a long time. One is asleep with her legs spread forward; another lies across a chair. I turn back toward the door and shake the handle. It is locked. One of the women giggles then nods her head.

I find an empty seat to pile my gear on then sit next to it. The room is so quiet, we can't hear the noise from the airport. I cross my arms and stare. Why was I put here? Where is my driver? Does the embassy know that I am here? No one comes; nothing happens. I don't know where my passport is. Every word of Arabic I had ever heard at home runs through my head. All of it seems useless--parents words to children, "Pick up your clothes." "Go to your room." "It's time for dinner." I want to pound my head against the wall and shake some Arabic loose--Arabic that will help me, that will make me understood to the soldiers. Rising I pull my purse onto my shoulder and march over to the door. I bang on it over and over. Finally the same soldier appears. "Why am I here?" I shout. He begins to close the door, but I block it with my foot. "I want to make a phone call."

He directs me to a phone in the hallway. Here I am, my first day in Saudi Arabia, and I am given a pay phone to use. "I have no Saudi money!" I shout.

He sends me back to the detention room and closes the door.

I want to break his neck. My face is burning. I pound on the
door again and again until the soldier returns with another. My
body is hot and tight. I put up my fist. "I want a phone, a driver,
and my passport." They lead me to an office filled with soldiers.
I grab the phone and start to dial the contact number for Tom
Dougherty, the cultural affairs officer at the embassy. One of
the soldiers leans forward but is stopped by another.

When a calm voice English speaking voice answers the line,
I breathe out. "Tom Dougherty, this is Elmaz Abinader." He
wants to know where I am. I explain I have been in Jeddah for
hours and they won't let me go. A driver, Abdullah Kareem, has
been waiting for me. Tom directs me to hand the phone over to
the soldiers. I snatch my American passport from the desk.

Brown Eyes
9 January 1993

Beautiful statues line the corniche along the Red Sea, but I
cannot leave the car and walk along the coast admiring them. In
Saudi Arabia the limits for women are official and enforced.
Fawzia, a woman who participated in the driving demonstration
during the Gulf War, told me she cannot sit down in Baskin
Robbins when she takes her children for ice cream. Lisa
Greenberg, a journalist for the Riyadh Daily, had a temporary
driver with her in the souq when the Mutaawa asked her to
leave. The driver locked the doors of the car to protect the five
children while Lisa called to report the incident. He was
deported for an act of aggression.

I begin to collect these stories and try to understand how a
woman who has a graduate degree from Indiana University like
Fawzia, or an American journalist, like Lisa live from day to
day depending on men to escort them to the market, to a store,
to the post office. I find myself creeping gingerly in and out of
my hotel, to and from my car, and onto the appointment of the
day. Lunches are arranged in the "family sections" of the hotel

31

restaurants where women can throw back their veils to eat .

Everyone I meet wants to hear my airport story. "You did the right thing" I am told, "because they would have left you there forever." And each has another tale of how a woman they knew was jailed in that dirty brown room for weeks. I ask Christine, a nurse from Australia, if she had ever been detained during her numerous trips in and out of the country.

"Me? No, I am blond."

I am confused, of course, until Tom tells me the conversation with the guards. "You look Arab," he says. "They didn't believe you were an American; they thought you were some loose woman from Lebanon or Syria. It's your eyes, you know."

The embassy instructs us that when we go to the market, we must go with our drivers, that wearing an abaya is a good idea, but we shouldn't cover our faces. "Do enough to seem cooperative but supporting sexual apartheid isn't our stance." When I walk with Jehan, Abdullah Kareem, and Sami Nawr who is restoring old Jeddah, I am wrapped in the black abaya. My cameras hang at my side. Sami points out the rehabilitated in-laid sidewalks, the reconstructed wooden windows, and rebuilt balconies. I shoot photos of a building that leans at a fifteen degree angle, and we talk about the Taos pueblo where Sami observed similar work. Suddenly I hear a voice yelling in Arabic and quickly turn to a man, bare headed, in a thobe. He is waving a stick at me and starts to strike my shoulders. "Cover your face." he shouts. Behind him, soldiers in brown uniforms approach. Sami is explaining that he is with the mayor's office and that I am a guest from America, but the Mutaween keeps looking at me, at my face. Abdullah Kareem moves between us while Sami pulls out an identity tag and waves it at the Mutaween. I feel a tug on my arm. A soldier is trying to take my camera. I yank the strap from his hand and jam my cameras into my purse and zip it up. He shouts at me in Arabic while more soldiers gather. Jehan draws me next to her. Abdullah

Kareem turns and leads us off to the car.

The contradictions are everywhere. Among groups of women I meet, once the abayas are shed at the door, the discussions are political, intense, without inhibitions. As a matter of fact, the women love each other in a very public way although they disagree on many fronts. The chair of the English department at the University for Women chided Fawzia and Munah for participating in the driving demonstration. The women, with the support of their husbands, got behind the wheels of their cars for the first time in Saudi Arabia, and drove a few blocks. "Look what happened to you fifty women; you've lost your jobs, your traveling privileges, everything the government provides." Both women had been professors of literature; now Fawzia writes for newspapers here and there. Munah has not found a new job.

Some women think the demonstrators made it worse for women; others believe the oppression has been steadily accelerating since the Iran-Iraq war. Sinful influences, western infidels, uncensored education contribute to decay. After all the crime rate is nearly non-existent in the country. At what price, the women wonder.

Wedding parties are held separately for women and men guests in private estates in remote desert towns where music can play without interference from authorities, where the Mutaawa are not combing through garbage cans looking for sign of drink or paying off taxi drivers to report when a woman hires a car to go somewhere alone.

In Riyadh, a city of modern architecture, western delights, and high technology, the ministry prohibits my visit to a women's university. As a matter of fact they tell the USIS that women speakers would not be invited anymore. Rebecca Idler is the embassy's women's program specialist. We found, sitting in the back of a bullet-proof car, that we were born in the same year in the same town. She wants to show me something positive about the women's culture in Saudi Arabia. We visit the Nahda Foundation--an extension school run by women from the royal family. It offers classes in languages, arts, and computers for women, and the profits support special programs for persons with Down's syndrome and other challenges. Inside a young director gives me coffee and a tour of the facilities. In one room I find three women with Down's beading and sewing in the traditional style. Their instructor is working hard at restoring an interest in native crafts and has traveled to the desert to find patterns of wedding dresses and pillow covers. Before we leave the building, I glimpse a sign at the door: "please put on an abaya before leaving."

## Buying A House In London
### 13 January 1993

CNN is the background noise of most gatherings. The big event in Dahran is a reading at the Consul General's house. When I arrive, a crowd has filled the main salon. The mixture of incomes, professions, and backgrounds illustrates the positive effects of the Aramco presence. Engineers and oil experts, teachers and doctors, embassy workers, including drivers are interested in poetry and the discussion is in full swing before I sit down. All the housing compounds connected with the oil industry are exempt from religious laws: men and women sit together and chat noisily.

I have selected some poetry that details cultural conflict and an excerpt from my prose works. I tell the audience stories of growing up Arab-American. The last poem is named "The Burden of History," a story in three parts of my family in Lebanon, on Ellis Island and then in the United States. I clear my throat to begin to read when a roar rumbles in the sky above us. Everyone looks at the ceiling in silence and the noise continues—jets in pairs, one set after another. Someone counts sixteen. When the commotion dies down, the Consul General slips out of the room to the study where CNN is already broadcasting. I know what has happened; everyone does. Someone whispers quietly, much quieter than the jets. "Please read now."

The discussions continue until the early morning hours. Before we leave we know about the strike at Iraq and the destruction of the Al-Rashid Hotel. Someone recited Ozymandias, a poem about a decayed and destroyed kingdom in the middle of the desert. I thought about Alex, a nurse I had met on the flight from Riyadh to Dahran. In the airport I saw her sitting alone and asked if I could join her. Eight months a year she works in a government clinic as a mid-wife on the Iraqi border. The work is demanding and the medical staff live in dorms surrounded by eight feet of barbed wire. The women have curfews, of course. Alex talks about how much she misses her boyfriend when she's in the desert. "How can you take it?" I wondered. "It's necessary," she replied. "I'm buying a house in London and it's the only way I can afford it."

Yemen

Poetry Everyday
17 January 1995

I cannot get the qat to cooperate. The men sitting in the "mufrage" have balls of the leaves in their mouths, and they smoke, drink Canada Dry, and talk at the same time. Sadeeq, whose cheek is the size of a racketball, instructs, "Chew the leaves and flip them in your cheek at the same time." I pull off the top tender leaves of this mild stimulant that yield the most juice. As I chew the bitter tang makes me want to spit it out or swallow it. I am handed a tissue and I cover my mouth and expel the weed. Embarrassed I want to try again, to make it clear to my host that I accept his hospitality, that I am honored to be there, and like all guests, I am willing to partake in this

35

Yemeni ritual.

Qat is a traditional and inexorable part of Yemeni culture. The mufrage is a special room in the house, usually on the top floor, designed for qat chews. Pillows for the seat, back, and arms are arranged around the perimeters of the room. A tray which holds water, soda, tissue, and biscuits, is shared by two people. Between them on the floor is the bush with the qat leaves. After they finish cleaning the branches of the leaves, they throw them into the middle of the room.

A qat chew lasts hours and is at least a weekly ceremony for all adults: women have their own chews where they dance and talk. Men have pleasure chews and business chews. When I was invited to a qat chew at Muhammad Safady's house, I understood the difference between Saudi Arabia and Yemen. All the poets, all these men, accepted my presence without much fuss. Safady, the leading poet in the country, writes about women's issues. He has been denounced and praised as a feminist. All the writers in the mufrage are politically oriented, two are members of parliament. Each day the newspapers print poetry and other literary articles. People heap books and tapes on me with poems, information about Yemen, and history.

The new is obscured by the old in Sanaa. The city is ancient and its architecture is a testimony to the unique artistic qualities that exist in Yemen. In the city, the buildings are old stone structures of about three stories. Above each window and door arches a half moon of stained glass. As I wind into the streets of the souq with Minnesotans, Carol and Ryan LaHurd who was teaching at the University of Sanaa, every dirt covered pathway leads to elegant archways and alabaster "takhrim" windows. We go first to find a money changer. In the hotel the exchange rate is twelve riyals to the dollar; in the street, it is forty-four. We walk along until a man in a leather jacket approaches us and asks if we need money; he raises a briefcase. I want to exchange one hundred dollars. He hands me forty four hundred all in twenty riyal notes--stack after stack which I stuff into my purse.

The souq is in the old city and is a maze of shops and pathways. The merchants sit in open rooms on the floor with their merchandise around them. Shoppers crowd down the center of the market until a car honks to get through. I want to buy a jambiya, the curved dagger that all men in Yemen wear hanging in the center of their bodies from a special belt. The curved tip always faces the right. Whether a man is wearing a futa, a skirt of wrapped material or an ordinary western suit, his jambiya is part of his clothing. I pick one with an inlaid wooden handle and an elaborate belt made of purple and gold threads. A man beckons me to follow him through the souq to an alleyway. He crouches among the garbage of pink and blue plastic bags and animal carcasses. With a small hammer and tacks he attaches the sheath and leather extender to the belt. Afterwards he puts out his palm where I place forty riyals.

Men walk around the streets holding each other's hands. When they greet they often touch each other's faces tenderly. The LaHurds explain that this is an act of friendship. I enjoy the groups of men who look at me as I pass and the different wraps the women wear. Some are completely covered but wear printed fabrics that look like batik. Most have their eyes or face visible. When Ryan was busy bargaining and Carol and I were examining the cones of spices on the trays in front of the stands, an old woman dressed in black and red, came up and touched our faces and talked to us. She wanted to know if we were teachers and she told us about her son in Brooklyn. When Ryan joined us, she turned around and walked away without a word.

In the Souq al-milh, the salt market, the alleys are specifically designated for particular products. In the silver market, rows of antique and new pieces with lapis lazuli, garnet, coral and other local stones dangle from the windows and hang on the walls. As we exit the market, we see boys standing in a line displaying lengths of material--often ten or

37

twelve feet long. As we step through the archway to the street, we have returned to the buzz of cars, traffic, minibuses called Dubaabs and more shoppers going to the electronics store on the main street.

A New Democracy<br>18 January 1993

In front of government buildings and schools, crowds of men wait to be picked as election officials. Since the unification of North and South Yemen in 1991, the promise of elections has been postponed. North Yemen, Yemen Arab Republic has been under the leadership of Abdullah Saleh and is related to Saudi Arabia politically. South Yemen, the People's Democratic Republic of Yemen, broke from the British influences of British Petroleum and became a socialist state with influences from the Soviet Union.

The new unification means fresh ideas according to the numerous officials and ministers I had met. The country is excited and responding to the unification as a new freedom. Political parties have popped up right and left and pursue their causes with vigor. One day we could not drive down a street east of Tahrir Square because the troops of Abdullah Saleh and the Baathists were having a shoot out. The week before I arrived, I am told by my translator, a thief hands were hanging in the square. It's the wild west, a junior officer surmises.

At the airport as I check my bags for the flight to Aden in South Yemen, the man in front of me is checking his rifle which is tagged and sent through with the rest of the luggage. Safady and other writers describe death threats against them. An editor of a prominent newspaper who sits next to me at a mufrage jokes about the hundred days he spent in solitary confinement. Everyone expresses a political view and waits for the results. They whispered to each other, "I saw your article today." They tease each other about the Baathists, Saleh's

38

people, or the fanatics coming to get them; except it is not a joke.

After I read, I take questions from the audiences. The same ones come up persistently: "Why don't you speak Arabic? Why don't you live in an Arab country?" I try to explain the age of assimilation and the pressure. My parents were the only Arabs in their small coal-mining town and they wanted us to fit in, to be successful Americans. But the Yeminis press me--they don't feel compelled to learn English and many resent all things American. The questions persist. My translator begins to answer these questions without me because he knows by the fifth time what I will say. He comforts me by saying that if they didn't care for me, like a sister, they wouldn't ask at all; they'd treat me just like another American.

Aden's architecture is dominated by rectangular apartment buildings with colored window panels. The traditional architecture was replaced with functional buildings by the socialists. Only a few monuments to that era remain--in particular a statue of a man and woman, arms raised, clutching a hammer and sickle. The traffic is more orderly than Sanaa and there is no need for the constant patrolling of traffic cops. Bart Marcois, my embassy escort, prefers Aden because it's more organized. He is not fascinated by souqs and native clothing. On the way into the city, he explained that the Aden Moevenpick where we are staying had a bomb scare when the marines were there. "As a matter of fact," he added, "we had a missile fired at the embassy the night you arrived in Sanaa."

I look out to the Gulf of Aden and the calm blue waters and the rocky shore. Here, unlike in Saudi Arabia, strollers fill the sea shore, some crouch on rocks examining the crustaceans. Shoppers populate the streets, and we drive through neighborhoods of Somalian refuges, Sudanese professionals, and Sri Lankan laborers; we pass shepherds walking their flock to market, see camels pulling carts of fruits and grain, and stands of mango, tangerines and banana hanging off the roofs.

While many Yeminis from the north are soliciting for jobs in Saudi Arabia, Africans and Asians are coming to Aden.

## Who Are You?
20 January 1993

The final event is scheduled back in Sanaa at a theater festival. Twenty plays are being produced, two each evening. The following day the audience critiques the piece to the writer and the director. Lines of participants wait for their opportunity to stand at the microphone to discuss Bye Bye London. After this segment, I am to read and take questions. Members of the audience come and snap my picture while I wait.

Muhammad Safady motions to me to join him on stage with my translator Muhammad Sharafuddin. In his introduction he explains about Doctora Elmaz, the sha`ira from the United States for almost ten minutes. I have no idea what he is telling the audience. I read two pieces which Mohammed translates. As he is reading a line of people forms at the microphone. The first is an old man, wearing his futa, a jambiya, and a gutra on his head.

"What is your name?" he asks.

"Elmaz Abinader."

He turns to the audience and then back. "What is your mother's name?"

"Elizabeth Abinader."

"What is your father's name?" his hands are folded in front of him.

"Jean Abinader."

He looks at me for a moment, glances at the audience, then turns back to the microphone. He raises a fist and shake it. "Why don't you speak Arabic? You are an Abinader! A daughter of Arabs! And you don't speak Arabic?" His face is reddening and the audience behind him is yelling in support.

40

"What kind of daughter are you?"

I am shaken for a moment, gather my wits about me, and tell him a little story of my childhood, about going to school the first day and having the administrators change my name to something more American because Elmaz was too difficult and probably not a saint's name. He is not satisfied with this answer and neither am I.

The flight for Frankfurt leaves Sanaa at three in the morning. I meet some oil workers going back home for their month-long break. Rick, a tall blond with a cowboy walk, offers me a Coke. He sits down next to me and crosses his legs. "So," he says. "Have you been here visiting family?" Suddenly the question seemed so complicated. What did he see when he asked it? Brown eyes? Dark hair? Can he imagine me inside a veil, yearning for release? Is that what the old man at the theater festival wanted from me? I pat my jacket pocket for my U. S. passport. I do not pull it out to prove who I am--no one believes me anyway. Not the soldiers in Saudi Arabia and not the grammar school nuns.

As the plane descends, I sit back and watch the other passengers huddle around the small windows. The skies over New York are clear; it is mid-afternoon and the traffic on the Van Wyck is light. Across the aisle from me are two women, heads wrapped in scarves, bodies draped in long dresses. They are chattering nervously in Arabic as they view the city. Turning to see out the other side, one catches my glances and gives me a smile. I see her dark complexion, her kohl-lined eyes and return her smile in recognition.

# Munir Akash

# THE LOWER ORGANS OF BEIRUT

*for Ghassan Kanafani*

The dead blow in the wind, flap like white flags
under a sky that hasn't seen war.
The dead are born in donkey-drawn carts
pouring into alleys of  night.
They buzz like bees inside the glass cage of time.
They still graze with gazelles
and go to the river to die again, afraid of what the
    water reflects.

Death itself utters the words of the sea
and the myths of original ships.
Death crowds the shore
and wraps Tal al-Za`tar with rising fog.
Death hides in ships sunk since the first invasion,
stalks stars dancing over waves
and the moon pouring silver over fishermen's nets.
Death writes the history of the coast,
dwells in deep caves, in undulating blue meadows.
Death stirs the waves and recites to our brides
    and to our fertile seasons
the first "books of the dead."

Its eyes peer at masts
and its tongue licks the lower organs of Beirut.

Even the "Horse Shoe" Café, where I sit now, descends with me
into sea holes and secret green watery corridors,
descends into death's guts that burst like lava from the sea.

All eyes follow the windows of cars that traverse a rainbow,
faces get born behind windows and die like white bubbles
    exhaled by sea creatures.
Death acquires the marks of love here,
and I spy it coming, flying over the seasons,
metamorphosing into flowers and birds,
even dreams and children's swings.
When people get tired of smoking cigarettes
they carve carts for caravans of tears
    out of the "Lord's Cedar."
What land will they import their tongues from,
as I lie like an overturned train, my
    wheels turning in the wind?

There is no language for my sorrow.
My sorrow is the corpse of an archeological cannon.
I was born with the dead in a place resembling the night,
    and we all blew in the wind
under a sky that hasn't seen a war.

There is a child whose braids are burning
waving with her hand from a high window pane.
There is a soldier closing the window
crushing her fingers between window and frame.
There is a caravan of donkeys, piles of shapeless faces,
pots and mats, weeping eyes, clucking chickens, bombs.
There is an abyss waiting for bulls' horns,
for shards flying at dawn.

The wind has teeth.
There is a wild goat running alongside us
    on rugged mountain peaks,
bleeding feet, large drops of rain.
There is death jumping from the furnaces of Europe
to the lighthouses of our harbors.
There is someone laughing like glass breaking,
streets to run through, tanks and tents for all seasons.
There are those who sold their blood to the absurd.
There is a sky being uprooted from the eye
    and a country escaping like a wave.
There are the dead and myths and a volcano erupting
from the sea vomiting its gods of death.
I was born there with the dead.
There are dead in yachts and private jets,
dead mounting donkeys, dead princes, dead kings,
dead generals and drunkards, dead criminals and victims,
dead hippies, dead bourgeoisie,
dead philosophers and madmen,
dead patients and doctors, dead students and professors,
dead progressives and reactionaries, dead capitalists and Maoists,
dead anarchists and surrealists, dead modernizers and traditionalists,
dead in caftans and dead in hoods.
Dead in a class struggle,
dead in a bloody competition for survival,
and dead lined up like racehorses in front of interested bidders.

Every time I weep for them I find myself one of them.
They died but did not journey.
I see them in mirrors and water.
I smell them on roads, among shadows and fields
    like oxeye daisies.

They died
but they still breathe like us.

They have become refugees like us.
They hang from our palm trees like date clusters.

All the dead are my body and the earth is my cells.
All the dead are my kin and death is my country.

By the fireplace sorrow comes and twists its tail under your feet.
This time it arrived from the snows of Galilee without saying a word.
Your fire has put on blue skin, suffusing your lungs
    with the aroma of roasted tents.
Tell me: Will you build a castle in your throat
  so you can fight the language of death?
Will you wrap the sea inside your bread pouch
and listen to it roar between your teeth?
Don't you see that your bones fill the sea,
and that you've embarrassed your memory?

This coffin mounted on top of your neck is heavier than a mountain.
Why don't you play a trick on it and flee?
Why don't you turn it into a fireplace, a cottage for lovers
    migrating in winter?
They haven't left a single tree standing for you to carve your name
    on its trunk.
They promised you a day
when all the arms that collected wood for coffins would be cut,
when all the forests would go around hungry and naked,
begging for handouts on the streets.

Blood stains the mountain snow.
The sky at the border crossing dozes on the branches of a tree.
Crystal creatures hang from the boughs and dance in the sun,
their cells sparkling with rainbows before their bodies hit the ground
    breaking like migrating comets.
Noble creatures formed from crystal
kill themselves over pools of blood.

Crystals and supernova erase the face of night from heaven's memory,
explode and launch the substance of our life into the Milky Way.
Why can't we fall from our branches with such grace and grandeur?
Why can't we return to our elements like all other forms of life
and close our eyelids on our death as if we were dreaming?

You asked me: "Is it true that death swims in water,
metamorphoses into flowers and birds?"
I spoke to her while my eyes descended to where death is transformed
    into a cave of velvet and fire.
I told her about America
when the continent swam naked in the streams of its dreams,
when Tula and the sun lay together in the same bed.

She said: "I don't remember where I killed you before."

I said: "on the banks of the Missouri River."

The plain of the sea was boundless.
The sun in the refugee camp played with the children and
    the chickens,
and shone on the open sewers.

All that is around me drinks the language of death.
Gets drunk. *D r u nnn k!*

There it is, running like a mare,
neighing because it catches the scent of its mother.

*1972*
*"Horse Shoe" Café / Beirut*
*(Translated by Sharif S. Elmusa)*

# Khaled Mattawa

# FREEWAYS AND REST HOUSES
## towards an arab location
## on the american cultural map

*Ignition/See the Light of Day*

At a particular curve just beyond the Hollywood hills on I-405 North the road descends into the San Fernando Valley. The whole northern part of Los Angeles appears. At night a million lights blend into each other creating a luminous blur, and alternately fragmenting into sparkling motes. The driver's eyes shift between the two offerings of the image until the descent is completed into a sprawl of asphalt and palms, a concrete churn of automobiles and human words and desires.

I drove down that stretch of freeway, and saw that view hundreds of times when I lived in the Los Angeles area two years ago. Some nights I failed to notice it, but when I did pay attention the vastness of it never failed to exhilarate me. Yet that same drive, that fall into a wide and seemingly endless expanse, also filled me with a burning urge to flee the city, and the United States altogether, to a more humane architecture, to a belonging wider than the property I rented.

I have never quite fulfilled those urges... Because home, the country of my birth and upbringing, is no longer home, because by many accounts the United States remains a lucrative and attractive option, because there is nowhere else to go. Within the minds of many immigrants these reasons have for centuries reworked themselves into enthusiasm for the U.S. as an adopted home. That has not been the case for me, and my sense of

49

malcontent with my adopted country has agonized me in very profound ways. Many ArabAmericans can cite the political causes: Unfair policies, demonization, and racism directed at Arab and Islamic populations on the national and international fronts. This is undeniably true and extremely important. But it is not the only reason. The truth is that I, and many ArabAmericans, do have a philosophical contention with America, one based on what we value, not on how we, or my cultural background, are evaluated. I think this argument with our surroundings is crucial, and can in turn transform our disaffection into a source of positive strength and creativity.

## *Vista 1*

On a tape of old songs from my native Libya one song always holds my attention. The singer is the late Ali Shaalia; the song is from a concert in the fifties not long after the country gained independence, ten years or so after the Italian occupation ended with Allied victory. The small band of violin, oud, tabla, and qanoon players, chugs its way into the melody. Once they catch their groove, the singer begins a love song about meeting the beloved on the street. He is burned by love and no ointment can heal him. He sings a few more lines, then the song halts to a *mawal*, a vocal solo accompanied by spontaneous musical responses to the singer's improvised lines. He addresses Night (lail) and Eye (ain) stretching the words, shortening them, alternating between high and low pitches. And here is what I always find remarkable: Shaalia ends his *mawal* with these lines:

> We've waited, and the end
> of our waiting was sweet.
> Thirty years have passed,
> and a great sadness ended:
> the armies of our enemy have left.

The audience cheers wildly at this and the band clumsily resumes the melody it began. Then Shaalia addresses his love wounds again.

### Vista 2

This song, and the change of subject matter, illuminated me in a different concern. While translating a poem by the Iraqi poet Saadi Youssef, a short lyric called "Freedom," I was uncomfortable with how easily the poet stated his purpose. The word "freedom" itself is bothersome, the way I hear it now in the Arab world, and in America--, so much invested in it, it has become like a gutted mine, a sound ringing empty in my ear. I knew the poem was an attempt to reclaim the word. Yet, I kept thinking what does a poem like this mean really? Does it offers a truly new definition, or is it a formula that only pertains to Saadi's surroundings, useless in America?    Here is the poem:

FREEDOM

> Alone now, you are free.
> You pick a sky and name it
>      a sky to live in
>      a sky to refuse.
> But to know that you are free
> to remain free
> you must steady yourself on a foothold of earth
> so that the earth may rise
> so that you may give wings to all
> the children of the earth.

The poem is full of clues, every word adds to the definition Saadi gives to freedom. *Huriya*, the Arabic word for freedom, means to be un-slaved, and also to consecrate, to clarify, and to kindle. Freedom suggests the fulfillment of a potential, not a

51

void but a process. Dedicated to a friend who finally made it out of Saddam Hussain's reach, the poem celebrates the newly gained freedom of the addressee. Alone now, you can live anywhere, any sky, the poet tells his friend. You may even be capricious in choosing your place. This sort of freedom, however, is a kind of prelapsarian innocence that cannot not last. Freedom demands awareness for its continuance. Freedom means nothing outside the earth; it is meaningless without a commitment to place and to people. Without others it becomes something else altogether.

Saadi's assignation of freedom as a kind of sky does not simply send us back to earth and leave us there. The poet is aware of our longing for the sky, for freedom from our bodies, from each other, from the earth, and from time. To be free then means to enable everyone to explore the sky, and this is how the earth will rise. This notion of freedom, captured in such visual terms, voices Saadi's idealism. Its braiding of transcendental yearnings recapitulates his years of commitment to writing from the earth.

### Quranic Vista

Saadi's switch from the individual to the communal and Shaalia's non-sequitur change of subject from love to current politics, point to an important ethical component in Arabo-Islamic esthetics. The highly charged timeless and placeless encounters with beauty, whether the delight of love or freedom, have to touch in some fashion the tangibles of daily life. Saadi's poem draws on the definition of the Good as an act of spawning. We find this notion stated in the shortest chapter of the Quran (Surat *Al-Asr*). The sura is made up of the following declaration:

> By the forenoon, for man is in a state of loss except those who believe and do good deeds and conjoin in righteousness and conjoin in perseverance.

The central message of these verses have their basis in the syntactical arrangement of this one sentence chapter. In principle, the sura declares that the human being, as an individual, is in a state of loss. But there are exceptions. The primary route to salvation for the human being begins in the transformation from the singular to the plural. The emphasis on this switch to the plural carries the rest of the sentence, and is emphatically underlined with the use of the verb *tawassu*. The Arabic verb of the English equivalent of "conjoin," *tawassu* also suggests to counsel, to bid, to recommend. In a sense, the way to individual salvation entails a conversation about ethics and values.

❏

Another short chapter of the Quran emphasizes this kind of melding in a more detailed fashion. An incident during the time of Muhammad's prophecy mitigated a clearer definition of the dynamics of individual salvation and social engagement. Surat *Al-Duha* (Morning Light) was revealed to Muhammad after a long period during which no revelations came to him. His antagonists in Mecca derided him for being abandoned by his god. The sura addresses Muhammad's pain caused by his detractors, and in an inspiring fashion redirects Muhammad toward his mission.

> By the glorious morning light and by the night when it is still, your guardian lord has not forsaken you, nor is he displeased. For in truth the hereafter will be better for you than the present life, and soon your lord will give you until you are satisfied. Did he not find you an orphan and give you shelter and care? and found you wandering and gave you guidance? and found you in need, and gave you until you came to your own? Therefore, treat not the orphan with harshness, nor rebuff those who seek your aid. And of the bounty of your lord, articulate and proclaim.

Before the revelation of this sura Muhammad had experienced a deep sense of anguish at being without visitation from the angel Gabriel. This incident is the closest thing the Quran comes to addressing existential isolation, the feeling of emptiness in the face of a vast and non-communicative universe. And while in Islamic dogma no such emotions ought to exist, I find this sura illuminating in how it addresses that sensation. Muhammad, to be remedied of feeling lonely and abandoned, is told a series of advice on how to live in the world with others. To feel the presence of God, the prophet is told to help those in need and to declare God's bounty and praise his creation. The first call urges engagement in social action; the second a call to pay attention to what surrounds us, to open one's senses to beauty and the sublime.

## Vista 4

The Quran, of course, while it formally compressed forms of Arabic expression, as in the chapters discussed earlier, it did not invent this fusion of the self, the world, and the other. The *mualaqa* (suspended ode) of Zuhair, written at the poet's old age, and considered one of the wisest of the pre-Islamic odes, weaves poetic sub-genres and tones to discuss a variety subjects. This *qassida* was auspiciously written as a eulogy for two leaders who paid a large ransom to settle a long and contentious tribal war. Yet Zuhair, at the age of eighty, begins his ode by recalling a woman he loved (unrequitedly). He asks

> Are these the only traces of the lovely Om Awfa?
> Are these the silent ruins of her mansion
> in the rough plains of Derraj and Mutathallam?

The poem, as the convention of the qassida dictates, begins at the beloved's abandoned campsite then goes on to lament her absence. After the initial description, the poet, overwhelmed by his memories of her, begins to envision a group of maidens, his beloved among them, as they journey away from him. Three lines later, and conveniently so, the campsite where the poet's beloved once stayed and where the poet had his vision of her, turns out to be the site of the great peace offering that the two noble leaders made the ransom to end the war among their tribes.

> The locks of stained wool, that fall from their carriages
> whenever they alight resemble the scarlet berries
> of night-shade not yet crushed...
> In this place, how nobly did the two descendants of Gaith,
> the son of Morra, labor to unite the tribes,
> which a fatal effusion of blood had long divided

This is one of the best and most cleverly structured transitions in all of poetry. It offers a clearly visualized setting that generates a continuum of dramatic moments. The poet reveals his vulnerability in bemoaning a loss. Then he undermines his credibility as a narrator by describing a doubtable vision. Yet, he does affirm the clarity of his vision with the precision of his imagery. Later he begins praising the peace making sheikhs and the poem assumes the role assigned by its occasion.

These changes in tone, as the various subjects raised demand, consolidate the poet's authority. He is a complex persona that has demonstrated knowledge of love, loss and pain, and one that appreciates beauty and has known the value of peace. A few lines into the poem he earns our trust and we grant him the right to speak on whatever he wishes. After the praise verses he begins an eloquent, imagistically laden polemic against war, then concludes with an associatively linked series of axioms as a distillation of his wisdom.

It would be a mistake though to see the change in subject matter, and the demonstration of a wide expertise as a mere rhetorical strategy. In locating the beloved's former camp as the site of the peacemaking offer, Zuhair comes close to creating a cohesive conceit to thematically unite the poem. This is of course antithetical to the poetics of layering that characterize the *qassida* where gaps are created by continuously changing the subject. The poem is unified, however, by its music, its metrical consistency and its mono-rhyme. The qassida operates on this constant tension between its divergent parts and its musical unity in the same way the that the poet's focus twines his most personal concerns with those of his people and his region.

### Rest Stop

In discussing Saadi Youssef's "Freedom" I argued that the poet's psycho-social logic originates in an Arabo-Islamic basis. This should help explain Saadi's socialist leanings, and the general attraction of socialism to modern Arab intellectuals and masses. It also helps explain why realism (sometimes of a blunt, didactic kind) remains the operative mode of the Arabic novel, and why a kind of activist zeal still permeates much of ArabAmerican writing from its most complex to its most banal and earnest. At a more personal level, it explains to me why I find the American style *laissez faire* rhetoric with its talk of the market as the ultimate social solution, and its promotion of greed as a positive value, completely disorienting coming from an Arab, and in the Arabic language in general.

This esthetic and ethical orientation most eloquently explored in the passages quoted earlier is the baggage (the heritage) that I, and many Arab Americans bring to the United States and continue to contend with. Aspects of this orientation can arguably be seen from within the old modernity and traditionalism discourse. Or it can simply be designated as an aspect of Medievalism, postmodernism, or even as a stage within the evolution of cultural production in capitalism. It is difficult to anticipate these arguments in full. What I am pointing to, however, as seen in Saadi's poem, is an ethical stance, and the manifestations of a tradition that are fully aware of Modernist and post-industrial global cultural developments.

This communitarian idealism persists, even as it confronts religious, social and political repression imposed upon individuals in the Arab world. It persists despite the reckless governance that permeates Arab countries, and the utter lack of institutional apparatus for individuals to engage with their cultural ideals. Clearly, what we see now in the Arab world is the nonchalance and vandalism that permeate societies deprived of participating in the making of their own futures. Yet, in spite of the hopelessness that drove so many out of the Arab world, this sensibility still persists, and it is what leaves so many of those related to Arabo-Islamic culture lost within the centrifugal sociopolitical landscape of the United States.

### The Lay of the Land

And understandably so. The spread of American cultural motifs and paradigms are causing crises all over the world. America is a different history, and a different present. Its impulses emerge from different experiences, legacies, and world view.

The three legacies that still contend within the American psyche are the mindsets of the religious refugee, the economic opportunist, and the slave. For the refugee, America is a place where one comes to be left alone. For the capitalist it is a place where one becomes engaged in the economy of exchange. For the slave it was the place of rootlessness, an absolute disconnection not only with one's cultural origins but even with future familial links. The mindset of the native American, the fourth dimension of the American psyche, is a sense of irredeemable loss coupled with acute alienation, an ongoing and deeply repressed ache.

The combination of the capitalist's adoption of exchange as a mode of social interaction and the Puritan's isolationism have created an architecture of expediency, one that minimizes intersections. The capitalist's ongoing search for new commodities and markets coupled with the slave's rootlessness have made the Americas a space of action not a place of belonging per se. This mode of operation remains with us today. Capital still searches for other markets, and in its pursuit of lower costs continues to crush weaker people by bidding them against even more impoverished pools of labor. Employees have to either relocate or be exchanged. Individuals, laborers of all sorts, like capital, can no longer afford to belong to a place; they must continuously move about in space.

## *Fellow Rovers*

Exchange, Mobility, Rootlessness, Isolation. Undoubtedly, such demanding conditions on the human soul have taken their toll, and subsequently have resulted in astoundingly positive outcomes. American competitiveness as an economic incentive, as well as an internalized abstract value, have contributed to the development of technological advancements unparalleled in human history. And the leisure granted by the Americas' wealth of natural resources and their individuals' isolationist propensity have created great opportunities for introspection. A healthy tradition of spirituality can be witnessed throughout the Americas. The continents' literary traditions of great compassion, candor, and imaginativeness have been one of the most powerful humanist forces of this century.

It must be remembered that these American spiritual quests and literary movements are essentially contrarian. Literary projects in America have not had a harmonious coexistence with capital. The greatest American poets of the 19th century, Walt Whitman and Emily Dickinson, were marginalized individuals--, a cloistered woman and a gay reclusive artisan. The generation that followed (James, Pound, Eliot, and H.D.) opted for living in Europe. Even the sophisticated provincialism of the New Agrarians' New Criticism held at its center an attempt to nourish a humanist opposition to ceaseless industrialization. The most influential American voices at the latter half of the century, Allen Ginsburg, Robert Lowell and Toni Morrison, have made their careers denouncing alienation, racial inequality, and imperialism while advocating pacifism, revisionist historicism, and social justice.

As an ArabAmerican I find great affinity and solace in these contrary and compassionate voices. These lucid critiques of capitalist dehumanization of all kinds denote various idealistic strains that can be engaged in exciting and fruitful ways with the Arabo-Islamic communitarian, activist sensibility that I explored earlier. To be sure, I am not suggesting a return of any sorts, neither to a particular place nor a particular era. I am advocating that ArabAmerican artists and intellectuals become seriously engaged in enriching the cultural tableau of the ArabAmerican experience.

### An Imagined Destination

Let me offer a two-fold approach for rethinking the Arab heritage and its role in the fashioning of an Arab cultural identity in America. When we face our Arab literary and cultural heritage we will encounter misogyny, racism, and superstition, ideas that simply cannot survive in our time. For works like the ones quoted earlier and others to have true pertinence to our lives in the U.S. we need to develop a more complicated relationship with them. Like all of literature and all of art, our Arab literary heritage is there to be grafted upon and to generate new art and new modes of thinking. Our heritage is there for its palempsistic potential.

In our efforts to develop a cultural identity rather than mere ethnic identification, I think it is possible, and certainly worth our while, to engage the tribal, religious, and Medievalist perspectives of the Arabo-Islamic literary heritage in ways as to transmute them into forms of existential idealism suitable for a secular, multicultural, democratic setting. Attempts at deriving abstractions from dogma, and genuine spiritualism from hollow cultural practices, were part and parcel of the revolutionary Sufi projects. Similar humanist ambitions have been part of the modern Arabic literary experience since the middle of 19th century. In more recent practices the works of Fatima Mernissi and Assia Djebar have engaged Islamic history to evolve indigenous and historically based forms of feminism.

### Pot Holes

The three major factors that characterize Arab life in the U.S. are continuous contact with Arab culture through the homelands, an ambivalent relationship with American mainstream culture, and a struggle with Arab culture in the U.S. context. These are the tributaries that feed our sense of ourselves. These currents seem to be pulling us in opposite directions, each demanding absolute loyalty. No simple solution is possible in this condition. Absolute return and going forward unfettered are both impossible.

Our sense of self emerges from a multiple critique of these forces. We deplore the repressive social structures of our native lands, but appreciate a great many of the values we and our parents were reared upon. We object to the consumer values of the American mainstream, but we appreciate the basic democratic spirit of America. We believe in the importance of individual initiative and drive, but we also believe in social cohesion and in preserving the well being of all. We do not want to become Americans in any traditional sense, but we are sure that we are not only Arab.

Arab identity in the U.S. is tentative precisely because we have not determined these choices as a valid position per se. Admittedly, we stand in the crosscurrent of many strong stances, but this is the position we occupy and it is the place where we wish to remain. To be solidified, this ArabAmerican identity needs a basis of eloquent and thorough social critiques of its own subculture. And it needs an intellectual and artistic tradition that draws on its vast humanistic heritage for ethical and esthetic foundations that can comprehend the wider American culture in which it maneuvers and that can be comprehended by it. We need to find ways of voicing the multiple critique of the ideological streams that swirl around our lives.

As it stands now, the staples of grandmotherly aphorisms, thickly accented patriarchal traditionalism, culinary nostalgia, religious dogma, belly dancing and adoration for Kahlil Gibran are meager nourishments for cultural identity, let alone a cultural revival and a subsequent engagement with the larger American culture.

### The Enigma of Non-Arrival

One October night a few years ago I took I-405 upon returning from an ArabAmerican event. I still remember the despondency and utter emptiness I felt on the way back from that banquet. Various speakers gave the usual cries of victimization, protests against media misrepresentation, kindly appeals to the Bill of Rights and clichéd calls for equality. The hall was full of handsome faces touched by affluence.

Yet there was nothing to delight into, nothing to hold onto firmly and affirmatively, and say this is mine, ours. The old was dead and shrouded in its intransigence, and the new pubescent and incoherent. Then the music began. The bodies swayed refuting any claims for fashioning an identity out of catastrophe and helplessness. The songs' words were like the sails of unreachable boats; the pulse of the music was all there is to cling to. And I thought how could they, how could I, be drowning here when there is so much poetry in the air, so much poetry in our blood.

ODE TO MEJNOON

You're creeping into the lexicon.
Soon I'll find you in Webster's
somewhere between mad
and melancholy. Mejnoon.
A million Iranians in LA
despite Saddam and Van Damme
Lewinsky and Tarantino
and the tanks of fake blood
and the pools of real blood
gang bangers and neo-Reganites
killer cops and evangelical sodomites
despite O. J. and McVeigh
they think of you Mejnoon
somewhere between jejune and moon
struck roaming San Fernando
starved and crazy about your cousin
and your uncle will not let you
marry the girl because Mejnoon
has no future in a rinky dink outfit
telemarketing your life away
soaking Sylvia and Baudelaire oiling
your midnights with Poe's forevermore,
putting a million frequent flyer miles
on red eye after red eye feeding
on atrocious turkey sandwiches
devouring a thousand movies,
a thousand mediocre acting careers,
billions of clouds and golf magazines
business people at their spread sheets
and the flight attendants' preowned kindness,
their dyed hair and crows' feet,
Mejnoon not leaving the girl alone
despite her indifference

her many things to do and Mejnoon
raving mad, her face in front of his
as if trapped under a virtual reality helmet,
unable to update the software.  Mejnoon
why does everything seem like a joke
and when all the networks jam
why are there no messages on the  machine,
no email.  Only chiropractors
and rough handed masseurs.  Mejnoon
in the coffee shops they don't talk to you
just whispering new ideas for Baywatch
sketching sit-com scripts about coming out
turning in their heroine syringes
turning in their abusive fathers
and Lester Thurow the only philosopher
and Bukowski is the only poet.
Mejnoon, now the woman next door
begs you to talk to her blind husband
lying there in his underwear, his skin
so pale, veins like slugs on his legs
and broken vessels like pieces of lint
and the old man ranting about poor health
and ill luck and the heartless universe
and there you are Mejnoon saying everything
will be all right, let's just all  go to the beach
despite the jammed highways and the insane
drivers, somewhere between pathetic
and pathological, on acid, cell phones and Zantac
and the ocean is so far  and so enormous
even the mighty sun falls there and bleeds
all over the clouds and falls and falls
until the sea and the sky are one  massive abyss
where colossal planets are no more than salt
and there you are Mejnoon, a blind man
beside you, a latter day oracle mumbling

curses at the all-mighty, and his old lady
too stunned and tired to talk.
This is what the skies have allotted you
somewhere between restless and thankless
and all you have is this heart abeating,
and this girl who's not keen on you,
and many days  to live that will pass in a blink.


GILGAMESH

Tablet:  (Red eye, Vegas stop)

First light of early morning dawning,
Tony Bennet at the ivory gate with a tune.
Stand on the right, Enkidu, or you'll fall
on your ass.  In the bathroom I stand
at an American Standard urinal as Boston College
does pretty well this year beating Notre Dame.
Leaving you who are the door
through which the cold wind gets in.
Leaving Vegas with the light of early morning dawning.
May the garbage of that City be what you eat.
A man slips a dollar in the slot machine.
Do you have aspirin?  I live in San Diego
and I have a girl now, the last three weeks
at the end of the ninth league, the rough tongue
of the North wind licking our faces, we began hitting it off.
I contain a vomiting multitude in the plane's emergency bag
and they order Buds those Japanese youths
whose laughter sounds like wads of paper being torn.
Moist decadence hovered above us

like a lioness watching her brood.
Please become familiar with the operation.
They met in Amherst those two and got married
three years later.  The last few weeks
the Nether world seized us but I knew
she was going back to her ex.
It could be easy to take these hours alighting
in the early dawning and wrap them in Styrofoam
to ensure safe passage through fear.
If you open this door you will have no home;
you will sleep on the city doorsteps.
Someone will tell you when to wear the mask
and all men will curse and revile you and turn away.
The planets stand in their upright positions
and the law prohibits tampering with the insects
that leave their cocoons to live but a minute
or disabling the terror and the Wild Ox.
Early morning is dawning above your seat.
There's a light that won't hesitate to call on you.

# Lisa Suhair Majaj

# NEW DIRECTIONS
### arab-american writing at century's end

Arab-American literature has gone through many shifts since the early decades of the twentieth century, when Khalil Gibran and other *Mahjar*, or emigre, writers in New York formed *Ar-Rabitah*, the Writer's Guild, and began to publish poetry and prose that changed the face of Arabic literature even as it initiated a century of Arab-American literary endeavors. But in many ways the issues that confronted the Mahjar writers continue to confront us as Arab-American writers today. Whether or not we struggle with the choice to write in Arabic or in English (for many of us the choice is not ours to make) we, like the Mahjar writers, inhabit multiple cultures and write for multiple audiences: American, Arab, Arab-American. While the details of our personal experiences differ, for many of us this negotiation of cultures results in a form of split vision[1]: even as we turn one eye to our American context, the other eye is always turned toward the Middle East. As hyphenated Americans we seek to integrate the different facets of our selves, our experiences, and our heritages into a unified whole. But the schism in our vision often affects our balance: as we turn our gaze in two directions at once, we sometimes lose sight of the ground beneath our feet.

This split vision is often expressed in Arab American literature through a tilt toward either Arab or American identification. For instance, although the Mahjar writers were influenced by their American literary and social contexts in ways which have still to be fully explored, they were nonetheless primarily expatriate writers, exiles whose vision was trained on the Middle East and its literary and political contexts. Conversely, immigrant autobiographers before 1950 were oriented toward the American context: indeed, their texts, which draw on the conventions of American immigrant autobiography, provided a vehicle through which authors could write themselves into existence as Americans. In their autobiographies Arab identity is mediated through strategies of containment and situated within a broad claim to American identity.

The focus on Americanization led, by mid-century, to second-generation writing exhibiting a deep-seated ambivalence toward Arab ethnicity. But the late 1960s and 1970s saw the rise of a body of second-generation Arab-American literature, primarily poetry, that engaged and affirmed ethnicity, and that paralleled the emergence of a pan-ethnic Arab-American identity bridging the different national and religious identities of immigrants and ethnics of Arabic-speaking background. Situating both this literature and this pan-ethnic identification were two cultural currents: 1) the ethnic "roots" phenomenon which gained ground in the 1970s, providing the foundation for the current celebration of multiculturalism in the U.S, and 2) the growing politicization of the Arab American community under the influence of new Arab immigrants to the U.S, and as a result of wars and other political events in the Middle East (most notably the 1967 Arab-Israeli war, the oil embargoes of the 1970s, the 17-year Lebanese war, the Israel invasions of Lebanon, especially that of 1982, the 1990-1 Gulf crisis and war, and the demonization of Arabs and Muslims in the wake of hijackings and bombings in the 1980s and 1990s).

This dual context of, on the one hand, the domestic

affirmation of ethnicity, and on the other hand, Middle Eastern political events, has shaped not only the thematic content of Arab-American literature, but also its form. The fact that Arab-American literary production has leaned heavily toward poetry has often been noted. The usual explanation put forward is that of an intrinsic Arab cultural propensity towards poetry. That is, it has been implied that we have, as a group, produced more poetry than prose because poetry is somehow "in our blood" -- even when the writers in question do not read Arabic and have no direct relationship to the tradition of Arabic poetry. But although there is something to be said for the Arab cultural validation of poetry, this explanation is perhaps too essentialist, especially given the significant influence of American literary forms on Arab-American poetry.

A second explanation sometimes put forward is more sociological in focus: we have produced more poetry than prose because as a small and beleaguered ethnic group we have only recently begun to feel established enough to turn to serious literary endeavors, and we have not, therefore, set in place for ourselves the kind of support systems, both economic and social, needed for the writing of fiction. It is arguably true that as a genre, fiction is more demanding than poetry in terms of time-commitment and focus: while it is possible to write a poem in an evening or a weekend, the same is not true of a novel. It is also true that publishing novels is far more difficult than publishing individual poems. However, despite the particular problems confronting the novel writer, this theory does not explain why have we as a group produced not only so few novels, but also so little short fiction as well.

There is another explanation, however, one connected to the ways in which our literature, like the rest of our experience, has been shaped by our split vision. It is possible that we have produced mainly poetry because poetry as a genre is particularly suited to both celebration and the expression of grief. Arab Americans have throughout this century been situated between an ethnic identity defined largely through familial relationships, and an intense engagement with Middle Eastern political events. These dual orientations are linked by the literary genre typically used to articulate both: that of the lyric. As a literary mode the lyric is particularly suited to moments of intensity and illumination. Love songs are lyrics, as are elegies. The lyric provides a ready vehicle both for nostalgic celebrations of family and community, and for anguished depictions of war and suffering, both of which have played a large role in Arab American poet

What the lyric mode does less well, though, is to provide a broader forum for representation, analysis, discussion and critique. Its poetic compression favors vignettes rather than narratives, moments of insight over sustained analysis. Its imagery tends to work by juxtaposition, with the result that lyric poetry tends to evoke rather than explain. The predominance of the lyric mode in Arab-American literature at a time when we, as Arab-Americans, have been engaged in articulating and consolidating a sense of our own group identity, is indicative: it suggests that we have, in large part, been asserting our identity and giving voice to our emotions rather than analyzing and probing.

Given our history of both exclusion and invisibility, it is no surprise that Arab-American writers have felt the need to celebrate who we are and to mourn what we have lost. But as a genre, poetry has not always provided a forum within which we have been able to probe the full complexity of our experience as Arab-Americans, or to levy a sustained critique of our internal community dynamics. As our Arabness has become more visible on the American landscape -- because of increased Arab migration, technological advances that allow the importation of Arab culture, negative attention directed at us in response to political events in the Middle East as well as to unrelated domestic events (such as the bombing of the Oklahoma Federal Building) and our own growing self-awareness and community organization--the task confronting us increasingly becomes not simply one of celebration, but of self-analysis and self-criticism.

Simply to be Arab-American is not an anomaly anymore, despite the fact that our identity is often held against us. National and professional organizations such as AAUG (Association of Arab American University Graduates) ADC (American-Arab Anti-Discrimination Committee), RAWI (Radius of Arab American Writers, Inc.), AAMA (Arab-American Medical Association) and others have begun to provide an institutional foundation for our communal life. At the same time, the increasing accomplishments of Arab-Americans across a range of professions have brought individual Arab-Americans into national visibility. While the task of asserting Arab-American identity remains crucial, it is important to recognize that we are not raising our voices in a vacuum. As we continue to strengthen our networks and develop our group identity, we need to expand our vision and to move beyond cultural preservation toward transformation. We need to probe the American as well as the Arab dimensions of our Arab American identity, and to engage not only in self-assertion, but also in self-criticism. As we near century's end, we need to take a hard look not only at who we are, but at who we hope to become.

In moving toward this new thematic terrain, a move to new literary genres is both necessary and unavoidable. As Khaled Mattawa points out his call for submissions to this special issue, "Changes in form are important signifiers of changes in subject matter and in fact." It is noticeable, for instance, that the growing emergence of a body of feminist Arab-American writing corresponds with a shift toward prose writing, fiction as well as non-fiction. It is as if the turn away from nostalgic celebration toward more rigorous and self-critical explorations mandates a move away from the lyric compression of poetry toward the more expansive and explanatory medium of prose.

71

As we seek to re-envision our own communities while situating ourselves more firmly within our American context, the need for alternative languages and forms in which to give voice to alternative realities becomes increasingly clear.

Hand in hand with the expansion of theme and genre has come a growing attention to literary analysis and criticism. The publication of several anthologies of Arab-American literature in the past decade -- notably, Gregory Orfalea and Sharif Elmusa's *Grape Leaves: A Century of Arab American Writing* (1988), and Joanna Kadi's *Food for our Grandmothers: Writings by Arab-American and Arab-Canadian Feminists* (1994) --played a crucial role forging a sense of connection and community among Arab-American writers, and in asserting the existence of a body of Arab American literature. However, critical discussion of this literature has remained limited, with much of it remaining at the level of the survey. The scarcity of critical discussion has meant that we have often written without self-consciousness of our debts to the diverse literary traditions upon which we draw.

This scarcity of critical discussion has also accentuated the problem of reception. Given the political pressures facing Arab-Americans, and the omnipresent stereotypes of Arab culture, writers may feel (and readers may expect) that their task is to affirm Arab identity and to translate this identity to outsiders. But while these concerns are part of our literary endeavors, they should not limit them. A body of informed and nuanced literary criticism would play a significant role in situating Arab-American literature for both Arab and non-Arab readers, thereby lessening somewhat the pressure on Arab-American writers to serve as "translators" of their culture. Literary criticism also has a crucial role to play in highlighting not just the cultural and sociological, but the literary dimension of our writing, reminding us that we are, first and foremost, writers.

I want now to outline some areas in which I think

Arab-American literature should increasingly move:

We need to move away from nostalgia and toward a more direct confrontation with our Arab-American past. Our history is not limited to upward mobility on the one hand (the classic American success story favored in our autobiographies) and cultural loss through assimilation on the other. Nor can it be depicted through a straightforward celebration of community. Rather, our experiences have been at once more complex and more painful. We need to explore experiences not just of ethnic familial warmth and of entry into white middle class America, but of marginalization, poverty and exclusion, not only from American society but from Arab communities as well.

We need more attention to the ways in which we have been racialized in the American context. For too long we have tried to escape into white ethnicity. But our experience has shown us, time and again, that our formal status as white is merely honorary, and is quickly revoked in the wake of political events in the Middle East as well as in the U.S. We need more explorations of the implications of this racialization. At the same time, we need to probe links with other groups of color, and to explore the ways in which our racialization can provide new grounds for solidarity and activism.

We need a stronger, more nuanced and less defensive articulation of feminism. Arab-American feminist critique has been hampered by the overwhelming array of orientalist stereotypes about Arab culture. When Arab and Arab-American women give voice to feminist concerns, they are often assumed, both by their own communities and by outside observers, to be rejecting their own cultural traditions in favor of a more "liberated" western culture. Depending on the stance of the observer, this is viewed either as an escape or as a betrayal. The result of such overdetermined discourse has typically been a pressure toward silence, with community censure of those writers who do attempt to explore more negative aspects of Arab and Arab-American culture. As we move toward a more public discussion of Arab-American culture, and as our writing is read by a widening audience of readers with no prior knowledge of Arab culture, these representational difficulties increase. Yet to succumb to silence in order to prevent our words from being misunderstood is in its own way a form of self-betrayal. What we need is not less but more representation -- for only when there is a wide array of depictions of Arab-American experience and culture will writing that is self-critical be understood for what it is: not a betrayal, but an attempt at self-transformation.

We need more social criticism in general. Although we have often liked to celebrate ourselves on our law-abiding record and strong family structures, we confront, as much as any other community, internal problems linked both to our Arab and our American identities and contexts. We are not free of domestic violence, drug use, gang participation or so-called "honor killings". We too often allow our own racism, homophobia and classism to go unquestioned. While literary texts are not social exposés, they nonetheless provide a forum within which social questions may be probed. Our writing needs to move beyond celebrations of identity and complaints about misrepresentation to grapple with the ways in which we have fallen short of our own ideals.

We need to take a closer look at the the complexity of Arab-American identity. We are not simply Arabs in the U.S., nor are we simply Americans of Arab heritage, although we are both of these things. Rather, our culture is the result of what anthropologists call "ethnogenesis"-- the creation of a new culture that draws on both Arab and American contexts and identities. Our legacy of split vision, of being torn between the Middle East and the U.S., has had direct and pragmatic impact on us. But when we write we do not simply write "Arab poems in English," as was once suggested to me. Our writing needs to explore our ethnicity not simply as a translation from the old, but as something altogether new.

We need to pay more attention to who is excluded by existing definitions. When we talk about Arab-Americans, are we including people of mixed heritage, religious and racial as well as national? Are we including Arab Jews who identify with their Arabness? Are we including gays and lesbians, whose experience has been for all practical purposes silenced in discussions of both Arab and Arab-American culture? Are we including those who don't know any Arabic? Are we including those originating from all the Arab countries, not just from Lebanon, Syria and Palestine? Does our literature reflect this diversity of experience and identification?

We need to infuse our writing with new cultural forms. Not only do we need more novels and dramas, we also need more screenplays, multi-media pieces and performance art. We need to pay more attention to the ways in which contemporary American cultural forms -- for instance, rap music -- affect our work. At the same time, we need to explore the possibilities of bilingualism in our work, along the lines suggested by contemporary Latino/a literature. What happens when Arabic enters our writing, both on a linguistic and a visual level? We need to become more self-conscious about the diverse literary traditions within which we are writing, and we need to turn more consciously to literary experimentation.

We need to keep in mind our multiple audiences without being stymied by them. When we write and publish, we speak both to and for Arab-Americans, and we address as well readers both within and without of our many other communities -- national, gendered, cultural, political and literary. This diversity of readers has a significant impact on how and what we write. The pressure to represent Arab culture in a positive light can have significant impact on our willingness to experiment. But despite the often overwhelming demands of communal representation, we need to remember that our literary and activist concerns are interrelated but not identical.

At the same time, however, we need to acknowledge our

activist role. As Arab-American writers we have the language that will allow us to speak in this country and perhaps to be heard. But what use are we making of our skills as writers? We need to write texts -- especially novels -- that will translate political realities into human terms, and that will create a space for empathy on the part of readers who might otherwise remain indifferent. Given the depth of ignorance and misinformation about the Arab world, we are particularly in need of prose-- of writing that is capacious enough in form to convey fact as well as emotion. We need historically-grounded novels that will narrate Arab realities to American readers without sacrificing literary quality to didacticism, that will tell a compelling but also informative story. But in taking on such projects, we need to make sure that we're not writing tracts, but are writing literature.

We need more children's literature that portrays the Middle East in human terms. Similarly, we need more children's literature depicting Arab-American experiences. Children in this country, both Arab-American and non-Arab, are barraged with negative images of Arabs in comic books, cartoons and textbooks. There has been until recently practically no literature geared at younger readers that could offset these images, although Naomi Shihab Nye's publications (most notably, her picture book *Sitti's Secrets*, her novel for teenagers, *Habibi*, and her collection of poetry and art from the Middle East, *The Space Between Our Footsteps*) have been groundbreaking. In addition to the activist project of portraying Arab-Americans and the Arab world in non-stereotypical ways, children's literature offers exciting possibilities for collaboration between writers and visual artists, collaborations that might lead to other kinds of aesthetic experiments and innovations.

And finally, we need, as Khaled Mattawa has suggested, to reclaim the personal. As Arab-Americans we have many concerns, and not all of them can be contained within the rubric of the communal. While Arab-American identification has had a huge impact on us, we need to recognize the ways in which the personal dimensions of our experience can also illuminate our understanding of communal concerns. Our lives are inflected and informed by ethnicity, but not limited by it. In segregating those aspects of our lives which do not seem "Arab" from our definition of Arab-American identity, as we so often do, we diminish both our writing and ourselves.

As we approach the end of the century we need not stronger and more definitive boundaries of identity, but rather an expansion and a transformation of these boundaries. In broadening and deepening our understanding of ethnicity, we are not abandoning our Arabness, but making room for the complexity of our experiences. To shift our focus from preservation to transformation is not to dilute our Arab-American identity but to make it more viable. At century's end, our split vision may be our most important legacy, forcing us to direct our gaze not only backwards, to the past, but forward, to an as-yet-unwritten future.

1. Edmund Ghareeb's book *Split Vision* uses the term in a slightly different way, to describe the ways in which Arabs have been misrepresented and stereotyped in the American media.

77

POPPIES                    .

                    what longing
        thrust me into the wind.
                searching for poppies
                    as if they could save me?
            they wouldn't last: a week,
                maybe two, and exuberant
            earth would be silenced
                a gift retaken

                        I'd need
                to depend on memory

        *smooth taste*
            *of sun, those brilliant*
                    *cries, those red-tongued*
                *mouths, wild*
                *with surprise*

            so I hoard memories
                sort them for seeds
        to plant, pray they root

            *pine shrubs on stony slopes*
                *blossoms startling a hill*

                        \*\*\*

                fierce tongues beneath transient
                    skies, those stars of imploding
            songs, those poppies now

78

## DEPARTURE

*Every time I think of leaving, my heart wrinkles*
*--Samira Atallah*

Leaving is always
like this. Years
of hours and days
ticked off like
a body count:
what's left but
shards of memory
smoothed and hoarded,
shrapnel griefs,
a few regrets?
It should be simple
to leave, land
falling away
like fear,
old skylines
erasing.

But lines
etched into skin
after years
of weather
chart boundaries
we cannot cross:
tangles of blood ties,
history's scars,
love's sidelines
of salt.

After leavetakings
planned and unplanned,
deaths you're forced

to move on from,
you learn these
things: how
to say goodbye
quickly, how
to choose what
to take when
you go, how
to live without
what you leave
behind. You learn
to like empty
spaces, blank
walls, shadowless
light; learn
to pour loss
like coarse salt
through your fingers.

Some things
you take when
you go: light
no one can capture,
voices that sing
alone, the touch
of snow on air.

Some things are lost
in the leaving. Some
remain. Some seeds
planted in brine
still grow.

SEA BONES

Before my mother died she confessed,
"My body's gone bad on me."
Her hands, delicate fins, arched a curve of despair.

Days later, she sank
before the morning light had fully rolled in.
I cast out net after net,
came up with a litter of shells,
empty and salt-crusted.

At the shore there's only the fierce crescendo
of waves. What we cast out as anchor returns,
fragments of bone in our nets, hard white *glossa--
tongue of the squid--* the calcium rib
left after sea strips flesh.

It's an old fisherman's secret:
ground to white powder,
*glossa* staunches the bleeding of wounds.

# Patricia Sarrafian Ward

# *"THE BULLET COLLECTION"*
## excerpts*

### THE QUALITY OF TWILIGHT

Between the Armenian hotel and Uncle Haig's house in the mountains lay a small house surrounded by trees so that it was always in shadow. A foreign woman lived there; no one knew who she was or what she did, but she read a lot, I saw through her window on summer evenings, and many times she would look out as if she were waiting. It happened one day that as I watched her stare out the window with her palms on the open pages of her book, the sound of hooves galloping on the road below the hotel startled me and she must have heard them too because she stood up, book sliding to the floor. She did not leave the room, but remained quite still, listening, and within moments a man on a white horse appeared at her door. Her house was swimming in long twilight shadows and the ghost-like horse pawed the ground as the man leaned down and knocked on the door. I held my breath, I had never seen anything so beautiful, and when she appeared I heard her laugh drifting through the silence as he bent down and kissed her. I felt ashamed for watching them; lying there behind the trees in the soft pine needles, I had no part in this.

It was through one of Uncle Haig's big meals that I met the man who had visited the foreign woman; I was twelve, and this was the summer my breasts were touched for the first time by someone other than myself.

The food that I relished the most were the sweetmeats, grilled in lemon juice and garnished with parsley, and on that Sunday my request was granted. My uncle swiftly sliced the sweetmeats with a sharp knife and squirted lemon juice as they sizzled on the grill on the west terrace overlooking the road. The fire sputtered and for a moment ashes were held aloft by the heat. As we prepared the table, we saw in the distance, beyond the slope of the hill, a cloud of yellow dust that signalled a car, and then a small Renault appeared, blue, all the windows rolled down, and as it charged up the road my uncle shouted: "It's Ziad, at last!"

When the young man stepped out of the car and slammed the door, my face burned as it did when I bent over the grill, and I turned away to hide the memory of him leaning down to kiss the foreign woman a few days before. As he marched towards us, he disrupted everything with his tallness and his big white smile, and my frail fantasies were crushed by the reality of his presence. This moment would never leave my memory: it would return again and again, long after he mysteriously died and long after I had discovered the truth of that death and the lies it had bred. Daddy rose from his chair and even the recalcitrant and gloomy Alaine moved aside, and then Ziad arrived, came to a standstill with his feet apart and hands on his hips, like a hero coming home.

I maneuvered so that my back was against the wall. Ziad threw himself at Uncle Haig and they hugged and shook hands and slapped each other's backs. When my hand, for an instant, was in his during our introduction, the shuddering in my belly started and I did not eat well for weeks afterwards, and that was how I lost the last bit of plumpness I had been carrying from childhood.

As they ate and I tried to quell my nausea, Ziad spoke about how he would build a disco in his barn that once had been filled with horses. He leaned over his plate and waved his fork describing the lights, the dance floor, and his presence was abnormal in our usually quiet gathering. He spoke of things that happened elsewhere, in other worlds and with other kinds of people, and Mummy and Daddy were obviously taken aback. Mummy kept looking down, as if embarrassed by this talk of dancing and drinking, of parties that lasted all night. Alaine toyed with her food, never looking up, her long curly hair jumbled around her face.

His eyes were black like jewels, I thought. Like opals. What color is an opal? Words jammed each other in my head. A fleeting, shameful image of touching his face, kissing! almost destroyed my show of calm. Everyone could see. Could they see? I crossed my legs and tried to look demure, a word that meant something mysterious but necessary right then. I smiled. In the middle of this rapid, excited talk, he invited everyone to come look at the barn, "So why don't you come down? Anytime you want. Just come see."

He waved his arm at the circle, grinning. And in the moment of silence after this invitation, without thinking, I said very politely, "That would be nice."

Then I realized I was the only one who had spoken and Mummy was smiling crookedly, that certain look of indulgence that I loathed and admired at the same time, and my insides shriveled.

"Yes, tomorrow?" he said, and I was so surprised I said nothing, but he was off again on the subject of his disco, and I kept my eyes away from him and pretended to be only vaguely interested.

When the food was gone and Ziad had finished his third beer, he leaned back and stretched, yawning. His belt buckle, a cowboy twirling a lasso on a galloping horse, was huge. Where did he get such a buckle? It was exotic. Ziad did not shake our hands again. He treated us like old friends. He shaped his hand into a pistol, pointed it at me, "See you tomorrow, kiddo!" and my thoughts lurched. Kiddo.

As the Renault sped away, Daddy said words I did not yet understand, "Ziad's dreaming big dreams for this place. Too big for a war. He thinks he can rein it in to suit him."

Mummy nodded with characteristic solemnity, and Auntie Firyal said, "I don't understand who he thinks will go dance there. In the middle of a war."

I did not care about the war. I worried that my breasts, knobs poking at my tee shirt, were too small to be of consequence, that I had only had my period a total of four times now, and that if I said anything at all on my visit he would think I was silly. Maybe he didn't mean it, that I should go visit. It was just a comment. I was simultaneously relieved and terrorized by the thought that this might be true.

Alaine suddenly emerged from her darkness to sing, "You're in love, you're in love."

"What?" Daddy said, and his expression of bewilderment made everyone laugh and I laughed, too, jabbing Alaine's ankle under the table. I wanted them to think it wasn't that exciting for me, to go see Ziad, indeed, that I might not go at all.

His house was about twenty minutes away and I walked slowly, as if this was a usual walk and should anyone see me they would think I was always doing this, walking along. Ziad had spoken by C.B. to Uncle Haig early in the morning and had said he expected me around one or two "if possible," as if I might have an agenda, which pleased me. I had pretended to mull it over. Uncle Haig had given me a Tupperware container of fried meat and rice. "Ziad doesn't eat enough," he had said. "He is too excited about his disco."

At the door to the house, I hesitated and as I contemplated turning back I heard rapid footsteps and then the door flew open and there he was, in boots and riding breeches.

"Good afternoon!" he said dramatically, and I sensed instantly with that instinct for self protection that he knew exactly how I felt and exactly how I saw him. Covered in shame, I barely managed a greeting before he took the Tupperware and guided me through the opulent house to the back.

"There!" he exclaimed, and I stared at the dilapidated barn whose roof sagged in the center and whose windows were all broken. Grass grew tall and yellow and vines had crept half way up the walls. An old white car was parked next to the barn, the tarp bunched on its hood. The car had no wheels. The scene was draped in warm silence, with the hum of insects rising and falling, and then I knew that whatever Daddy had said was true.

"Come see," he commanded, and I realized he must be a little drunk because his steps were just off, just a little too bouncy.

"Where is your horse?" I asked, and he explained over his shoulder that he boarded it at a neighbor's stable. I was disappointed, I had imagined touching the animal, stroking its warm, soft muzzle, even riding in a circle. But the fence around the paddock was falling apart and the grass had grown high, and now it seemed his horse did not belong here, had never lived here.

The interior of the barn was dim and smelled of air that had travelled for centuries through rotting wood and dry earth. Beyond the eight stalls, stacked against the wall where the tack should have been, were tables and chairs with velvet upholstery and several boxes of different shaped glasses. Toeing one box with his foot, Ziad announced, "I got all this for a bargain price from a hotel downtown." I pictured a burned out, shelled hotel, any one of many in the city, and then Ziad hauling these boxes and furniture into his Renault. Impossible. He must have rented a truck.

"The bar will go there," he said, pointing at the opposite wall. "The stalls will be booths," he continued, "and the front will be the dance area."

After every gesture he glanced at me and winked and I saw

the black hair that kept falling over his eyes and the way his shirt was open to his chest. I dug small holes in the dirt with my shoe every time I moved into a different spot, and kept my hands behind my back, as if showing them would weaken me. I wanted to go outside, away from this dim, gray place which seemed to me would never become a disco, because where would people park, first of all, and how would he ever be rid of the smell of animals living in the rafters, and then one cigarette thrown aside and the whole place would burst into flame.

"You seem to have lost interest." He had interrupted himself, and I shook my head and smiled, but when he eyed me seriously instead of continuing, I scrambled for something to say and then he opened a cooler and offered me a beer.

"No thanks," I said, which made me feel foolish so I said, "Who's going to come dance in the middle of a war?" This sounded important, adult. It was a good question. "These are big dreams," I added.

Immediately I knew I had said too much. He raised his eyebrows and then started to laugh and I focused on my feet.

"You're adorable," he said suddenly, and then he walked over to me and I remained rooted to my place on the floor. He tipped my shoulders. He rocked on his heels a little and his expression was sad and handsome.

"What is needed is a revolution," he explained. "This," he waved at the expanse of the barn, "will be a revolution."

His hands, falling from my shoulders, singed the tips of my breasts so that they would never again be the same. His palms were held still against them, as if stopped in surprise, for only two heartbeats, the briefest of moments, but so hot that later I would search the soft wrinkled skin around my nipples, the eyes of the nipples themselves, for burn marks. For now I was immobile, my mind populated with absurd thoughts, such as the swirl of vines on the outside of the barn and the humming of cicadas in trees and the forlorn and naked sight of a car without wheels.

"Sorry," he mumbled, and I saw that he seemed confused. He moved away, shrugged. "I think I should take a nap."

When I reached the door I turned and stared openly at him, devouring the sight of this young man who had inadvertently touched me and who now sat against the door of a stall, hands resting on his knees. He looked at me and smiled a little, just enough to make me feel a certain triumph, because the smile was so tired and drained and made me pity him and his revolution of circling lights and wine-colored leather and women with feather dresses and gold shoes.

For the rest of the summer I lay on the hill smoking cigarettes and imagining Ziad on his white horse, Ziad in his breeches, Ziad in a suit coming to take me away, to elope. He did not visit again. Uncle Haig went to see him a few times, and reported that the disco was coming along, but it was always with sadness that he said this, and later, as everyone had always predicted, the project would be subsumed by the war that even then was moving to the mountains. Sometimes I heard the cropping of hooves on the asphalt road through the village, but the firs obscured the road, and it was too far to run to catch a glimpse of him.

The foreign woman was hardly to be seen and I pretended they had fought, that their love affair was irrevocably finished and that it was only a matter of waiting on this hill, waiting in the car as everyone went into the shop to buy ice cream, *Marianna, What's the matter with you? Come inside*, waiting on the side of the road as Alaine scrambled though the thorns to pick thyme, her face determined and perspiring, waiting until he found me, by chance, on his way somewhere.

It so happened one day, as the girl was watching from behind rocks and trees, I was sitting still with my palms on the open pages of my book when the sound of hooves galloping on the road below the hotel startled me and I stood up suddenly, my book sliding to the floor. I did not leave the room, but remained quite still, listening, and within moments Ziad appeared at the door. My house was swimming in long twilight shadows and I saw through the arched window of the door the ghost-like horse pawing the ground as he leaned down and knocked. I held my breath, I had never seen anything so beautiful, and when I opened the door I laughed, a sound that drifted to the girl through the silence, and Ziad bent down and kissed me. I was embarrassed by my awe of the quality of twilight, predestiner of nostalgia, for after all, I had a part in this.

I sat on the hill and smoked cigarettes and watched the stone house. He arrived twice: once in a jeep and the second time on the horse. He stayed with her a long time, too long for me to wait, my head throbbing and places beneath my skin driving me away in confusion. There is nothing more to remember yet, not in this summer: no image of Ziad turning his head at the sound of a doorbell ringing, of Ziad opening the door and greeting someone, of the surprise on his sunburned face at the discovery that he has been shot.

Or: Ziad sits at a table, swallowing the despair of plans undone by circumstance, of land that has been lost and of houses torn down by soldiers, sold stone by stone to profiteers, and the spinning chamber of a revolver the only sound in the room.

## THE STORY OF THE COUNTRY

"Never mind Ziad," I say to Alaine. "It's everything else, too." This whole place, I want to say, frightens me. The way it is erasing our past. Every day spent within this American wooden house is dulling. I sneak a glance out at Hamish, the gas station attendant across the street, and he stares back through his window above the cash register.

"He's watching us again," I whisper, as if he might hear.

But Alaine has become fascinated by Ziad. She wants to convince me of what she knows to be true. "He died cleaning his gun," she insists. She does not listen when I offer other versions. She says she knows the truth, and that it is as she told me, and so Ziad sits on the edge of his bed, peering into the barrel of a shotgun, one eye squeezed shut, an oily rag in his hand. The apartment is small, a few rooms, furnished with the same kind of furniture that was in the barn where I met him. He pulls the trigger, just to hear the click.

"It's impossible," I repeat. "How can someone so experienced make such a stupid mistake?"

"And Russian Roulette is what? You can't play Russian Roulette with a clip, anyway," she adds, and I am surprised by this illogical resistance to truth.

"He must have had a revolver," I explain.

"He didn't."

How does she know this with certainty? I argue, but she is resolute.

I give in. There is no way to convey how things happened unless one was there. And even then, things get distorted, perhaps even more so. Maybe he did not play this terrible game. Maybe it was as she said, he was cleaning the gun.

"I want to leave," I say. "I could go to Rome and stay with Armen." He is my mother's cousin, and Alaine and I visited him when we were younger.

"You're crazy," she says.

Alaine works in the garden, and her body is thin and muscular. All morning I watch her hands churning through the dark earth, I have had worms thrown at me for being so lazy, I have been amazed by her ability to make this a beautiful place. She looks up from her patch of American land. A clump of earth sticks to her jeans. Her dark, curly hair is tied into a bun with a piece of cloth.

"What's your problem?" she says. "Go do something."

I squat beside her. "The point is," I say, "no one remembers.

Or, at least, everybody remembers a different version." I'm going to get her now. I'm going to prove my point. I ask, "What about the body you found on Crystal Mountain? No one knows if you really found it or not."

Her face becomes a mask. Her face says, "It was half-decomposed. I buried it with my hands."

"I remember." That is all my mouth can form. I stay with her in the garden, rocking back on my heels and holding my knees, while my sister's hands turn over this new earth, drop tulip bulbs into dark holes, pat them into hiding. She is counting on them all the way from now, from Autumn. She says they're for me, to see from my window next spring. She can see below the surface, even after it has been smoothed and the basket of bulbs, the trowel, the bottle of water for drinking have all been carried away. To me, the ground looks empty. From my window, this patch of ground looks like a brown rectangle, nothing more, and my footprints trace its outline, single-file. I am astonished by Alaine's hands. They wind over one another under a stream of water in this aluminum American sink, the dirt from our garden swirling into the drain. She has finished planting all the bulbs. She has finished preparing our garden for spring with the resolute trust that spring will come. Her hands, I understand this now, have always been reaching into the earth and leaving treasures there.

Alaine climbs Crystal Mountain. We called it Crystal Mountain for the many-colored stones jutting from the earth, for the nuggets within them catching the sun. I am eighteen years old and it all happened long ago, but in my dreams she is still so thin, so angry, and me struggling in my sleep, awakened by nothing with the sheets on the floor, exhausted. My mother brings me coffee in the morning. I hardly eat, and my hips jut like Alaine's always have, and at night I lie wide awake, smoking, concentrating.

My mother takes me grocery shopping. I pause at the

beginning of an aisle, overwhelmed by the rows of colors and shapes yawning away towards the frozen meats in the distance, smooth yellow-white floor. My mother disappears. I start crying like a child. I wait outside on the curb. I stare at my ankles and feet through my hair, listening for the approach of strangers, but no one comes to help me. After some time, my mother emerges, dragging behind her the two-wheeled metal cart packed with groceries. We walk the twenty minutes home, the cart rattling and banging behind us. It shames me, this cart, which is all we have in a land of cars. The cart folds into a flat version of itself and stands on its two rubber wheels behind the kitchen door. Occasionally it loses its balance and falls over, pushing the door closed. I kick it. I kick it all over the floor and into the wall until my father runs in and rescues it, like saving a bent and bruised pet. I cry at the way he examines it with such worry.

America: This is the land where people want to be, that is what my mother tells me now, all these years later. She tells me, "There is nothing wrong with liking it; after all, why do you think so many people want to live here?" The truth of this disturbs me. But if I myself like it here, fully accept the black shining streets, the smell of grass early in the morning, the absence of dirt, I will relinquish the last faded hope of going back. That hope can only subsist on the feeling of not belonging, of being a temporary visitor. I have my expired membership to the beach club, my university I.D.s, my outdated identity card that says I belong there, that I am allowed to be there. First they stay in my wallet, then they lie rubber banded in a drawer, then a box, and finally I preserve them smooth and glossy beneath the plastic sheath in my album. I feel guilty when I look at these old creased cards. I once threw them on tables, or lost them carelessly and then replaced them, and now they are so precious that I collect them in a small monument, along with all my photographs, as if they are images themselves. These objects which had been so regular in their real life, when they served a commonplace purpose, are now relics to be worshipped, talismans that will guarantee a return one day, it is absurd. I must not think this way. It is as if there is a hidden law created in moving, a law against remembering, and I am breaking it.

Alaine climbs Crystal Mountain. She grapples with stones and dirt with the agility she has always had, winding her way through the clumps of prickly bushes and climbing higher and higher. I don't know who called it Crystal Mountain. The mountain had small muddy fossils and pieces of flint which waited there for us during the millennia after the oceans receded, now company to soldiers' cigarette butts and spent shells from machine guns and shrapnel near small craters where someone might have died. Alaine climbs grimly, leaving us behind, leaving us in the white house where we throw stones at stray sheep and practice shooting at the branches of the olive tree. At the top of the hill lies the soldier's camp, and just below, a flat area where she likes to hide and think and turn in on herself like an imploding device. Alaine's face is flushed with this voyage, dark eyes livid with sorrows we do not understand. She carries a knapsack with paper and pens, the GI Joe with the shaven face, a few bullets from her collection for good luck.

When she finds the soldier's corpse, at first she remains still, and then she looks back towards us, as if we might have disappeared in that second when her eyes first careened across the features of the dead. Sitting next to the corpse after it is buried, knees tucked under her chin and the spoils of his death ready to carry away, the story of the country is caught in the dirt on her hands and legs, that history of a place abandoned by a retreating sea that should never have left, that should have preserved this land in silence.

# THE DYING THAT IS COMING FOR HIM

I am fourteen and when the lawyer picks me up for Ziad's costume party, Mummy smiles and trusts him and we go, and it is in this way that history might be changed, because in this moment nothing has happened yet, there is still a year or two until his death.

The nightclub is by the sea. The road leading down the hill is decorated on either side with beautifully manicured cacti and white boulders, and palm trees rustle and the lights sparkle over the water and people in costumes push past when I stop to gape at the wonders. A tall woman swathed in great white feathers spins by, accompanied by a man in a cape, and more people, so many more, in glittering shoes and gowns and masks and gloves and the lawyer pulls me, Come on, it's time.

We enter the nightclub through a magnificent arched doorway and the lights reflected off the mirror ball speckle arms and faces and walls, going round and round, and Ziad is there, a drink in one hand and the other resting on a woman's shoulder. How do you describe the handsomeness of someone who will die in so many ways, his story distorted and ridiculed and retold? Possibly his hair is still black and curly, his skin dark from the sun that shines on an irresponsible, capricious lifestyle, and it could be that he is dressed in white since this is his farewell party and he is the prince. His silk shirt reflects the warm glow of the spinning lights, the radiance of his revolution so long in the making.

In the back office, the walls trembling with the beats of music, with the laughter and shouting and dancing outside, Ziad lowers his forehead to the desk, his temples sore with the headache of orchestrating such happiness in the midst of a war. The office smells of leather and cigarettes. I stand in the corner, the princess, waiting to be kissed.

"Do you remember," he says at last, "how the horse waited in the shade while I spent whole afternoons in her house?" and of course I do, these are not details to be discarded, and the horse's eyes are half shut, tail slapping at flies, and its great white wings are folded and the feathers flutter in a breeze scented with pine. Ziad stands up, he is more animated now that everything is coming back, that unrepressed joy at having invented a solution to the war. He cannot be restrained: he is destined to live and live and live, and the war means nothing to him nor to me, it is a figment, a kite streamer of contradictions and promises, of cease-fires and gunshots dismantling the sky, so he paces the room and his shirt dampens with sweat as he draws the fantastic images of the future in the air, his hands shaping this new world. He will steal for all this, he tells me, he will steal and steal and he does not care. Ziad is malicious, handsome: he is too much for this war that cannot contain him.

On the beach we slide the kayak into the water. I lie on my back while he paddles, and my head is at the prow and the sea rushes past my ears, sloshing onto our bodies, cold and unforgiving of what will come and of my frail attempt to avert it, and on the shore the party wails on, lighting up the waves and the rocks and the trees. When the sea is deep, when the party has become a flickering parade of lights, Ziad tucks the paddle between us, puts his arms around me, and I think I might have done it now, rescued him from the dying that is coming for him. His breath spreads and fades regularly on my damp cheek and he whispers, "There is nothing this country can do to me," and this might have been possible, for him to say such a thing.

The sky is vast. Before us, between our tangled feet, the mountains divide the stars from the earth, and behind us, for we are lying with our heads to the west, the mammoth battleships distort the line of the sea. We float here, Ziad and I, between the fierceness of his living and my memory of it, between the silence of the American fleet and the coming winter bombardment, between lips and hands and ink that is smudged in anger. If we could only stay here long enough.

None of this can be remembered. If it were to fit into history, then the killing of the foreign soldiers and the following bombardment of Souq al-Gharb by the American fleet is only months away, and soon the hotel in Dhour al-Shweir where my grandparents celebrated their wedding, scandalizing the proprietors, will be destroyed by the Syrians, or Phalanges, or Israelis, what does it matter, and the roads lined with firs and olive groves will be impassable. People will vanish, and Uncle Haig and Auntie Firyal will crawl along the side of Crystal Mountain, shooting chickens, scrounging for food, while Druze fighters fire rockets from the road below the Armenian hotel. The owner of the hotel, whose worried, silent daughters will be with us in Beirut, will beg these soldiers to arrange themselves elsewhere and they, surprisingly, will comply. Uncle Haig and Auntie Firyal will descend from the mountain in winter, alive as saints, thinner, full of anecdotes about stupid gunmen and vegetables and fruit growing in gardens that are wildly luxuriant, dumb to the war and left to flourish without restraint. In this time Ziad was there, and he too, grew wild and untended. But now, none of this matters, it is not important Ziad breathes against my cheek, his arms around me, and the sea that has no illusions rocks beneath us and the land waits for him to yield with the security of things ordained.

---

\* The narrator, Marianna, is located in the present time in the United States, where her
family has been living for a year. She moves between past and present as she recalls
the stories of her childhood in Lebanon and tries to come to terms with her new life.
These excerpts have been drawn together from different parts of the book.

# Sharif S. Elmusa

# THE LOVE SONG OF IBRAHIM ABDELMADI
## and other poems

NO STATUES WERE BUILT IN THE CAMP

And it came to pass,
we lost the war
and became refugees.
It is always the beginning.
My father lugged me on his arms,
a bundle of hope, of a country's pain,
and panted across plain
and up heaving mountain,
without a compass, heading east,
on his peasant feet
and adequate fear.

We set down in a desert
without the sinuous sands
of the movies, in a camp,
by the gateless Jericho.
In that flawed landscape,
under the shadow of the dark rocks
of the Mount of Temptation
the world was kind to us.
The United Nations, our godfather,

99

doled out flour and rice
and cheddar, "yellow," cheese--
sharp beyond our palettes.

My father remembered
his twelve olive trees
every day for ten years.
> *When the peasants told the olive tree*
> *if she felt for their toil,*
> *she'd yield not olives, but tears,*
> *the tree answered:*
> 'Tears you have enough; I give you oil
> to light your lamps, nourish, heal.'"
Then one day he let go. Let go.
My father was no Ulysses.
He found a new land
and stayed away on the farm,
eking out some rough happiness.

My mother stayed home,
shepherded a pack of twelve,
cleaned and yelled,
and, for punishment,
summoned father's shadow.
She stuffed our thin bones with sentiment,
as if to make us immobile.
The mud-brick hut wasn't hers.
The rain running barefoot in the streets
wasn't real. Her past was insatiable:
The new house they had just built,
with windows on four sides,
windows tall and arched
to let in the ample light,
to spread out the prayers;
how my father rushed to ask for her hand

the day after she had kept him in line
at the water well;
the sweet-scented blood of her brother
lying dead in the police station,
killed by the discriminate bullets
of the British soldiers.

No statues were built in the camp;
the dead would have been ashamed.
The living dreamed--
the dreams of the wounded.
In the shops and houses, the radio was the hearth,
and the news the oracle.

THE LOVE SONG OF
IBRAHIM ABDELMADI

*Tomorrow*, she says.
I roll back the calendar and wait.
The kisses are there, on my lips, waiting.
A man in love is a primal presence waiting.
She tosses and turns in my chest.
O how I suffer her constant motion.
But I slight the pain, like a mother,
and swaddle myself in silence.
I confuse my eyes with her eyes.
I see the crystal water behind the mirage.
Faith is the yeast of love,
and faith and love are in the waiting.

Tomorrow.
What does it matter where we are--
in a white grotto,
on a second-hand couch,
or on the edge of a knife.
Our words are lush like summer leaves.
Our bodies aren't thinking
about us. They merge without an edge
in the ancient rhythm of joy,
joy flowing to their eyelids.
Even the night can't contain their fire
and the herd of cries they unleash
to be quenched. Quenched.

Ah (the Ah doesn't delight that's not uttered),
my aches have been cleansed,
like the sins of an old man
who makes the pilgrimage to Mecca.
The earth feels so firm beneath my feet
I can walk on water.

Is this the everlasting?
Is this the woman I love?
Am I awake or dreaming?
*Tomorrow,* she says.

## JUXTAPOSITIONS

The Prophets have convinced us
if we (don't) believe in them,
we (don't) believe in God.
What a cosmic sleight of logic.
What a juxtaposition of God and Man.
The Surrealists, too, took a shot
at juxtaposition with their automatic hands.
Their *Marvelous* was the chance meeting
not of God and Man
but of *an umbrella and a sewing machine
on a dissection table.*
Poor Lautreamont! Poor Breton!
Their leap was a hop, their dream
are-arrangement of the real.
How many faithful can they count on?
How many would be willing to spill
their blood and the blood of others
on their dissection table?


## SOLILOQUY

When I was a boy I didn't want to die
before a woman with a candid body
filled my arms,
her tongue danced with my tongue,
her teeth crashed with my own
and passion flowed between us in the slow night.

When the likeness of her came
I was in college, away from home,
and I leapt out of bed

each time I thought I could die
and be flown back in a box,
unable to wave to my father at the airport
and hand him my fresh, family diploma.

Alas, there are always reasons to live for.

I have now causes that lose,
poems I've failed to write,
a wife and children-- a counterweight.
It's almost midnight, and they're asleep.
I'm downstairs, in the living-room,
rocking in the rocking chair,
smoking a pipe. I stuff the bowl,
a pinch at a time,
sniff the aroma, and strike a match.
I bask, like the smoke, in my own dissolution.
Last night my dead cousin called
and said he and grandmother had found a house,
a pleasant white house on a hilltop,
then asked me to join them for dinner.
Tomorrow I'll race up and down
        the steep
          subway
        stairs
          to test
            my breath.

REQUEST

Poets, critics,
members of other tribes,
please, let's not reduce the poetry
of the tribe
 into a sheepskin of poems
about the tribe.

# Evelyn Accad

# ALL AROUND STILL
## from my *cancer journal*

*Urbana, March 20th, 1996*

Since I was diagnosed with cancer, I have begun noticing more acutely people who truly achieve things in life, though remaining virtually anonymous, as opposed to those who boast all the time but achieve little. It is fortunate that such people exist on this earth. It makes it worthwhile to be alive.

For example, there is Rod, my neighbor. He lives to help others. He has divested himself of all material possessions, as much as he possibly can. I admire the way he lives. I feel less sympathetic for those surrounding me in academia, who seem to succeed better in the system, by making more money, and getting invited to all kinds of prestigious places. Many of them complain to me, but their recriminations do not touch me any more. I look at what Rod and Alban manage to achieve in humility and silence, without the constant boasting I hear from others. There is also Théophile who lives the true message of the Gospel.

Among the women I admire, there is Marianne F. who was able to move to high positions in academia, within her field, and even in administrative posts, without losing sight of the really important issues, without taking herself too seriously, remaining humble and attentive to others, and there is Andrée Chedid always so humble, in spite of her success, her many awards and achievements, she truly practices what she writes:

*THE JOURNEY*

From obstacles to terraces
From branches to darkness
The journey is merciless
Go    hand in hand
with so many others
Their fire    your fire
will be allied
Move on
The earth will take your shape
It abolishes only your mirrors!
In spite of our enclosures,
       our Babels, our ravages, somewhere
             the word converges and unites us.

These beautiful people are the role models I look up to, the ones I would like to emulate, I feel there is quite a ways to go.

*Urbana, April 8th, 1996*

I have had many dreams lately, about Mother. In the first one I was adopting a little girl, between 6 and 9 years old in Lebanon. She was chubby, wore glasses and had a walkman on. Her parents, a couple I had actually met while visiting Lebanon, had been forced to get married because the wife had got pregnant, and at present they no longer had the financial means to meet the expenses of raising the child. Adelaide told them I would be willing to take her on condition she bore my name. I wanted her to have my name. Mother and Adelaide were happy about my decision and were telling the couple: "We told you she would take her." But I was thinking: "How am I going to raise that child who will not want to listen to me because of her walkman, and who will not want to communicate. How will I manage? I see Juanita with Laxsmi, she has quite a few problems even though her daughter is extraordinarily intelligent and charming. But how will I manage, what should I do?"

Another dream, another night. I was in my Paris apartment. Lots of people wanted me to put them up, among them Mother and Adelaide. I was telling Mother: "What shall I do to find space for everyone?" Mother was reassuring me: "We have already found our place, we have settled in." There were lots of beds stacked up on two or more levels. I later narrated my dreams over the phone to Mother. She said to me: "How nice, what beautiful dreams!" I was told that after my call, they found her still holding the receiver smiling and talking. She thought I was still on the other end talking to her! My sweet mother, I hope she will still be alive this summer when I go to Lebanon. I am told she sleeps most of the time and barely wakes up for one or two hours a day. I was also told she often talks to Father as if he were sleeping next to her!

Zohreh lent me the April 1996 issue of *Time* magazine on prostate cancer. It is a real epidemic. One in five men are expected to get it and soon there will be as many deaths every year from it as with breast cancer, about 50,000 deaths! Most of the treatments lead to some form of impotence and incontinence. And hormonotherapy works only for a certain time. After that, cancerous cells manage to circumscribe the treatment. It makes one shiver to read all that. There has not been much progress for this plague; no absolutely reliable tests to detect how aggressive the cancer is, no progress in the therapies. It is a terrible disease which men are barely starting to talk about.

General Schwartzcoff, who led the Gulf war, made the front cover of the magazine, represented as leading the war against prostate cancer! Always war vocabulary and images to deal with cancer! He had his tumor completely excised, the most reliable procedure if there is no metastasis, but also a risky operation because in a very delicate place connected to other organs.

A reassuring telephone call from Miriam today. Her eye

operation to remove skin cancer on her eyelid had gone very well. It was a small, rather mild type of cancer and it did not disfigure her. What a relief! I had worried so much, she had sounded in such panic when first diagnosed!

I am reading *A Woman's Decision: Breast Cancer* by Karen Berger and John Bostwick. It was loaned to me by Dr. de Camara whom I went to consult about possible reconstruction. I would like to have read this book before my treatment and the decisions I thought I had been given. It would have helped a lot to have all the information this book provides and to see pictures of reconstructed breasts less frightening and more esthetically acceptable than anything I have seen so far.

*Urbana, April 15th, 1996*

Séverine came for lunch today. She was quite depressed. She has pain in her bladder. She knows her days are numbered. She needs solitude and not everybody understands that. There are some people she avoids and whose messages she does not answer. Alban told her about the Chinese doctor he had seen this weekend for a problem with his hand and who had helped him so much. He practices both traditional and alternative medicine, is very soft-mannered, and made a great impression on Alban as well as help him with the pain in his hand. Alban thought Séverine ought to try to get in touch with this doctor. Séverine told me Resa's cancer had come back. She is only 42 and had been free of her first cancer for more than 10 years. I never thought she would have to hurt and go through that hell again. She has no insurance since she had been treated in France. What is she going to do?

I am also depressed because Israel is bombarding the South of Lebanon. There are 300,000 refugees who do not know where to go. It is supposed to represent a cleaning up of the Hizbollah. But why are they attacking civilians? They have killed almost a hundred women and children who had taken refuge in a United Nations compound. It is like a cancer coming back into my dear country, Lebanon.

Today I was telling myself: "Stop the world, I want to get off." I find it too hard to live in times like these. I realize what a toll the Lebanese war has taken on my life. I could not bear its recurrence just as I cannot bear to hear of cancer recurrences in my friends.

Fighting an all-out war and aggressively fighting cancer both serve only to shift the problem from the source to the symptoms. Both situations are preventable, both are expressions of failure to resolve imbalances while there is still time. Cancer and wars of mass destructions are the hallmarks of this century, of a world bursting at the seams with contradictions and spiraling conflict.

*O'Hare Airport, May 15th, 1996*

My life always unfolds in airports, planes, trains, ships, meeting places, arrival and departure spots. Not so long ago, I was going to meet my parents. They were in Switzerland. Not so long ago, they were in relatively good shape, very young at heart, full of life and projects. Now Father is dead and Mother is close to death.

Life goes by too quickly.

Not so long ago, I had just been hired at the University of Illinois. Zohreh was holding one of her young boys in her arms. We were both at the beginning of our careers. Now she has undergone three operations and a heavy chemotherapy treatment. The last operation was for horrible pains in her stomach caused by skin adhesions strangling her intestines. They are the result of her ovariectomy but are also caused by stress and nervousness. We must both learn to relax and avoid stress, but it is very difficult to do so in the academic system.

We had a very difficult winter, icy and freezing cold and no springtime. I am glad to be leaving for a while. I am anxious to be with Alban.

*Tunis, May 26th, 1996*

I understand why my play, *The Daughters of Taher Haddad*, could not be performed in Tunis again. There are too many tensions and dissensions between the women acting in it. Everything is so hard here! I wonder how it ever managed to get produced in the first place. It came to fruition the first time around on an impulse of the heart, a surge of enthusiasm. Now the heart is gone, the quarrels have wounded and erased it. The play had to stop.

We celebrated Azza's birthday. Her father came to share the birthday cake. He spoke about illness as of an evil one programs in oneself. His remarks made me angry and revolted. I said that such remarks were intended to victimize the victim, that I was surprised to hear such comments from a former Marxist. But I should not have been so astonished because reformed Marxists, like most converts, are often worse than others because they have had to fight against the very thing they believed in, were hooked on, or practised before. He said to me: "Before, we used to suffer for the workers, the miners, etc., we got sick fighting for them, but it was useless since there was nothing we could do anyway. Now we try to transform things from ourselves, from our own wounds. It is much more effective." I replied that one ought to do both, work on and from the inside and the outside.

I thought of Séverine, who is suffering so much, who is dying of the same ovarian cancer that killed her mother, and of her daughter who screams every time she hears anyone mention cancer or recurrences. I thought of the letter Séverine wrote to Eric Siegel and other positive thinkers, all those who think that miracles spring from one's conscience, that they come about because one wills them to do so through working spiritually on the conscience.

As my sweet Deirdre (who had come along with Cindy on this trip) well remarked: "It is easy to speak about healing oneself from the inside when one has not been sick. It is a

112

completely different story when devastating diseases hit us in our flesh."

*Tunis, May 29th, 1996*

I am on the train going from Tunis to La Marsa with Cindy and Deedee. Yesterday we visited Manoubia in a popular district between Gammarth and La Marsa. It was thanks to Deirdre who made special contact with Manoubia, Meriem's cleaning lady, that we were able to go. It was an incredible experience, the height of our stay in Tunis.

Manoubia bought a piece of land in that district with some help from her father. She started building parts of her house slowly with the help of some neighbors who also provided her with an electric line since she does not have electricity yet. She was so excited about receiving us even though she felt sick and had temperature. She got all kinds of things out for us: jewelry, different objects, incense she burnt on her *kanoun*, music she played on a boombox flashing psychedelic lights, a great number of cassettes, talismans like an old dried up chameleon whose head she cut to put in her doorlock. She danced with Meriem. It was very moving. Deirdre had brought her a white big towel from the States. She gave her an African-Arab dress. Deedee put it on and Meriem placed a cushion at the belly emplacement, screaming ululations. And they were making wishes for a baby to be conceived.

Manoubia was full of an incredible exhuberance. She showed us her driver's license, the paper for her land acquisition. She told us that her brother had asked for half of her land to build on. She had refused telling him she did not get along with his wife. He said he would stop talking to her if she did not accept. She replied he did not really love her if he loved her only for the things she could give him. He no longer speaks to her. He even refuses to see her if she goes to visit them, pretending he is not there.

What strength this woman has! What courage! She told us

that the people of her district talk behind her back because she lives alone. She was married and divorced after seven years. Now she prefers to live alone. She is making all kinds of future plans to enlarge her yard, get a shower, improve her rooms. When she gets home, she sews, she listens to music, she is happy to be alone. Her only anxiety is to die alone in the house without anybody noticing. Her mother died when she was fifteen. Her father remarried. He backs her up and gives her all the support he can. She showed us his picture kissing it to express her deep love for him. She invited Deedee and her husband to come and stay with her the next time they visit Tunisia.

I was remembering Umm Ashraf and some other women I had visited in the popular districts of Cairo. They were not as independent and had not been able to assert themselves like Manoubia. Their condition seemed much more desperate, and the environment they lived in quite sordid compared to Manoubia.

*Tunis, May 30th, 1996*

I did a kynesthesiology session with Amel. She made me go back to untie the knots of my past, first in my mother's womb, my feeling of well-being as well as my fear of hurting her; then at nine, the negative image I had of myself as too plump, my desire to be different; at 33, my divorce, the war in Lebanon; at 50, cancer and my fear to hurt other people. What came back over and over again was my fear of hurting other people while I should be thinking more about myself, remarked Amel. I had read it was important to understand and untie those knots which represent the unresolved dramas of my past, I must undo them in order to heal completely. I was thankful to Amel for making me do this work and helping me find these wounds.

Amel tells me it is incredible and strange how my fear of hurting other people keeps coming back. I believe that the session I had with her also reflects my relationship with her.

114

When I learnt that she had suffered so much at the announcement of my illness that she had felt as if the earth was shaking under her feet, it hurt me to be hurting her that much. It is true that I do not like to cause pain in other people especially the ones I love.

*Paris, June 17th, 1996*

Joy and Joël are here in Paris with me, Augustus is arriving to-morrow. I got closer to Joy because we had time together alone. She told me about her life. Her father martyrized her mother so much, by taking a second wife and throwing her out of the house, that she lost her mind. She is considered clinically insane, but Joy thinks her condition is the result of her suffering. She reacts as if she had lost her mind. Joy was raised in an orphanage with two of her sisters. The orphanage was Chinese Methodist and they taught her the Bible and about Christianity, even if it was quite superficial according to her.

One of her sisters and her best friend left the orphanage to enter prostitution, a move Joy did not understand. She believes that one can make money in Singapore through work other than prostitution. She has convinced her sister to get out of it, she has let her use apartment. She would like to convince her best friend to do the same, but it will not be easy. Joy was crying telling me about how her mother had been forced to live in an asylum and on the street, with only a plastic bag containing all of her belongings; she would carry it everywhere, sleeping during the last years of her life on the steps of the temple, her only refuge. She remembers her mother, coming to the orphanage to see them, and bringing them rice and chicken, and how much it must have cost her to get such a dish! She watch her three daughters eat, making sure they had equal portions.

I told Joy I understood why Augustus was so concerned about helping orphans and why he had told me one day that if anything happened to him he wanted us to take care of Joy. Joy started crying again; she does not like to remember all these

115

painful memories and rarely talks about them.

Augustus told her that I would include her story in one of my books if she agreed to open up about it, which is what I am presently doing, not only to keep that promise, but to provide yet another example that the diseases that women suffer are often social diseases, from spousal abuse, to prostitution to total rejection by society. Joy's case is not an isolated one, but is painfully familiar: she confesses to us that her father was completely irresponsible and abusive, that he never cared for any of his children, including those of a third wife that was discovered by Joy's family only after his death. Home is where the hurt is among many of the women of the world.

I had a lot of joy getting to know Joy better. She has a beautiful dimension and is very warm. I used to think she was rather cold, but it was probably due to shyness rather than distance. We got much closer this time and I love the way she is raising Joël. She is so calm and attentive. The little boy reflects this calmness and assurance. He looks very secure and at ease.

*On the plane, Beirut-Paris, June 25th, 1996*
Théophile said to me: "Don't put off for too long your trip to see Mother," so when Ghassan Tuéni sent me a ticket to go help organize a conference on Mediterranean poetry, I seized the opportunity to travel to Lebanon, even though I am scheduled to go there again in July to take care of Mother. Théophile is not one to be alarmist. If he thinks Mother has little time left to live, it must be true.

Alban had hoped that his doctor would tell him he could stop taking the anti-testosterone treatment, since it is making him impotent, but his doctor said he should not stop. His PSA has dropped to 0.3 which is good, and shows that the cancerous cells are reacting to the treatment, but there may still be some left, escaping and traveling around, ready to metastasize. There is no absolutely reliable control for them. This disease is really frightening.

Can we call it "to make love" when only one of us has an orgasm and when the other is prevented from reaching those heights?

Alban tells me he gets a lot of pleasure out of giving me pleasure, but I get frustrated because I cannot satisfy him the way I used to. I find it so unfair. It is just one more of the many forms of "collateral damage" that this unjust cancer war has inflicted upon us.

Jane told me to recall that the killing of Iraqi civilians during the Gulf War was euphemistically referred to by the military as "collateral damage"!

My trip to Lebanon was painful but essential. Mother has only skin left on her bones. She weighs 48 kilos. Some of her bones are even showing through in certain places. Adelaide is very sweet with her. She puts her in fetal position in the bed for more comfort. She changes her bed sheets and her clothes several times a week and sometimes twice a day to make her feel better. Mother has to be spoon-fed and I did that for her. I also sang which made her very happy. She, who used to love singing and from whom I inherited my voice, can barely speak, let alone sing. I could tell hearing me was almost like singing herself again, her whole face beamed with joy in spite of the pain she suffers all over her body. So I sang and I sang, religious and folk songs, Swiss and French songs from Piaf to Brel, songs in English and Arabic, whatever came to mind. I did my entire repertory for my mother. I find it so therapeutic to sing!

The house in the mountains where the organization of the conference took place, the Nadia Tuéni Foundation in Beit Merri, is a dream place. Located in a pine forest, it overlooks Beirut and the Mediterranean. Faraway from pollution and car noises, I can imagine how Nadia Tuéni got inspired to write her poignant poetry in such surroundings. I found Ghassan Tuéni touching with his fidelity to the memory of this woman, this extraordinary Lebanese Francophone poet I teach in my classes in the States. Her text, *June and the Miscreants* adapted for the theater by Roger Assaf, was being played at the Beirut theater during the time I was there. Four women, four different Lebanese identities, four religions representing Lebanon (the Druze, the Christian, the Muslim and the Jewish), four voices and four ways, four wounds, expressing their despair, their suffering, their joys and their sorrow against the background of the outbreak of war:

> Can one keep the desert from leaving with one's body
> naked as a prayer
> O sumptuous rottenness
> each day is a resurrection
> with the earth's complicity
> all those unconcerned with the sun
> make a liquid noise
> the nights
> here and there
> have the flight of birds in their eyes
> and I cry the time of a star
> the one who stole my death

(p. 125, Naḍia Tuéni, Juin et les mécréantes, in *Les œuvres poétiques complètes*, my translation)

It was very moving to be in Lebanon, center of culture, crossroads of fascinating exchanges, a country which has suffered so much, to be with people I communicate with at the deepest level.

*On the plane, Beirut-Paris, July 20th, 1996*

I went back to Lebanon a month later to be with Mother, and to take care of her. I walked around the campus of the Beirut University College in Ras-Beirut. In my childhood and adolescence, these hills were still wild, covered with field flowers, birds singing and little torrents of water flowing downhill whenever it rained. Now they are disfigured with

118

luxurious concrete buildings, empty because few people can afford them. It is sad to see Beirut transformed into a huge construction monster.

Some young people came to see me. We had coffee several times at the CityCafé right below BUC. It is a very polluted and noisy spot, but I was glad to visit with them. I told them about my life, how and what I had lived in my adolescence, expressed in my novel *L'excisée*. I told them I believed that Christ had come to liberate and not to chain people with rules and dogmas. I felt things had not really changed since my youth; rather, the bleaker side of history seemed to be repeating itself and spiraling out of control. The promises of modernization had not been kept, the specter of chaos and disease looms greater than ever.

I got interrupted in my writing by a conversation with my cabin neighbor, Fatima, a woman from Saïda, in the South of Lebanon. It is the first time she has traveled on an airplane. Her brothers in Canada sent her a ticket to cheer her up after her husband died of liver cancer at the age of 41, two years ago. She has four children, the youngest of whom is three years old. Her mother is taking care of her. She cries while talking to me about how much she misses her husband. They had loved each other since childhood and got along so well. She also lost her father to cancer when she was quite young. Her mother raised the family by herself.

Her husband had been feeling well until the disease hit him suddenly. Nothing could save him. She is now very conscious of food and the environment. She gave me the title of a book in Arabic, *Al-Shifa' Bi 'Ayat Al Qur'an*, about healing through herbs and verses cited in the Qur'an. She told me that *habb al baraka*, the anti-cancer grains Maria had given me to take, were cited in the Qur'an. (Alban tells me it is a medicinal plant described in many medical books).

Fatima explained to me how it needs to be washed and browned in a pan; it produces its own oil. In Saudi Arabia, oil is extracted from it and sold on the market. One can also grind it to make a paste. It can be used in all kinds of dishes, as a rubbing ointment or taken as medicine. She tells me about dates, supposed to be excellent against cancer, and garlic. One should eat a raw piece of garlic at least once a day. One should avoid meats, eat only fish. (Her husband did not like fish). I tell her about cabbage, carrots, lemons. I was deeply moved by this woman from the south of my country. We cried when we parted company. I guided her to the plane she was to take in Paris for Canada.

Cancer is really everywhere.

*On the plane, Paris-Chicago, August 30th, 1996*
We saw doctors for Alban because of his headaches and of how diminished he had been feeling, as a result of the medical treatment he was undergoing. The doctor told us that one could not suppress a hormone like Alban's treatment does without "side" effects: fatigue, aging, etc. Alban said: "It is hard to be deprived of sexuality the way I am!" The doctor suggested Prozac to "improve his mood" (I could hardly believe it!) and painkillers for his headaches. I was glad Alban could express himself, but I thought of the impasse we are in and the "solutions" proposed by doctors. What can we do? Where to turn?

The day before I had gone shopping. I saw lots of bras with little pockets to fill underneath the breasts; it lifts and pushes the breasts up. They are called WonderBras (or something to that effect). It is a new popular fashion to show round breasts overflowing the bras. I noticed there were no bras with pockets for prostheses. No consciousness for the disease hitting a tenth of the population! I looked at these bras I could no longer wear.

I can hardly believe it. I knew it had to happen, but I kept hoping for a miracle. My little sister Séverine died, yesterday morning at 8:30 in the morning. It was Zohreh who called me to let me know. She left a message on my answering machine telling me it would be healing for them to have me there for the various ceremonies that are going to take place to-morrow back in the U. S.

I was glad to be extremely busy packing, but I could not help thinking about Séverine all the time anyway. Her death hurts me deeply. She wanted so much to live to see her daughter at least through high-school, but even that was not granted her! I will miss her terribly. It is hard and so unjust!

*Beirut Airport, Dec. 30th, 1996*
So much is happening all the time in Lebanon. My heart is heavy and light from all the wounds, slowly healing, reopening quickly with the slightest movement of wings, with any aggressivity, with every harsh word, with each painful image, with each nailing dogma, with all the reminiscences this country holds for me.

Mother is no longer here. She died in September, a few days before her birthday (Father had also died the month of his birthday.) I hope they are together now, united in their eternal love!

Noureddine Aba also died a few days after Mother. He certainly is one of the most human and touching of North Africa's writers, poets and playwrights I know. I remember when Emile had given me his ninety-page-long dramatic poem on Palestine. I was a student at Indiana University. I had been so moved by it, I had cried and cried reading it; I translated it in one stretch (Noureddine also wrote it in one stretch after viewing films of Palestinians burnt with napalm by Israëlis during the 1967 war), and Jay illustrated it with very fine, incredibly elaborate pen and ink drawings.

I was very inexperienced and shy at the time. Emile had encouraged me to go meet the writer as I had a stop in Paris on my way to Lebanon. And this is how I developed a long friendship with Noureddine Aba and his wife Madeleine. My translation subsequently got published into a bilingual edition,

*Montjoie Palestine! or Last Year in Jerusalem* (L'Harmattan, 1980.) The Abas came several times to the States for conferences and to teach. And I visited them in Algeria.

Aba had recently started a Foundation that gave prizes to Francophone writers, a courageous act in light of the very intransigent, Arabo-Islamic nationalistic atmosphere prevalent in Algeria. He could not get his money out of his country and decided that giving prizes to Francophone writers and researchers would be his contribution to struggling against intolerance and obscurantism in the country he loved so much, whose violence was tearing him apart.

Madeleine sent to people who knew him and had written her, in lieu of an *adieu*, a few lines from, *Le chant perdu au pays retrouvé*. They express Noureddine's deep faith, a message of hope; Madeleine believes it must absolutely be transmitted:

.....And so that everything will be said, I add:
that it is not the origins which make man
but man which gives to the origins
their value, their richness,
that it is not the country which makes a man
but man who gives to countries
their prestige and their light and their spirit,
that it is he, the quality of his love,
the strength of his faith,
which are its ligneous and indestructible stem
which gives birth to its branches
which carry hope
of a unique fraternity
in tune with the universe...

....Tomorrow I will depart
before the sun
is high in the sky....
(my translation)

It was hard to see Mother's empty bed, and even harder to see the painful expression of Sana, the fiancée of one of my nephews, as she gazed at my Mother's empty bed. Father's place has already been empty for more than two years, since my cancer started.

We are all here in Lebanon, we, the five children of this incredible couple that were my parents. We are making plans. We have all kinds of projects to start fulfilling our parents' dreams. We talk as if we still had more than half of our lives to live. But I believe it is more like a quarter of it that remains, if we are lucky!!

Nevertheless it is good to be making these plans, to start building structures, in both the concrete and spiritual sense of the term, and to mobilize people to work and live within them to help the abused, those whose lives have been thrown into disorder by the war and an endless series of aggressions of all kinds. It is good to be all here, united in wanting to realize our parents' vision, in building Bridges of Peace so much needed, to be constructed between the various communities, in this part of the world. Will my nieces and nephews be as careful with my wishes? Can I count on them as Father counted on me?

While in Lebanon I visited the women's prison in Ba'abdat with Agnès and her daughter Anne. We were bringing them Christmas presents, and Agnès asked me to bring my guitar to sing. The prison is right next to the hospital. There are four rooms, approximately twenty to thirty square meters each, with between twelve to twenty women in each room. The women were all lined up next to each other. Most of them were chain-smoking and it was quite unbearable and impossible to breathe in these rooms where only a tiny dormer window close to the ceiling lets in barely a ray of light and air. Stifling rooms, wounded humanity, most of the women came from the most disadvantaged levels of society.

There were a few foreign women, a small group of Sri-Lankans, thrown in jail for lack of proper papers

123

("*sans-papiers*"!). The group was not smoking and I thought of how hard it probably was for them to be suffocating in such an atmosphere without the means or possibility to say anything, or go out to breathe some fresh air.

Agnès told me that the food was atrocious, looked more like vomit than food. The women who have families get their food from their families and they often share it with other prisoners. I thought of these poor foreign women often persecuted in their own countries, hoping to earn a little money through slave work in Lebanon, ending up in these prisons were they are left to rot.

We distributed some presents and sweets, we sang and talked with the women. There was one woman whose presence struck me. Very beautiful, all dressed in black, all hunched up in a corner, crying, refusing to talk. Her beautiful white face with a halo of jet black shining hair, was all puffed up from crying. The women around her were trying to console her, feeling sorry for her. They told us she had been there for only a short time. According to them, she was innocent; a dancer in a cabaret, there had been a police raid the night she was stopped and thrown into jail. Her back hurt because she had been beaten up.

Towards the end, as we were leaving, she accepted to talk to us. I said to her: "Soon you will be out, your brother has come to get you out. The women here told me you were innocent. You did not do anything bad." She said to me: "I did something bad." I asked her what: "I threw out this bastard who was trying to abuse me!" She reminded me of Ferdaws, the character of Nawal El Saadawi's *Woman at Point Zero*. I wonder what happened to her.

I am thinking of Yvette's niece. She was kidnapped and strangled one day when she was going to school in Philadelphia. A beautiful young teen-age girl, innocent, trusting, opening up to life, brutally crushed in the prime of her youth. Yvette is crying rivers of tears, tears that will never run dry.

I am thinking of Séverine's burial ceremony. It was surrealistic. I could not believe Séverine was in that little box filled with her ashes. Two pastors talked about her beauty, her strength, her straightforwardness. Samira had brought three red flowers, a kind Séverine liked. I asked her for one of them. We walked together towards the box and deposited them on top of it. Séverine's daughter let a red balloon fly above us in the sky. It happily climbed... and disappeared. My eyes too became rivers, rivers that flowed into the sea of our common tears.

# LONG OVERDUE

A gardener stares at our raggedy front yard. More weeds than grass. The star jasmine vine has died in the drought, leaving its bony spine woven through the frets of the wire fence. A young hackberry presses too close to the house. A bedraggled pomegranate tree crowds the banana palms.

The gardener shakes his head. Hands on hips. He is large and blonde as a Viking. He wears no shirt. When I ask what he thinks about laying flat stones on the beaten path from driveway to porch so we don't track in mud when it rains, he nods silently, then puts his arms out to embrace this troubled yard. "Long overdue."

Excuse me? And the trimming? What would he charge to take out that tree? Could he edge this flowerbed with smooth rounded river rocks while he's at it? He stares into my face.

*Long, long, long overdue.*

I laugh out loud.

His few well-chosen words come back to me for days.
That's how I feel about lives bereft of poetry.
That's how I feel about the whole Middle East.

The words we didn't say. How many times? Stones stuck in the throat. Endlessly revised silence. *What was wrong with me?*

*How could I, a person whose entire vocation has been dedicated one way or another to "the use of words," lose words completely when I needed them? Where does vocal paralysis come from? Why does regret have such a long life-span?* My favorite poet William Stafford used to say, "Think of something you said. Now write what you *wish you* had said."

But I am always thinking of the times I said nothing.

In England, attending a play by myself, I was happy when the elderly woman next to me began speaking at intermission. Our arms had been touching lightly on the arm rest between our seats.

"Smashingly talented," she said of Ben Kingsley, whose brilliant monologue we'd been watching. "I don't know how he does it--transporting us so effortlessly, he's a genius. Not many in the world like him." I agreed. But then she sighed and made an odd turn. "You know what's wrong with the world today? It's Arabs. I blame it all on the Arabs. Most world problems can really be traced to them."

My blood froze. Why was she saying this? The play wasn't about Arabs. Ben Kingsley was hardly your blueblooded Englishman, either, so what brought it up? Nothing terrible relating to Arabs had happened lately in the news. I wasn't wearing a *Keffiyah* around my neck.

But my mouth would not open.

"Why *did so* many of them come to England?" she continued, muttering as if we were sharing a confidence. "A ruination, that's what it is."

It struck me then she might be a landlady having trouble with tenants. I tried and tried to part my lips. *Where is the end of the tangled thread? How will we roll it into a ball if we can't find an end?*

She chitted on about something less consequential, never seeming to mind our utterly one-sided conversation, till the lights went down. Of course I couldn't concentrate on the rest of the play. My precious ticket felt wasted. I twisted my icy hands together while my cheeks burned.

Even worse, she and I rode the same train afterwards. I had plenty of time to respond, to find a vocabulary for prejudice and fear. The dark night buildings flew by. I could have said, "Madam, I am half Arab. I pray your heart grows larger someday." I could have sent her off, stunned and embarrassed, into the dark.

My father would say, *People like that can't be embarrassed.*

But what would he say *back to her?*

*Oh I was ashamed for my silence and I have carried that shame across oceans, through a summer when it never rained, in my secret pocket, till now. I will never feel better about it. Like my reckless angry last words to the one who took his own life.*

Years later my son and I were sitting on an American island with a dear friend, the only African-American living among 80 or so residents. A brilliant artist and poet in his 70's, he has made a beautiful lifetime of painting picture books, celebrating expression, encouraging the human spirit, reciting poems of other African-American heroes, delighting children and adults alike.

We had spent a peaceful day riding bicycles, visiting the few students at the schoolhouse, picking up rounded stones on the beach, digging peat moss in the woods. We had sung hymns together in the resonant little church. Our friend had purchased a live lobster down at the dock for supper. My son and I became sad when it seemed to be knocking on the lid of the pot of boiling water. "Let me out!" We vowed quietly to one another never to eat a lobster again.

After dinner a friend of our friend dropped in, returned to the island from her traveling life as an anthropologist. We asked if she had heard anything about the elections in Israel--that was the day Shimon Peres and Benjamin Netanyahu vied for Prime Minister and we had been unable to pick up a final tally on the radio.

She thought Netanyahu had won. The election was very close. But then she said, "Good thing! He'll put those Arabs in their places. Arabs always want more than they deserve."

My face froze. Was it possible I had heard incorrectly? *An anthropologist speaking. Not a teenager, not a blithering idiot.* I didn't speak another word during her visit. I wanted to, I should have, but I couldn't. My plate littered with red shells.

After she left, my friend put his gentle hand on my shoulder. He said simply, "Now you know a little more what it feels like to be black."

*So what happens to my words when the going gets rough? In a world where certain equities for human beings seem long, long, long, overdue, where is the magic sentence to act as a tool? Where is the hoe, the tiller, the rake?*

Pontificating, proving, proselytizing leave me cold. So do endless political debates over coffee after dinner. I can't listen to talk radio, drowning in jabber.

The poetic impulse--to suggest, hint, shape a little picture, to find a story, metaphor, scene--abides as a kind of music inside. Nor can I forget the journalist in Dubai who called me a donkey for talking about vegetables when there was injustice in the world.

*I can talk about sumac too.* When a friend asks what's that purple spice in the little shake-up jar at the Persian restaurant, tears cloud my eyes.

*Is it good for you?*

Are vegetables, in some indelible way, smarter than we are? Are animals?

130

But then the headlines take the power. The fanatical behaviour.

*Problem is, we can 't hear the voices of the moderates,* said the Israeli man, who assured me his home was built on a spot where Arabs had never lived. Where are *they?* Why *don't* they *speak louder?*

(They don't like to raise their voices.)

(Maybe they can't hear you either.)

The men haven't fixed it. Lose their turn. Their turn was long enough. Hanan stepped back. Anyone can understand why. Too many men. Pass the power to the women. And the children. And the eggplants. But it *was women who said stupid things both times to me.* No one exempt from stupidity. Is there a cure?

I love when the poet Wislawa said we have to honor anew those humble words *I don't know.*

Then we start out fresh. Like the soft dampness of a new morning.

I don't know. How. To tell the whole story. No one tells the whole story. No one knows it! *Still, don't those guys seem to talk forever?*

EVERY VIOLENT ACT SETS US BACK. SETS US BACK. Say it louder.

What to contain. To honor, leave unspoken. People will talk and talk while the almond tree is blooming. But something crucial is always too big, or too obvious, to say. Obviously, it is the thing which could save people, if we could only learn its name.

The gardener laid the stones. He cut the trees back. He turned over the soil around the plants so their roots could breathe. He used no language doing it. His skin glistened in the sun.

131

What he has suffered in his life remains a mystery to me. Rumors in the neighborhood say it has been much, and extreme. What did Aldous Huxley say toward the end of his life when someone asked him for advice? *After so much study, after so much research and discussion, it comes to this: Be a little kinder to one another.*

Before leaving, the gardener mentioned the grass would grow up soon between the stepping stones to help them look much nicer, as if they had been there for years.

# David Williams

# WE'RE HISTORY
## and other poems

BETWEEN WORDS
*refugee resettlement lessons*

our common language
not broken but
half formed

no facing page
translation but
what's inscribed in flesh

or brief as the notes
wind writes singing
across the face of the lake

eyes and lips reflect

no mirror but
what muscles translate
we learn again to read

slowly and slowly name

except for those glances
nothing erodes
and only still water can bear


INHERITANCE

You were a great one for building with scraps,
straightening nails to use them again.

Once I understood your poetic orations
were rhetoric--quotes, interchangeable parts--

I went back to listening like a child,
amazed at how the poem expanded

your ribcage, squared your shoulders, raised
your chin. That sonorous Arabic tone

began further back in your throat than English
and made you close your eyes.

I wanted you to tell me what really happened,
some story bigger than yourself.

Instead you left me scraps. Well maybe
we all put ourselves together like that.


To say that, to have at least that scrap,
is not to deny your cruelty.

It shook through every beam in the house
like a bassnote. We spoke of tradition, respect.

Denial was the family art. You couldn't
keep your hands off anyone. Where

does the damage end? I was afraid
to move; you did what you wanted. Did you

think you were beyond forgiveness?
Where did the damage begin? You cut

your *arak* with water, tossed off those milky
shots, and slapped the table.

We lay our hands on the wood
to stop its trembling.


That last year sleepwalking night after night
you wrestled the devil out the door

and still he returned to claim what was his.
Then you tore your proudly built cruelty down

and hurled it after him piece by piece
and kept death off until the job was done.

Anyway that's what I made of it,
watching you hang on, breathing hard.

Only during breaks in the work
could you recognize us and speak.

You wanted our forgiveness
in a voice we were shocked to recognize.

What we'd taken for silence was a murmuring sea
rocking the broken boards.


The sea enters, a gift, a surprise,
bigger than anything, wearing straight-cut, abandoned

quarry stones back to their old curve and slope,
and a green roots under the breakers.

I can't hear it pressed against chips of cement
in your garden, all your tenderness lost

on your blasted roses, nothing left
of their sex but pathetic stubble.

The midwife upstairs did abortions too,
and planted them here, like hermit crabs never

to take up abandoned shells.
But even those hard, empty chambers bloom

white as breakers with the voice of the sea:
the stubborn, fragile rhythm of my blood.

## WE'RE HISTORY

*1. for my neighbors*

When the Gulf War began,
Pham lacked the English
to understand the news,

but remembered home, and prayed
full of dread, as celebrity generals
cautioned against euphoria.

Felipe's nightmares came back.
All he sees is Nam.
But the tough guys at the VFW

who called him a prima donna
have got it all tied up
with yellow ribbons.

*2. arabesque*

Analogies break us. Analogies break.
(Reporters are on the scene, but only
quote official sources.)
*The target lit up like a Christmas tree*
*or the Fourth of July. A turkey shoot.*
Cancel history.

                The tyrant whipped
and in business, his anti-aircraft fire
clouding an empty night sky, his blackmarket
routes secured by sanctions. It goes
without saying children's bodies present
textbook signs of starvation.

# Nathalie Handal

# POETRY AS HOMELAND
## and two poems

## POETRY AS HOMELAND
A Letter to Lisa Suhair Majaj

> *"Wandering one's whole life among foreign tribes..."*
> *--Czeslaw Milosz*

The moon separates those who see with one eye. Perhaps we are among those who see with one eye? Perhaps we are fragments of wood that cannot be used to finish any single window? Perhaps we are masked birds in search of a face we think we are looking for or would like to think we are looking for?

You have often told me, dear Lisa, that sometimes even you don't know who you are. But is it really you who doesn't know or others who make you think that you do not know who you are-Arab or American, American or Palestinian, both or neither? I know that sometimes we lose our names as the traveling moves too rapidly and the handwriting on the name tags changes. Our handwriting, we even think, not recognizing the notion of scattered identity so anchored inside of us. I understand that we try so hard to understand that we risk never understanding. But why torture ourselves?

Maybe we need to live in this never ending state of drama or know no other way but to hang on the invisible strings of identity. You were born in America, grew up in Jordan, studied in Beirut, and the Arabs still make you feel American. And of course, the Americans consider you Arab. Thus, we are constantly left with the question, why do they persist on labeling us as the 'other.' This pounding 'other' which doesn't represent anything but empty space.

Of course, there is also the fact that we are Palestinian. What is it to be Palestinian? Is it being born there? We weren't. Is it having lived there? We haven't. Is it having a Palestinian passport? That didn't exist. Is it speaking Arabic? We can't really. Then why are we Palestinian?

Your father was born in Birzeit and grew up in Jerusalem. And my grandparents come from Bethlehem. I grew up in a house where Palestine was at every corner of our hearts. Through the years, I always went back to Mahmoud Darwish words:

"I have lost a sweet dream
I have lost the touch of tulips
And my night has been long
Upon the fences of gardens
But I have not lost my way."

I did not lose my way but didn't know when I would be back. I was present in my absence, an absence which was in itself absent... at least, that is what I felt. Palestine was so present in my memory, or rather in the memory of others that I borrowed. It seemed so right to belong to all those stories my grandfather spoke about. I even forgot they weren't moments I had lived. There was one certainty, those stories became real images and experiences in my mind, and I had found my place inside of them.

As I listened to my family speak of returning, it became my dream, and my way back was always for me a matter of time. Nothing seemed more beautiful to me than going to Palestine, and losing my eyes in corridors of endless olive trees without being concerned about their return. I always remember the first time I went to Bethlehem, and saw my name on a mosaic plate on the wall, later on store signs, bakeries, a hotel, an *arak* bottle... I come from this land, and my name and family was that proof to me. Once we are at peace with a part of our identity then we can start settling the other sides.

Although most of the time, I feel like we are hunting for the hunter who tried to capture us. Our endless discussion which never ceases to bring us to where we originally started, continues everytime we speak. We keep asking ourselves how we can be so Palestinian, and so American, and so whatever else that lies at the borders. Well, why do we only have to be one person? Why do we only have to have one homeland?

There is the homeland inside of us, the one we inhabit, the one in our dreams, maybe others. I forever thought of myself as being in the frame, when in fact, I was also everywhere in the painting... and I think it is the same for you. As I observe and continue to observe you searching and discovering, being lost then regaining the surface of yourself, disappearing and reappearing, breathing and remaining completely breathless, I have come to see a pattern-one that exist not only in you but in myself and in most of the Palestinians, most of the Arab-Americans that I meet. In our journey to finding this identity that we think can be settled, we confuse ourselves for I have come to believe that we will forever travel in margins. But margins of our own. And those margins are states where eternity also breaths.

And dearest Lisa, there is poetry. As you know, Darwish's work has always elevated me. And as I continue to read and reread his work, I have found an infinity after every one of his words. And as I lose and find myself in those infinities, I have come to discover whatever it is about poetry that I have always wanted to meet. I have come to meet the petal and the stone. I have come to meet the pure springs of poetry. A land open to us entirely.

In poetry we are everything and everyone that we are. A

country between the real and reality. A universe of bread and water, imagination and the imagined, cosmic unity in the world of words, the harmony of words with no end. In poetry we find each other and lose each other. We meet love between ourselves. We cross at times our past or our future-we forget the leaking of water and remember only the verses in its drops. Lisa, remember when we saw each other in the middle of the river, the river between Palestine and poetry... remember how the sky was memory, how green, so green it all was... I remember this homeland. How can I forget it. How can we ever forget how it sings to us, opens its featured arms, telling us to stay. As poets our words are our home, poetry our homeland. And so how fortunate we are to have found this place, this tiny place, this tiny infinity.

This might all seem contradictory and confusing—well it is and it isn't depending on how you look at things. It's not confusing if you consider that anything pertaining to identity is a bag of contradictions. It is confusing if you consider that such opposing sides should not exist inside of someone. In my case, I have finally come to the end, although deep inside I know that the end always seems to be the beginning of everything in my life.Can anything really be defined and remain fixed? Isn't everything always changing? Even as I claim to be an Arab-American that definition is changing as I write. Is it the passport one holds? In that case, when speaking of poetry, why is Sargon Boulos never referred to as an Arab-American poet although he is a US citizen? Is it because he writes in Arabic? In that case, is it the linguistic patterns or the cultural implications in poetics which determine where we belong? What is the real definition of an Arab-American? an Arab-American poet? Should there be fixed rules if someone claims this identity? Can anyone contest another's claim even if that person doesn't always fit in the margins of that inconsistent definition? The fact that inconsistency exists concerning identity, doesn't that in a way answer the question that nothing can be categorized so definitely?

I dreamt of going back, today I dream for those who dream of going back. I said I know who I am-that I am an Arab, a Palestinian and that has not changed, except I am also American, French, and anything else that I feel that I am. I dreamt of going back, and will, maybe. And so in fact Lisa, I have resolved the problem which has no real solution. As for you, even the silence beyond you is Palestinian. I will always remember that afternoon, the winter of our first encounter, your Palestinian map around your neck, telling me who you are.

If you ask me now what being Palestinian means to me? I will say it means being from somewhere where I constantly have extra luggage, constantly live on the edges of what I believe and what I think I believe... being Palestinian is always living in between skylines. It is "wandering one's whole life among foreign tribes..."

Except in our land of poetry, poetry as homeland.


A BUTTERFLY'S GAZE

The night floats, the world chokes
a sip of betrayal stuck in my throat...

I walk in Milos Jovanoviç's dream
barefoot
with jokes under my feet, tears in my pockets...

143

I walk in a shallow midnight battle, toward a falling treetop
a drizzle and its cane, a memory,
a memory caught in jasmine and standing whispers...

I walk in days of strangeness murmuring
beside columns of spaces,
murmuring-echoes and ghosts belong to the same world...

A world surrendering to a butterfly's gaze
surrendering
for the nights are floating, the world choking

and we continue      remembering...


ESCAPE

*Time escapes us and gives us no time to escape*
Voices caught in the narrow distance between two raindrops.

*Time escapes us and gives us no escape*
Voyage, that instant when you realize you've landed.

*Time escapes us and gives us no escape*
and we continue listening to the rumbling of passing travelers,
the slope of our tragedy ending with nothing but bare hands,
memorizing the journey...

# Etel Adnan

# LIKE A CHRISTMAS TREE
## a play in one act, three scenes

### About the play

*Like a Christmas Tree* involves two characters, and a guard who interferes but remains invisible.

An American journalist and an Iraqi, butcher by profession, are in a jail, in the basement of the Ministry of Justice building, in Baghdad, at the beginning of the war which followed the invasion of Kuwait and the massive retaliation by America. The American journalist was arrested in the streets of Baghdad and thrown hurriedly in the jail "for his own safety." The butcher had killed his wife a few days prior to the war and was "momentarily" thrown in that jail, pending his trial.

When Baghdad was burning under bombs one of the American pilots said over his radio (and newspapers all over the world related it) that "Baghdad was burning like a Christmas tree!"

### The Characters

Badr: An Iraqi butcher
Jim: An American journalist in Baghdad
Guard: (heard as an over-voice, but not seen).

### Staging Suggestions

The lateral walls of the *theatre* could be equipped with television sets which, *before the play*, would run images of Iraq, not synchronized, and mostly of deserts, palm trees forests, marsh lands, cities, and rivers. Just before the end of the play and while the people leave the theatre the sets will show the fires of Kuwait and Iraq (which are actually recorded and have been shown on television and as a special documentary) with their sound, on the screens, at different moments, so that they are not synchronized either, while the T.V.

145

sets show these fires the front curtain becomes a big screen on which the fires are shown, completing thus a full environment of apocalyptic scale.


(*A room in the basement of the Ministry of Justice in Baghdad. The room is dark and unfurnished. Two men are inside: Jim is an American journalist. Badr is an Iraqi-butcher by profession*).


## Scene 1


**JIM:** What's your name?

**BADR:** Who, me?

**JIM:** You have a name, don't you?

**BADR:** You speak my language?

**JIM** (*looks at his watch*): It's two o'clock. Already a whole day!

**BADR:** If you start counting the hours the days will get *very* heavy. Watches do something to people's minds.

**JIM:** You have been here for how long?

**BADR:** My name is Badr.

**JIM:** Okay. You're Badr.

**BADR** (*looks carefully at Jim*): If you speak my language, here, in the dark, you must be a spy.

**JIM:** I wish spies were in the dark! Let's not get into that. How many days have you ... (*he's interrupted*)

**BADR:** I am Badr. An ordinary prisoner in this prison. It has been a long time. It's always very long. Everything takes a long time because new things keep happening and they forget about you. Before they threw you in here the guard told me: "Here: I'm bringing you two olives and more bread. One doesn't know what's next. There will be war." "Which war," I asked, and he said:"I don't know. War against everybody." Where are you from, did you come to bring war with you, to this country?

146

**JIM:** No. I have been here for a couple of years, at least.

**BADR:** And what were you doing? What are you doing in my cell, so well dressed, staring at me? Did you do something about this war and they want to punish you? Beware, they're going to be tough.

**JIM:** I'm telling you. Wars are old buddies of mine, I seem to be always running after them. I am what you would call a correspondent. Wherever there's trouble, I am there writing about it.

**BADR:** They arrested you because you know how to write on wars? We don't do that here. You must be writing very well. My mother says that writing is something that *we* have invented. Some other times she says that that's an invention of the devil. She can't write. Not at all. Neither can I. But I can count as much as I want.

**JIM:** And what have you done to be stuck in this darkness?

**BADR:** I ... I killed. That's it. (*Badr whistles a song, softly... takes his time*). I haven't felt like singing since I came down into this pit. I'm messy and you're clean, but don't sneer at me, you'll get messy too, and pretty fast. There's no water, just a little to drink. But when I'm telling you that one gets messy, *very* messy in jail, that's not the whole truth. There are many messes, much more important ones, that one sheds, little by little, like a snake's skin, in these dark doghouses, and one forgets, no, you don't forget, on the contrary you remember with such a clarity and such an obsession that everything burns, disappears. This is why everyone who is in a prison cell, after a while, is innocent. Regardless of what he has done, because his mind is itself washed out.

**JIM:** Did you guess where I come from?

**BADR:** You're an American, of course, like the people who must be creating this war.

**JIM:** I am not doing this war.

**BADR:** You did it yesterday, the day before yesterday, ever since I can remember, always. Don't look at me like that, there's nothing funny to be afraid of. You're locked, like me, the two of us, you're not any better than I am, and you are in the House of Justice! (*Badr has a fit of laughter*). Nobody gets out from the claws of the House of Justice. Who would have said that Badr would share a bedroom with an American! If you are a spy I will have to kill you, here and now. In war everyone is the government. I am more than the government. I'm Iraq, the rivers of the south and the mountains of the north. *Akh*, if my mother were to see you she'll spit on you.

**JIM:** I want you to shut up, Badr, to shut up! (*The American sits, remains silent. He stands up, decides to make some relaxation exercises, does stretches, bends, lies on his back. Stands, sits. Starts talking as if to himself*): I refuse to be struck by lightning, quiet, keep quiet, my heart, stop beating so fast, learn to be patient, think of something precise, focus on it, describe your desk in Washington, tell yourself that you're not in a prison but in your office, writing a sensitive paper, imagine this coming war, describe it in its most intimate details, think of the Pulitzer Prize that you so much desire... The war, the reel one, the final onslaught, when it will come will not last. Nobody and nothing will resist its absolute power. It will be worst than God's anger. And faster. And then, you will get out of here. This prison is just a nuisance; it will be over, there's nothing they can do against you because they're scared, they will always be scared...

**BADR:** You're talking to yourself now, we're only two and that's too many for you?

**JIM:** What's there to be said... (*he yawns!*). My wife, my children (*he's interrupted*).

**BADR:** You have a wife? A pretty one? Where did you find her? And children! Me, Badr, no wife anymore, no children, only my mother. I have only a mother, but the best one. And I have Baghdad, the whole of it, what a world! Baghdad knows me in each of its corners. I was dealing dope and a jerk started taking my clients away, then denounced me to the police, so one day I shook him hard, pressed the button, hard, very hard, and he dropped stone dead. That's it.

**JIM:** (*The American unbuttons his shirt and moves a bit away from Badr. The guard pushes into the cell some water in a tin cup and some bread*).

**BADR** (*goes to the door and speaks through the opening in the door to the guard-who will not answer*): No olives today? Some for the guest? (*he waits a little then turns towards Jim*): It must be late afternoon. Then it will be nighttime. So what? Who could tell the difference! Wait, let me drink first, I was here before you, then you'll drink the rest. That's not much water, though; well... eat! (*the two prisoners eat. They both eat very slowly, to make it last*). He didn't give us any olives today. Olives are good, they give olive oil, but the guard is stingy today, he didn't give anything good today anyway, he doesn't give olives often. Give him something, your handkerchief, your shoes he may give us... well, bread, bread, bread, what I used to give to beggars (*Badr keeps suddenly quiet*).

**JIM:** Are you sleepy?

**BADR:** Why? You need anything?

**JIM:** No, just asking

**BADR:** By the way, did the guard take you to the toilets this morning?

**JIM:** Yes, he did

**BADR:** I didn't see you go out this door with him.

**JIM:** You were sleeping. Snoring. That's getting hard. He takes us once a day, in the morning. (*sneering*): No morning promenade!

**BADR:** He must have orders, or he's afraid. People are just afraid, of anything, of their shadows, people are even afraid of

149

themselves. Fear, fear, you can breathe it, it's all over.

**JIM:** The latrines stink. That's not a toilet over there, that's an open sewer.

**BADR:** What do you mean? A toilet is not a perfume shop, is it? It stinks. It's done for that. Unless you Americans find a way to prevent humanity from shitting... you can do anything you want, don't you?

**JIM:** We're going to shut up. I need to think about something else.

**BADR:** Think of your wife?

**JIM** (*raising the tone of his voice, arrogant*): I want to think about something you will never never understand.

**BADR:** You're in a jail and why should you think. Here it's nothing added to nothing. You just sit.

(*The American lies on the floor,on his back, with arms and legs spread out*).

**BADR:** I will do my prayers

**JIM** (*The American is startled, gets off the ground, sits straight*): Your prayers?

**BADR:** What's going on? Are you surprised that I will perform my prayers because there's no water? Lie down, don't look. I will rub my hands against my clothes and it will be as if there was water and it will be alright. No choice. In the desert we can use sand for that. Nobody told you?

(*Jim doesn't move. Badr can't figure out his thoughts*).

**BADR:** I see questions in your eyes. Why do I pray? Because we do. Since I've been here I have had a lot of time, nothing but time, to think, and I thought about praying and found out that God really exists and fills the world, He can do as He pleases, He will have pity on me. People are ruthless. The world is made of dogs which bite and howl. But God, up there, is generous. My mother used to tell me that every morning. You don't believe in God? Then you're certainly a spy, spies are vipers and there is plenty of that in Iraq. Every possible country, even the tiniest one, sends us some spies. The hotels are full of these birds of ill omen. You would think that they hide in our palm trees, that they melt in the Tigris, eating our dates and enlisting the sun for their schemes.

**JIM:** It's very dangerous to believe that there are spies all around. That's a disease; we have a name for it.

**BADR:** Why don't you sleep, or pretend to sleep? I'm going to perform my prayers.

(*Badr turns towards the South, bends, kneels, stands, recites the ritual verses of the Qor`an, in a rather low voice. The sounds of airplanes buzzing penetrates the cell. One hears sirens.*)

## Scene 2

**JIM:** It's clearer in here, in this windowless room. What's happening?

**BADR:** Your eyes are getting used to the obscurity. Already! That's good. You may have to keep me company for a long while.

**JIM:** No. I know that I won't. This war will not last. That's not a war. It will be a race in which all the horses come first together at the finish line. A blitzkrieg. It will be over before it starts.

**BADR:** How do you know all these things?

**JIM:** I said that it's getting clearer but it's still so dark.

**BADR:** You're lucky to be in the dark. There are jails which are so bright, so lit—as if the whole of the sun was in one big bulb, and brains fry like eggs. Iraqis have too much sun. In the summer we sweat and we boil, we jitter like boiling water.

**JIM:** I spent a few summers in the country and it felt like being in a volcano's mouth. Now all I want is to get out as soon as this is over, and it will be, pretty soon...

**BADR:** Who told you that you'll get out? The war against Iran took eight years. We gave my brother to it and I know. At best this will take four. And I may even be out before you.

**JIM:** When would you speak of something else, something which makes sense?

**BADR:** The world is full of fools.

**JIM:** And then?

**BADR:** More fools.

**JIM** (*A little silence. Jim brings his attaché-case and takes out a notebook, a pencil... then his flashlight, gets ready*): I am going to have an interview with you. I will ask you questions and you will answer and when I will be out of here I'll send the whole thing to my newspaper: "An Iraqi's point of view on the war." Better, "An Iraqi witness to the war." Well. The title can come after, when I know how this will come out.

**BADR**: And what if they kill you before?

**JIM:** They won't have the time. They won't dare.

**BADR**: When·one thinks like that one has no business being in this country.

**JIM**:   Shall we start?

**BADR**: You mean you will write on me, in a big newspaper, and why?

**JIM**:  It's my job. I will write only what you say, trust me.

**BADR**: In your own language?

**JIM:** Yes.

**BADR:** What good would that do to me, bring more trouble?

**JIM:** Shall we start?

**BADR:** Start? Yes, alright. But wait a minute. We cannot talk man to man. You wish ill to my people so how could we be friends, unless...

**JIM**: unless?

**BADR**: you tell me first if, at least for one day, you loved this country.

**JIM**: I don't care if it burns out of existence, it has burned me already. A dead man doesn't cry over death.

**BADR**: Who's this dead man? What's happening to you? You speak funny. You want to see the sun, no, you want to work, you just said it.

**JIM**: Yeah. You're right. Let's return to my question. Since when are you in this hole?

(*all along the interview Jim will use his flashlight—not continuously—directing the light on his notebook*).

**BADR**: I don't know. I feel like being in front of the doctor. It was in the summer. It was very hot. You know.

**JIM**: Why are you in this building's basement and not in an ordinary prison?

**BADR**: That's how it is. They interrogated me then threw me here. Maybe they forgot about me. It happens.

**JIM**: You killed a fellow drug dealer.

**BADR**: You sure will write all this?

**JIM**: All that you say.

**BADR**: Written... It's all going to be written, and it *was* all written. I can't lie. Things are written on God's books. I will tell the truth, I didn't kill that man, that's not the real story. Badr's story is going to be written and the story is that he killed *his* wife. I killed my wife. (*pause*) And you, how did you land here?

**JIM**: They stopped me at night, on the street, near my hotel, seized me and pushed me into here... But let's stick to you. Why did you kill her?

**BADR**: Badr came home one day because in his butcher's shop he cut his finger badly. His first accident, first serious one ever. He entered his house, then his bedroom and there he found his

153

wife naked in his bed with a policeman, making love. He ran down to the shop grabbed his best knife and came back to his place and slaughtered his wife. That bastard of a policeman was gone.

**JIM** ...(*puzzled, annoyed*)

**GUARD** (*with the tone of the over-voice one hears from an invisible narrator in movies*): The Americans are sending a storm over us like they send the monsoon over India! They are coming with their soldiers, their airplanes and their fleet. Oh Lord, it's going to rain hard!

**BADR**: Rain! water! water! the Great Flood! We're going to drown and the whole world will sink with us!

**GUARD**: Stupid! A rain of bombs, rockets, missiles.

**BADR**: Like the gods of Babel.

**GUARD**: O stupid! A rain of fire.

**BADR**: Tell us more, you have the radio, tell us, come in, tell us.

**GUARD**: I'm not allowed!

**BADR**: You're an ass. This is chaos. War. Who's going to allow and not allow?

**GUARD**: I am law and order. Enough. (*The guard closes the little opening*).

**BADR**: So it must be true that there is war, war and nothing else. So you will write in your paper that there's a brand new war.

**JIM**: The news is already published, instantly. What I want to know is what's going on in *your* mind.

**BADR**: Why? Do I have a mind? Yes, I do. I don't know waht's happening in my mind, or to it, but I know that we will win sooner or later.

**JIM** (*arrogant*): And what if you don't, what would you say?

**BADR**: I will kill you; a little, a single victory it will be, at

154

least, isn't it?

(*The American is startled. Moves back a bit. Stops writing, or trying to write*).

**BADR**: Look at you! You're already scared. How do you start wars if you're scared! The eagle is scared of the lamb he'll eat! (*Badr goes to the door. Pounds on it to call the guard's attention. Nobody answers. He comes back and sits in front of Jim*).

**JIM**: Let's start for good this time. Why is there so much sadness in you, this is work... What do you think of your government?

**BADR**: I will tell you what I think of my government and also what *you* think of *your* government... When my government manifests itself in Nassiriyah I would rather be in Mossul; when it is in Kirkuk I find myself in Basrah; when it flies in the air I swim in the Tigris or the Euphrates. With you, it's the opposite: everything scares you and you have no love but for your government. It's upside down.

**JIM**: Why do Iraqis not like Americans?

**BADR**: Why do Americans always ask this question?

**JIM**: Good. Let's go. Do you think that after their defeat Iraqis will still buy American cars?

**BADR**: Whose defeat? I just told you that we'll win this war, this Mother of all Battles!

**JIM**: And if you didn't?

**BADR**: Me, I only love Mercedes-Benz. I can't answer you.

**JIM**: I am a newsman and I'm doing my job. If I got you out of here, soon, would you love me?

**BADR**: You'll never see me again if I got out of here. I'll go immediately to my mother.

**JIM** (*very serious*): Is Saddam Hussein the friend or the enemy of the people?

155

**BADR** (*startled, then quieter*): Did he send you here to ask me this question? Do you wish my mother's death?

**JIM**: Do you agree with all he does, or with most of it?

**BADR**: What I think of Saddam? He put me here, although I have my honor. One of his policemen was in my own bed with my own wife, I already told you that. I had to save my honor. Otherwise I would have gone raving mad, would have been a barking dog if I didn't get her, once and for all.

**JIM**: So he's a bad man?

**BADR**: In my case, yes. But you're trying to gouge something out from me, don't you fool me, you're clear as water and I will tell you that he has his honor, too, write it down, he has to fight even to the last of us if it needs to be. We, for thousands of years, are raised on pride, vengeance, and punishment. And you, you're raised on what? Food and money? We should have never talked together, not on *this* earth.

**JIM** (*getting angry*): You dare say that we have no honor?'

**BADR**: Yes. Badr says so. Where is your honor, going after a city like Baghdad? My city. We're flies, no, good targets for your airplanes?

**JIM**: Little flies can disturb the world more than you know.

**BADR**: Is death the kind of order you want?

**JIM**: If it has to be it should be. There's something worst than the body's or the soul's death and that's anarchy, chaos, disobedience...

**BADR**: ...then, good. You must obey me because, within these walls—and don't forget it—you're on my territory, the territory of my will and of my muscles and (*looking at Jim attentively*) I can flatten you in no time.

**JIM**: Do you have the slightest idea about what power is about?

**BADR**: If I want to love you, I will, and if I have to kill you, I can. It's up to Badr to decide.

**JIM**: There isn't much that I can add to that. Badr, listen, we're talking seriously. Power is energy and it makes things happen, like... air!  It's invisible, but we see it. Air can produce tornadoes and power can generate storms. That's what we do. When America blows its storms, it's awesome.

**BADR**: And why do you blow so much air?

**JIM**: So much fire.

**BADR**: So much fire?

**JIM**: Because nobody can do nothing about it.

**BADR**: Would that give you something?

**JIM**: Power brings power. It feeds on itself. And grows. It's a cancer with no cure. Terminal cancer.

**BADR**: If you believe it's so bad why do you need it?

**JIM**: Why do you need to eat, and sleep? Because you need it. That's all.

**BADR**:  You're sure, so sure of everything, you. Listen, we have greatness and misery, and when you cook these two ingredients together you get madness. You too are crazy, we have petroleum and petroleum makes you go crazy. It goes to your head like a rotten perfume.

**JIM**: That's richness.

**BADR**: Whatever is useful to you brings ill fate to others.

**JIM**: Have you ever gambled? Life is a gamble.

**BADR**: You cannot drink oil. It will make you sick, and vomit.

**JIM**: You gamble? We are masters of the game. We can play it alone.

**BADR**: That's why you're so happy.

**JIM**: So strong, (*and lowering his voice*) so full of sorrow, at times, so desperate.

**BADR**: You're already cheating. Play fair!

**JIM**: Good Lord, how long am I going to stand this darkness (*the American stretches, tries a few exercises lies flat on his back, legs and arms stretched apart ... a little silence*).

**GUARD** (*slides food to them, makes noise*).

**JIM**: Damn this prison! There's less water than yesterday. Less and less. (*He pushes everything towards Badr*). Some bread and a little water! I refuse to eat. He didn't take us to the toilet. When is he going to? It's stinking all over. We're breathing shit. I'll vomit. I'll die of disgust in this damn country!

**BADR**: Eat! I'll eat it all if you won't. Don't die of hunger on my hands!

**JIM**: Take all this fucking food away. Swallow it.

**BADR**: I drank your water too.

(*Jim prepares slowly and tiredly his notebook*).

**BADR**: I thought a lot about it. There's darkness in your brain. You are a bird of bad omen, I was sure when they threw you in like a bag full of worms. The darkness of this place is nothing compared to the one you brought over the world...

**JIM**: ...That's what you have to tell me? Aren't we suffering enough? Isn't this torture?

**BADR**   I have a radio in my butcher's shop and I used to have it on all day long and between the music there was Panama, Guatemala, Vietnam, death. It doesn't haunt you at all? Did you write on all that? I wish I could have traveled in all these places, like you did, but with no death in my baggage.

**JIM**: Who tells you these things?

**BADR**: I'm reciting the list of your victories, your mischiefs, they're all written on our tablets. Every child in Iraq knows that God used our mud to create the world...

**JIM** (*trying to find something to write on his notebook*): You went to school ...

**BADR**: To create you, too. God created good and evil and America.

**JIM** (exasperated): If only I could sleep and forget the war the...

**BADR**: Are you talking to yourself again? You want to forget, forget what, me, you? I will enter your dream, tonight, not later than tonight. It's always night here, a night which gets longer, monstrous like everything that touches us. Two monsters, that's what we are, two stinking beasts in one cage. You, because you came to see how we shall die, how a whole nation should disappear, and me because I killed in the dark, in a place like this. She had the curtains drawn, like now, in this lack of light, she barely had the time to shriek, she barely made a sound, her blood made a sound. I killed her with my butcher's knife, skillfully, like a nameless sheep. We are killers with no regrets, yes, say yes, admit it, and you would sleep much better.

(*They try to lie down and rest but they're too restless. Badr goes to the door, bangs on it and calls the guard*):

**BADR**: Hey cousin! What's going on out there, where is the war, for God's sake let us know, it's getting unbearable in here, give us good news and God will reward you (*no answer, a heavy silence*).

**JIM** (*uninterested, tired, trying to come back to his notes*): If you were free to go on a trip where would you go?

**BADR**: Where I'll go? for a trip I'll go to Mecca.

**JIM**: Why to Mecca?

**BADR**: Mecca is a holy city and I'll be closer to God. And I'm going!

**JIM**: How?

**BADR**: We will win the war and then there will be a general amnesty. Certainly. And I will be free.

**JIM** (*The American looks skeptical but goes on with the "interview"*): Would you stay in Baghdad? In fact, where is your home?

**BADR**: Deep down in the South there are marshes and palm trees and the world is made of water, it doesn't stand still, it quivers with the light and the seasons and the sun swims, and

Badr was born there.

**JIM** (*discouraged, increasingly discouraged*): Do you have any strong convictions besides... religion?

**BADR**: Like what?

**JIM**: Justice?

**BADR**: That's the biggest nonsense I ever heard. Good. You make me laugh; we need it. We're in the earth's belly, a cracking world, we're probably close to its end and you speak of justice? Your justice makes me want to be fierce, ferocious, to tear the skies apart. Airplanes understand it, yes? Ours, yours, they are all on screens in the movies. Wars are for television and for the dumb, who die in invisibility, and the earth is thirsty and it sucks blood. I witness it everyday. I slaughter a lamb and the blood is gone, finished, drunk by the soil, and what's justice for my poor lamb when it looks at me, once more, and dies, and makes a noise that no one hears save those who slaughter. Where do you think God is when I kill a lamb? And I will add that a lamb is a heroic animal. It has honor too. The morning of their execution they know they arrive with another lamb's blood on their buttock.

**JIM**: A few more questions: If you had your say, what form of government. would you have liked to have?

**BADR**: You're either too naive or too shrewd; I haven't figured it out. A government is a jail keeper, a prison guard. Have I chosen this guy sitting there behind this door? No! And you, have you chosen your boss at the newspaper? No. So?

**JIM**: I voted for my president.

**BADR**: I have a friend who voted for our president. Yes, I think so. Somebody else has also voted for him. What does it prove? I don't care for politics, I'm a night bird, I live in tavernas, coffee-houses, brothels. It's full of people and of stories. You should go there and see how people live. You are in the country of the Thousand Nights and One Night. Nothing here is what it

160

appears to be. That's not a place for the likes of you. Nobody reads newspapers at night.

**JIM**: If you were on the street and you were to meet an American soldier what would you do?

**BADR**: What would I do? I don't know. You're an American and you're in my cell and I didn't harm you. Right? (*suddenly his tone of voice changes*). A soldier, on the streets of Baghdad, an American one who's shooting at us, what do you want me to do? what would you do in my place: I'm in the streets of New York and I'm shooting you down! Oh! you're scared. What the hell, to be an American and to be always scared!...

**JIM** (*furious*): You will never be a soldier in the New York streets .

**BADR**: Write! and fast. Write that Badr inhabits the Earthly Paradise, under the shade of palm trees. In the city of the Thousand Nights. Manna falls from heavens. The day a man dared insult him the man got killed by Badr himself. Badr is in a black hole. They're telling him that birds made of iron are dropping death all over his country. He is incarcerated with his enemy with whom he shares his bread and his water. Badr believes everything because he knows everything. He who has killed with his own hands is a scholar because he has learned in his own flesh life and death and the line in-between. He sold to the world dream and desire and he's paid with gases and bombs. Write! Badr is a knower. He knows that the earth is round and that she will end in petroleum and fire. Make your readers read that the sky is darkening more and more and that you have already preceded them to the Day of Judgment. Write! What are you waiting for?

(*Intense sounds of bombardments heard within the cell. The destructions are very close. The top floors of the Ministry are totally destroyed*).

Scene 3

**JIM**: It hurts all over my body. I must have slept a few hours, at most. The stench has become more than unbearable. We haven't left this hole God knows for how long and the smell is suffocating me. The destruction is closing in on us. How can we ever get out? where's the guard? Is he still there? Did you hear him?

(*The American does some exercise, painfully, walks in a circle then sits down, wearily. Badr was lying on the floor, awake, he raises himself up, all broken*)

**BADR**: You did sleep some, don't worry.

**JIM**: I'm hungry, I'm thirsty. It seems that we are in a prison which is itself within a prison. It's endless.

**BADR**: You have never been imprisoned before, for anything? The whole world, to me, is a prison, God's prison for anything dead or alive. I wonder sometimes if Paradise itself is not a prison, God forgive me for saying so. My skin is a wall, my mind is stuck in here, in my head, a prison. When you clean out a lamb you can see how its brain is in a box, his eye, in a hole, his heart, in a cage. We are boxes within boxes, I see it every day!

**JIM**: You can talk all day long, go ahead. Nothing makes sense anymore. Is he going to bring us some water at least.

**BADR**: We didn't have any water yesterday. He said the pipes are broken and very little water trickles down to him. He has to drink too. It's neither day nor night in here. A tunnel with no end, right? Turn your back if you want, I'm going to say my prayers.

(*Badr's prayer is immediately interrupted by a knock on the door and some bread is pushed in*)

**JIM**: This is not bread, it's a piece of stone. I have no saliva in my mouth, nothing. No water. Is he going to give us some water? ask!

**BADR**: Eat. Just eat. Don't you see you're in a trap. Don't make it harder. It's like with God: one day He gives, one day He doesn't. O patience of Job! Why don't you go back to our game, asking me questions. I can give the whole story of my life. It will make me think of my mother. Come on.

**JIM**: No. Nothing. I want nothing from you or from anybody else, anymore.

**BADR**: There is nobody else.

**JIM**: Don't I know it! If only I could know what's going on, out there, there!

**BADR** (*gentle*): You want me to tell you about my wife and how I killed her?

**JIM** (*shouting*): NOOOOOOOO!

**BADR** (*angry, humiliated*): Cowards! all of you cowards! You burn whole countries and you can't stand the story of a single killing? But that story haunts me.

(*Both start biting on the little piece of bread without looking at each other*).

**JIM**: I am not a coward. I'm rather, in a peculiar way, a man destroyed. Don't think that I can't love. But why should I tell you *now* what I am going to say? Is it the darkness, the imprisonment? No. It's a weariness deeply buried that I never allowed to reach the surface. I had to be strong, which meant, for most of the time, indifferent. I'm bullet-proof, you should know, there's metal here, on my chest. Oh don't look surprised, this metal piece is invisible to all but to me because it's heavy on my soul. Badr, do care. Who knows? I may never reach home after this is over, this cataclysm like no other in your ancient history. Should I explain more?

**BADR**: I guess I will hear you because we're lonely, stuffed into a cage, but birds sing and we don't. We're similar to rats, although my mother would never compare me to a rat, not on

163

her death-bed. I'm king for her, and king I am, even if a pitiful one to you.

**JIM**: It's always the same story, the wall between nations, between people. (*looking straight ahead and not at Badr*): Years ago, when I wasn't yet twenty-five, I was sent to Iraq by my government for my first mission abroad, and they sent me up there, to the North, in the high-country, up through mountains, and a guerrilla war was being waged and I ended up as the chief adviser to the top Kurdish war-lord. He was in his forties, and America was promising help, and she did, we did, and for a few seasons, a couple of years, I shared his confidence. I believed in him and was astounded by his courage, the charismatic power he held over his men. These would dance for him, would give their lives, not for land, but for him alone. I gained all his trust. He told me one day, (don't I remember that day!) that I was the being that he came to trust most in the world.

**BADR** (*interrupting violently*): When I thought that I must be on my guard against you I wasn't wrong.

**JIM** (*raising his voice*): For once *somebody* has to hear me, you just have to. (*then Jim calms down, disenchanted, monotone*): So I loved that man and he made me realize acutely that I never got to know my father. I didn't have one, really. He had died toward the end of the second World War and came back in a coffin. We were living in northern Texas, a land of tornadoes, a dust bowl. I myself left home at thirteen and went to my grandmother, on a Mississippi farm, for a couple of years. And it was as if nothing was ever happening in my life until I found myself in the Iraqi mountains which could as well have been the Himalayas, an eagle's nest for meteorites, a refuge for prehistoric heroes. But in midcourse my government changed its policy towards that tribal prince of the North who then became an outlaw, again and again, a man I had instructions to betray and destroy... I can't stop now, my story has to be told the way it was lived, to its bitter end. Would it be that I was fated to find my peace in here? Prisons seem to be confessionals ... aren't they?

**BADR**(*suddenly touched, and friendly*): So this man replaced your father?

**JIM**: That man could have never become my father. He loved me, well, I became his lover and that was to double my betrayal.

**BADR**(*exceedingly surprised*): You're a woman too? You are *weird*, no way, a traitor against whom, against all, against me, against the Kurds, against your government, sleeping with their enemy, are you sure that you're a normal human being and not some kind of monster in a miserable jail with a miserable companion?

**JIM**: There isn't much more to my life that would interest you. Forget it, Badr, it's none of your business. This land of yours grips one and never lets go. But how can you understand me, you're part of it, you're lucky. You will die on it and go to your heaven and be received by your prophets. My own space is this earth, I will have it for as long as I can.

**BADR**: You never say prayers? You should. They will help.

**JIM**: No, I can't.

**BADR**: But you speak of God, no? Your president speaks of God on the radio, the television.

**JIM**: My president is maybe the Lord's cousin, for all I care. But me, I have been always on my own. I traveled a lot. I bet I know Iraq better than you do.

**BADR**: Of course, with all the terrible things you must have done.

**JIM** (*the American shakes his head, stretches on the floor, stares at the ceiling, silent. Badr in a corner tries to say his prayers but can't bend, tries, then comes back and sits next to Jim. Jim, still lying on the floor*): Don't sit that close to me as if

165

I were ill and you wanted to attend, I'm alright. And you stink!

**BADR**: Good brother, listen. We are here whether we want it or not. Now: you who are a great newspaper man, tell me the truth, you may have nothing to lose. Tell me about this war, what is it about, deep down, what is it?

**JIM**: Iraq has invaded Kuwait and that is unacceptable.

**BADR**: So we invaded Kuwait! We succeeded in getting Kuwait! That's a great piece of news. We need a good access to the Gulf. You're sure we got it?

**JIM**: We cannot let little countries be eaten by bigger ones. I'm certain that right now the Americans are liberating or have liberated Kuwait.

**BADR**: You're crazy? Liberate barrels of oil, kill people for oil?

**JIM**: It's about undoing an invasion; we have to keep the world in peace and quiet.

**BADR**: And who asked you to save the world?

**JIM**: There is morality, Badr, which is bigger than you and me.

**BADR**: What is this thing which is so big that it has to destroy nations!

**JIM** (*sarcastic*): The common good, Badr, the common good (*a terrible sound of bombardment*). I'm damn thirsty. No water... water, some water!

**BADR**: We better shut up and wait. It's better to be in here than outside under bombs.

**JIM**: If only my threat didn't choke me...

(*a muffled sound of bombardments and then, suddenly, crack! the impact is so violent that the door opens widely*).

**BADR**: Good Lord! The guard! Where is he?

(*Badr hurries out where it's as dark as inside, then hurries back*): He's wounded, the walls caved in, there's a mountain of rubble. No way out, not yet, wait, I'm going back to see him.

166

**JIM** (*takes out his notebook, speaks loudly but does not write his thoughts. Just stares at his notebook. He looks spaced-out*): I'm near my liberation. This whole building seems to have collapsed, I will soon get out. If we have zeroed in on this Interrogation Center it means that other public buildings have been blown out and that things are going very well for us! Let's wait and see if the guard is seriously put out of action so that he won't shoot at me when I'll escape. I'll go straight to Fayçal ben Youssef's and wait there for the Americans to rescue me. It'll be soon, I'm certain.

**BADR** (*comes back into the cell*): He's hurt, hurt on his legs. He was totally out of breath and I practically had to revive him. Anyway: *he* can't get out, *we* can't get out... the number of prisoners is growing over here.

**JIM**: I smell total war, I can tell. The flies are already feasting on human flesh.

**BADR**: You're smelling the foulness that we live in, for all these days, these excrements... But war is clean: the lies accumulate, swell and produce a huge belly, and then boom! The lies explode, the sky clears. It's lighter here, some light is creeping in like a worm. I can't stand it, it's too bright ... (*Badr hasn't seen much light for a long time so he can't stand the little bit of light which is seeping in through the door and the rubble*).

**JIM**: We'll soon be out. Take it easy, Badr.

**BADR** (*starting to get crazy*): Don't call me Badr. Call me Sir. (*then mumbles to himself*).

**JIM**: Alright Sir (*then in a soft voice, to himself*): Lord, should I go on my knees like Badr and pray before you? Americans don't pray on battlefields; they fight and win. Victory is their good old and reliable buddy, the only God we know.

**BADR** (*He can't concentrate on praying. He's agitated*): The earth is round, yes? so if the earth is round everything else is

167

round too, and comes full circle.

**JIM**: ..yeah!

**BADR**: if everything comes full circle I'm your boss and you'll obey.

**JIM**:...

**BADR**: Write! I don't see you doing it.

**JIM** (*Doesn't move. Looks unconcerned. Tired*).

**BADR**: Badr Ibn Hamdane son of Sulafah bint Hassan will take over America, cut its forests and build houses, houses, all over the Plains, and then he will burn the whole thing down. Write it down! You want to get out of here, *I* will take you out. Come with me. See. We are in the desert under a full sun, a thousand suns! It's empty as far as you can see and the horses are wild, unharnessed. We mount them, there we go, racing the sun. Write down that Badr Ibn Hamdane and Jim Mortimer the Third are going, are going to go and never look back.

**JIM** (*softly*) And never come back.

**BADR**: Write down: each moment is the end of the world and we are celebrating the dead, all the dead martyrs are resurrecting today.

**JIM** (*to himself*): Should victory always be accompanied by the smell of shit!

**BADR**: Can you do something about all this?

**JIM**: I want to live. I have a wife there, children.

**BADR**: I have a mother. Lord, is she well? Is she dead? Is she gone with the city? (*getting violent*): If my mother is dead why should *you* be alive? That's not going to be. You're a killer, a demon who escaped from hell. Paradise and hell make up Iraq, my country, and you're killing us. My mother, you're killing her, right this instant. I slaughtered enough sheep, cows, goats, oxen, and my own wife. I know where the bones are, glued to the flesh, the color of blood, the heart smells differently from the thighs, and I will smell your bones, I will have to, you called me a stinker, wait to find out how you will smell when you will be as dead as these walls (*Badr was almost breathing in Jim's face, that close*).

**GUARD** (*crawls to the door and in a distinct but faint voice with the same "over-voice"— he says*): The radio is saying over and over again that Baghdad is entirely burning, hell came to us, the waters of the Tigris are boiling. The American pilot said over and over again and the whole world heard him saying that Baghdad is burning like a Christmas tree, that a billion fires turned it into a Christmas tree, that it was mind-blowingly stupendous and that it was burning like a Christmas tree.

**BADR**: O thousands of suns, O Prophet Mohammad peace be on you, did you hear? All of you did you hear? The radios of the world are saying that Baghdad is burning, that my mother is a burning tree, and the radios are watching and repeating... (*turning towards Jim*): Did you burn Baghdad did you burn my mother? (*Badr bangs his head against the wall, utters a long shriek*): O God who knows death but doesn't die, help me so; make them blind, those who compete with you and light such fires. O my mother, where are you in those flames and this son of a bitch is looking at me, I will kill you demon who came straight out of hell to burn me and my mother, I'm killing you!

(*Badr throws himself on the American, aiming at his throat. The American is stronger than Badr thought and fights back. Both men are locked in battle. Badr is at the point of being strangled and Jim shouts with a hoarse voice*):

**JIM:** Badr, don't make me kill you!

**BADR**: (*with a hoarse, dying, but audible voice*): I am not Badr. I am the judgment of God!

(*The sound of a huge crash, of explosions. The building collapses on the three of them... Then a cloud of yellow dust falls like a yellow rain*).

# Amira El-Zein

# IS THIS DEVASTATION FOR ME ALONE?
## and an essay

*for my father*

Your grave is my blossom.
My childhood rained
when you died.
I cried:
"Were you dazed at the moment of death?"

How did you see your body
leaving you?
How did you bend over it?
How did you pat it
and bid it farewell?

You listened to people
whispering.
You heard their voices
 in a tunnel.
You rose to the ceiling
and looked at your body:
"Is this devastation for me alone?"

You said:
"It's the murmuring of ants

at my fingertips.
Ants are patiently pulling me to them."

O beloved,
when did mushrooms
blaze in
your head?
When did the whirlwind of tufted cotton
enfold you,
as you heard them
taking your body into the cold?

Moons were dripping blood.
Mosques arose
then were buried
three times.
And the priest of the temple came no more.

Beloved,
tell me:
What were you when you left?
Were you my androgynous tree
bending down to the ground?
Were you my perfect palm tree
blessing the maddened sun?
Did you work your way back
further
and further
to watch our forefathers
paint gazelles on cave-walls?

Tell me:
Where did your death come from?
From the saliva of your mouth?
From the sweat of your body?

From the ends of your hair?
Where,
O beloved?
How did those ants free your atoms?
How did they tell them:
"Turn around in all directions,
and let the water of the body
flow across every grave,
and salute death!"

How did your limbs
dwindle
to feathers,
Oh white feathers!
How did you cry out
when the iron melted, and you knew
it was death?

Tell me, how did you move from red to orange,
and Oh, to white?
How were you dazed
at the time of death
and how did you
utter: "IT IS DEATH"?

Tell me,
How did you pursue
your body,
then it evaded you,
then you caught it,
then it fled?

Love flowed from your failing form.
Your molecules laughed
and said:

"This is freedom!
All forms are mine,
and all beginnings!"

Did you hear the wailing
of my insects seeking you,
tribe after tribe?
And you said:
"It's like a lover's cup
shattering over the miles."

You said:
"It is death attending me.
It is birds that rave
at my fingertips
and beat at their cages."

You saw the birds
wail with their wings.
And you said:
"The time has come to leave."

Cough-wracked,
you saw the blazing bedouins of hell.
You saw thick ropes
dangling from their bellies
chanting:
"With us is Refuge."
You saw the eyes of hell
fall from their fingers.

Pain from the Arab hell attended you.

You heard ringing in your ears
from bedouin whistling,

as they parted spheres of water
then swallowed them.

Then you turned,
and saw them grasping
your coat-tails,
admonishing you:
"Chant,
chant,
chant!"
You fell down, then shook yourself,
then fell again,
when they pulled you toward the cold.

Did you see those in agony
spreading salt on their bodies?
Did you hear the mad bones
break the bridge of the neck?

What burns the eyes
and bleeds the body
came to me from you.
A swelling of your waters came to you
mixed with the salt of ants.

Why did you sleep, O beloved,
when they came to you?
Why did you surrender to death?

Threads of sobs veil you from me.
Are they threads?
Or a memory of plants,
or their voices?

You listened to the birds

echoing Amen. You heard the trusty dolphin
mourn you in deep waters.

You heard the bleating of your veins
melting,
you listened to the raven of your
throat croak
in agony.

Who sent waves of death to me?
Whom did you meet there?
Did grandma welcome you
in her white veil?
Did my little brother rush to you?

You said: "The lotus flower now ripens
in my soul."
You said: "My body falls
into the well of space,
and I must part."

How many a time you fainted,
then you awoke,
then fainted.
Someone whispered:
"Come quick!"
Who clapped his hands
and said: "Bring him!"
Who presided over the table,
and called the sufferers in
for the first supper after death?

O beloved,
you who sleep no more,
who does not wake,

who know neither hunger
nor thirst,
tell me,
how do you swim now
without a body?
Why do I see you everywhere, leaping?

Do you see me as a newborn
sees the instant of birth?
Do you see me dead,
and yourself alive?
Do you shine?

Now I turn off my light
and enter my tunnel.
Now I rise to the ceiling
and look at my body:

"Is this devastation for me alone?"
                    *(Translated by Karin C. Ryding)*

## THE MASKS OF *THE CRANE*

### *1. The Masks of Time*

Only one event takes place in Halim Barakat's novel, *The Crane*. One event in the present: the writer's mother falls down the basement steps of his house, and with her he tumbles into the past. The mother departs to a nebulous world where all the chapters of her life intermingle; the author, meanwhile, sets sail upon a wave of reality and illusion. *How does my mother forget the present and remember the distant past? I wonder, where are the frontiers between reality and illusion? How does illusion change into reality and reality into illusion?*(48)

His mother's fall to the basement floor brings chaos to the system of time. It elapses in every direction. As Proust discovered when his lips touched the slice of *Madeleine* in *Remembrance of Things Past*, the present can become a mere pretext for writing about days gone by. So it is with Halim Barakat. Directing his sight towards the backwards stream of time, he renders the present a means by which to evoke all that occurred before his mother's collapse.

He begins to *hover*, rising and descending. His color changes when he gazes upon the heights, loving and fearing them at once. He beats his wings across the pages, in search of *things past*.

With his mother's accident, the present becomes the most trivial period. The writer sees in it nothing but trifles—for instance, making small talk with a woman on the plane, or the elevator operator, or the airline stewardess over the phone. Those who live in the current era are also trivial, transient beings. The present enters the world of existence merely so that the author may ride it to the past.

Barakat's beloved wife strives to draw him out of this single temporal dimension by building a dialogue between them. Yet in the end, their dialogue resembles little more than a monologue. Her voice remains a captive of the present which she lives, while his voice traverses the wall of his past. *You are a prisoner of your comparisons. Forget Kafroon. It's a reference to everything. As long as you insist on making Kafroon a reference, you will never be capable of starting any new relationships or seeing any other kind of beauty!* (80)

Thus branches time into the lone bough of the past. The writer fell to the bottom story alongside his mother. She was transformed into an elapsed *epoch* or *decade* or *interval* which fills the present with life. Now, the son yearns to recapture her in any form. As long as she remains a bygone age he must travel in an inverse direction to retrieve her. He must allow himself to become one with her, for with her reside the days they lived together during his childhood in the country. In order not to lose her, he has to partake of her memories, to share with her the joy of being absent from the present and living in the past. The present becomes a distant illusion of tangled eras: *My mind rages with associations—I don't know how or why they proliferate, nor what their relation is to each other, images from the past I had thought entirely forgotten awaken in me as plants break through the earth's crust on a sunny day after an abundant rain.*(86)

This remote apparition also reconfigures the places of the past, for space accompanies time in its journey to yesteryear. If the present is merely an excuse for traveling to the past, then place, the eternal companion of time, likewise wears the cloak of elapsed hours. Thus Shenandoah becomes Kafroon: *And we escape together to Kafroon, in the direction of the towering mountains of Shenandoah.*(70)

As a result, the present becomes a weighty burden—I would almost call it *despair*—and a necessary evil. The novel ends with the narrator's rejection of today, his restlessness with it, his feverish desire to remain in the past. The book closes with these words: *Was a return inevitable?*(114)

Like the writer, we also return from our voyage to Kafroon and the past. The past fades with the novel's end in reality. The novel in this perspective is twice time. For there is the time of the thing told and the time of the novel.

In this manner we depart from the novel which, by the very temporal sequence of words, failed to triumph over time. Yet the piece succeeds in rendering the author's personal past our collective past. The bird, or author, circles between Kafroon and Shenandoah seeking an era from vanished days. He does this not only to recapture his own individual history, but to bring back the lost time of the human race, in the Jungian sense of the term. Halim Barakat repeats the journey toward the depths which so many *sons* have undertaken. It is a pilgrimage of sorts, a mission to resurrect the ancient feminine symbols which reigned over human civilization before the advent of male domination.

In his brilliant work *The Masks of Gods: Primitive Mythology*, Comparative Religion specialist Joseph Campbell claims:

> Woman, as the magical door from the other world, through which lives enter into this, stands naturally in counterpoise to the door of death, through which they leave. And no theology need be implied in this, but only mystery and the wonder of a stunned mind before an apprehended segment of the universe—together with a will to become linked to whatever power may inhabit such a wonder.[1]

The American scholar of religions Jane Harrison adds in her book *Themis:*

> His [the primitive man] calendar is at first seasonal, based not on observation of the heavenly bodies but on the waxing and waning of plants, of the fruits of the earth. The worship of the Earth in a word comes before the worship of Heaven.[2]

180

Barakat's recovery of his mother is a voyage to the deepest recesses of time, to humanity's distant past, to the age-old symbol which rendered mother and earth a perfect unity. Frontiers between *mother* and *country* fade: *We follow the news of the country's slow death like the death of my mother.*(15) In another place, he adds: *The death of the crane and the country and my mother...*(65) Later, he addresses the German composer: *I agree with you, Wagner; you are right that mother earth is the source of wisdom.*(24)

### 2. *The Masks of Divinity*

Barakat concurs with Wagner on many other issues as well. Indeed, this man of music takes hold of many strands of the novel, moving across all of its temporal phases. He ties the past to the earth, the present to exercises in futility, and the future to an insurrection against every form of tyranny. His potent symbols live throughout the body of the novel.

Thus Wagner unites the periods of Halim Barakat's life. This fact is particularly relevant in that the composer considered himself the new Dionysus, the messenger predicting an energy which could unify the world. In the composer's eyes, this force was exemplified in the mighty monuments of his German city Bayreuth. Now, Wagner invites Barakat to bend towards mother earth to summon back the past. And when he bids him arise, he reveals violence to be the driving force of everything in this life.

In return, we do not find Halim Barakat speaking or taking part in the present except for when his wife addresses him, or when he talks to Wagner or listens to him. Hence Wagner and his beloved spouse become the only two voices capable of pulling the writer from the depths of the past to the surface of the present—for a very limited period. He exits his memories to speak with the composer while hearing his music on the airplane. Once again, he is in accord with the musician's views: *I agree with you, Richard Wagner: the gods and their representatives on earth are, these days, and perhaps in different eras, sinners. It is humanity who will save them!*(35)

When Barakat emerges, briefly, on the surface of the present, he not only expresses allegiance to Wagner's beliefs, but conforms to them entirely. His position on violence and religions becomes clear. He calls for a continuous struggle in the present, criticizing Martin Luther King, Socrates, and Christ for their submission. Here the author approaches Nietzsche's critique of Christianity. Then, like the German composer, he lets forth a powerful cry for life to explode in all its myriad forms: *Violent pursuits are pleasurable. Even pleasure has become violence. Love is violence. Sports are violence. Writing is violence. The university is violence. Music is violence.*(46)

Wagner's music appears the antithesis of those ordinary people who, in the mundane encounters of daily life, drive the writer to the depths of the distant past. The author thus sees Wagner's ideas as complementary to those of Feurbach and Hegel. With him he demands the rupture of all life forces and energies. When we hear Halim Barakat invoking violence and battle without surrender, it is as if we almost see the shadow of Wagner crouching behind him, saying:

> I am mankind! I am millions of people. I am power incarnate, I am God turned man, hastening over mountains and valleys and plains to bring to the multitudes the gospel of joy.[3]

Or when Wagner calls for insurrection:

> I will destroy the order of things that turns millions to slaves of a few, and these few to slaves of their own might, own riches. I will destroy this order of things, that cuts enjoyment off labor, makes labor a load, enjoyment a vice, makes one man wretched through want, another though overflow.[4]

Here Wagner's music leads the writer to meditate upon expressions of violence not confined to a single time or place. Across the novel's pages unfold images of bloodthirst and predation, of those who devour and are devoured. Face to face, the executioner and his victim epitomize life. *Ra'if bounds forward as if he were a hungry tiger smelling its prey.*(10)

In spite of that, flocks of cranes still circle through the sky, *ignoring the hunters who left their homes and came over the hills and rooftops carrying rusted rifles, as cows and bulls roam through the wide prairie butting one another with their immense, curved horns.*(9)

The first section of the novel ends with the cranes' fall from the sky and the writer's mourning: *Of what use is this confrontation?*(18) Likewise, the penultimate portion finishes in near hopelessness: *Human history is a terrifying record of bloodthirst.*(108)

Between the despair of the beginning and end hovers the crane/human being. The example of Wagner had called for insurrection against all forms of divinity and authority. Here, however, rebellion is a shadow of despair. The mother's impending breakdown intensifies the revolt against godhood. In this manner Halim Barakat speaks to the god: *How can you forget how much she prayed to you in a single day? How many candles and how much incense she burned for you? How many vows she pledged to you?*(16) Later, he wonders: *How many times did she entreat her Lord, 'From my fall to my grave'? But He does not seem to hear her.*(17)

The desperate writer and his desperate revolt once again embrace Wagner's position on the issue of divinity: *I know well that human beings are responsible for the gods' salvation, just as they were responsible for their creation. God will not rescue my mother before I free her from His grip upon her fate—for I will save Him through my mother's death.*(23)

Ultimately, Barakat saves neither God nor his mother. People continue to offer themselves up as sacrifices to the gods.

Writing is the only consolation the author finds in this enduring human martyrdom. For in its own right, it is a testament—an undying testament of humanity's eternal sacrifice.

## 3. The Masks of Elements

So that his writing might serve as testimony of the fall of man and the rise of gods, Halim Barakat must journey through a wilderness of symbols which reveal the conflict between weakness and omnipotence. He is compelled to choose two symbols that wear this dual garb. The author has no choice but to ascend by himself, a crane, to the summit of the sky, and then plummet bloodstained to the earth. At times, he is forced to turn into a river of rage and revolt, only to subside to a mere trickle, surrendering to the limpid water's flow.

All who plumb Halim Barakat's writing cannot but notice one feature: his firm allegiance to the same symbols from one creative endeavor to another. In his study of literary works, the renowned French critic Gaston Bachelard emphasizes the repetition of particular symbols throughout a given author's corpus a tendency known as *Eléments*. Barakat's work exemplifies this practice. The elements of *water* and *air* recur through his various pieces; indeed, the author is in constant journey between them. The crane is the colleague of that other bird who returns to the sea[5]. Perhaps it is accurate to say that if Nietzsche is the writer of the mountains, the writer against the air as Bachelard calls him, then Halim Barakat is the writer of air and water together.

Like Rousseau, Nietzsche used to think while walking. "He made walking into a battle.... For it is walking that provides the rhythmic energy of Zarathustra."[6]

As for Halim Barakat, he rejects the elements of earth and fire, preferring liberation into the vast, lofty plains of outer space or the depths of the sea. If Bachelard is correct in viewing in the four material elements of water, air, fire, and earth as "four different types of provocation, four types of anger"[7] and if it is true that we see in these four elements a "four-tiered root of anger,"[7] then such provocation emerges to its fullest extent in the symbols of the bird and the river, or the elements of air and water....

Halim Barakat sees in the crane ultimate freedom. Along these lines, Bachelard says: "If images in the sky are sparse, movements are free."[8] And behold, the author speaks to the bird, dreaming that he, too, might fly: *When you soar above the earth, what is your relationship to the wind? What do you observe? And what do you seek?*(50)

He fixes his gaze upon this creature swimming through the boundless air. So often does he observe the bird ascending and falling that soon he himself takes on motions resembling flight. Indeed, the most significant aspect of Barakat's novel comes in his transformation into a crane. This cloaking is not merely symbolic; on the contrary, he describes for us the manner of his gradual metamorphosis from human to bird form. Each time he stands watching the birds from a high peak, his desire to soar with them mounts until he lifts his head and takes flight. Little by little, we see him escape from the gravity that compels him towards earth. The oppressive battle between his urge to fly and his fear of falling·dissipates. His yearning of falling dissipates. His yearning grows stronger and a new lightness spreads through his limbs. Only after raising his eyes many times to the heights and striving to follow the winged creatures on their natural course does he attain this state of weightlessness. For many years, Barakat has trained himself to become a bird; the natural world of Kafroon prepared him for such an undertaking

With regards to this matter, Nietzsche in *Thus Spoke Zarathusra* states:

Levitation requires lengthy training. Whoever wants to learn to fly one day must learn before anything else how to stand on his feet: how to run? How to jump? How to climb? How to dance... for human beings cannot fly with one simple push!⁹

Life in the country thus prepares the narrator to wear the crane's attire. He enters this state of metamorphosis expressing astonishment that his wife cannot fly with him: *Do you feel your heart bursting from your chest when you look down from a towering summit? I feel as though I were sprouting wings and soaring, dumbstruck. My heart leaps from its nest like a crane ascending, flapping its wings. Truly. What a marvelous experience for a human being to burst free, to grow wings and traverse the wide, wide sky.*(45)

Bachelard's discussion of the trial of flight pertains directly to the experience of Halim Barakat when he changes into a bird: "A man senses his wings when he no longer exerts any effort to fly. They appear suddenly, like an emblem of victory."¹⁰

The bird shades into the author; the transformation unfolds inside his body. And then, at once, he flies: *Something in my chest flutters. I feel it with all my strength. It is breaking free, taking flight like the crane. It rises, beating its wings against the outstretched sky, crossing the dense white clouds above the Atlas mountains.*(53)

In this way Halim Barakat, the bird, travels from America to Syria, to the valley of Kafroon, landing breathless and at peace. He calls to the crane as his colleague, and side by side they circle through the sky of Kafroon. *Like you, crane, I have crossed continents and soared above great summits.*(110)

With his flight, the author attains utmost accord with the novelistic element he has adopted. In this vein, Bachelard says: "Is this not the memory, awesome and without date, of the aerial state where all becomes weightless, where our inner matter takes on a native lightness?"¹¹

This transformation does not comprise the bird Barakat alone, for here we see him moving from individual time to shared time, to the past which is the earth. A single bird, he carries his transformation to other birds, the inhabitants of his village (for most of them are birds). Mansur, for instance, feels himself *riding on the wings of an eagle, soaring over valleys as deep as the wounds of his heart.*(38)

And Mikadu says to him: *I still walk and run and... fly, and we in our turn change into birds, we all sing in our cages, longing to take off into the spacious sky, to glide above peaks and valleys, to cross horizons, to die before our wings fall apart, to remain legend.* (56)

In this manner the crane carries between its wings the writer, the village inhabitants, and the human community at large. Hence it becomes a collective symbol in a shared place and an individual time.

Of interest in Barakat's novel is his deepening and enriching of the symbol on all levels. In his hands, the symbol—or element, as Bachelard likes to call it—takes on a complexity resembling myth.

The crane is a universal emblem of freedom. A legendary bird, it is in constant migration between north and south, traversing continents in its course. It has a long history with vast spans of earth and horizons in bloom. *Its neck is like a bridge between two islands.*(24) It is everywhere, in Kafroon and Shenandoah. But of what importance is place? The crane fills every site the writer is found. His wife has only to put her hand in his for him to feel that a bird has landed in his palm. The associations are always present. *Thus we were in Shenandoah watching the colorful leaves of the trees, gathering some as they fell like the feathers of a crane.*(88)

The bird is an individual time; it is also a collective place. It appears wherever falls the writer's gaze, yet belongs to the singular past of Kafroon. It is an elapsed era that the author alone possesses.

Likewise the bird cloaks itself in the writer's past—for the crane is also his father. Barakat describes how he approached his father: *I neared him in fear, just as I had neared the*

187

*bullet-ridden crane.*(99) The bird is his mother, too: *Her little body lies still above her head, and she breathes with pain. I tremble as I had neared in front of the wounded crane, not knowing what to do.*(100)

For Barakat, symbols of flight are not sufficient to enter the liberating phase of "weightlessness." Freedom is not enough for him. He seeks that which might purify and cleanse him of the world's filth. As he ascends into space, so we also see him wading in rivers in order to bathe in them. Hence the novel oscillates between flight and falling, ascent and descent. Barakat loves the heights as much as he hates them and he knows, as Bachelard says of Rilke, " The dream of flight is... a gradual collapse.... It is the synthesis of ascension and falling."[12] Only a soul such as Rilke's may unite the simultaneous joy of soaring and fear of falling.

Without a doubt, Barakat knows that the act of bending toward the earth implies its inherent antithesis. Rising signifies the straightening of our crooked bodies, so to speak. Through flight, Barakat triumphs over the watery depths. As Bachelard states, "the being who rises sees the outlines of the abyss fade away.... It dissolves, evaporates, grows cloudy."[13] In this manner the writer binds together depths and summits. Just as he undertook the trial of flight, now, by swimming, he merges with the water's current. *I run through the river, galloping like a horse defiant, broken free of its saddle and reins. Water splashes to my right and left, spraying my face and chest and shoulders. Water, water, water. The earth was once water. It will return to water.*(59)

Yet just as flight by itself proves insufficient, so does swimming. Having dressed as those winged creatures of the sky, he changed us too into birds. And here he becomes water: *I burst forth, as rapids running toward the deep valleys. I flow with them into the plain. I stream into the belly of the earth and the pores of its plants. I evaporate and journey in white, ashen mists.*(59)

Likewise he becomes the creatures of the river: *With my beloved's return after many years, the world changed into a river and we became colorful fish. Freely we swam in different directions and depths.*(42) And as the bird changed into a collective place, so flows the river toward this fate. *The world changes to a river. Everything stirs, grows, surges, storms, overflows. The currents toss us about. They raise us and set us down. Their salt penetrates our depths.*(42) And the world becomes a universal bird, and a universal river filled with the *ontological purity* of the element.

In exploring water as a dynamic medium that purifies and engulfs him at once, Barakat returns whence he came, tying the thread of the distant past where lies mother earth to the world of the river where his own mother is found. For the waters possess a *deep motherhood...* a feminine imprint.

The waters' domination of the novel reminds us once again of Wagner, Wagner whom Halim Barakat loves, whose vision he so admires—for the composer of *Percival* imagined the voices of singers as boats floating on an orchestral sea.

*(Translated by Paticia Khleif)*

Endnotes
1. Joseph Campbell, *The Masks of God: Primitive Mythology.* vol.1, New York, The Viking Press, 1959. p. 389.
2. Jane Ellen Harrison, *Themis: A Study of the Social Origins of Greek Religion.* New York, Meridian Books. 1962. p. 451.
3 *Wagner on Music and Drama: A Comprehensive Compendium of Richard Wagner's Prose Works,* translated by Ashton Ellis, New York, E. P. Dulton&Co., 1964. p. 72.
4. Ibid.,73
5. An allusion to Barakat's novel *The Bird's Return to the Sea*
6. Bachelard, *L'Eau et les rêves,*1943, Librairie José Corti. Paris 216-217.
7. Ibid., 214.
8. Bachelard, *L'Air et les songes*, 1972, Librairie José Corti. Paris, p. 74.
9. Ibid., Bachelard quotes Nietzsche , p.164.
10. Ibid., 72.
11. Ibid., 43.
12. Ibid., 45.
13. Ibid., 73.

# Halim Barakat

# *THE CRANE*
## excerpts

I have a childhood vision of quickly descending through thick black fog torn by flashes of lightning. It is my father's death that has come into my mind. He died suddenly when he was in his thirties without leaving us much except for our stone house with its clay roof, and a mule which he had used for transporting goods.

He died during harvest time at the end of spring. The men were working hard to reap golden stalks of wheat that swayed harmoniously on the rolling hills.

That hot day changed into a rainy night. The trees, roads, and houses were cleansed of their dust, and covered with cold air. My father washed away his daily fatigue and climbed to a sleeping hut set between two trees in front of our house. His friends Najeeb and Mighal came and talked to him for a long time about a dispute between that took place that day on who should have been first to irrigate his land.

When I got up the following morning, I didn't see my father. My mother explained that he had gone to Marmarita and that he would spend a day or two there as well as in Hab Namra to fetch a new saddle for his mule.

Two days later my father came back but he was ill, doubled over in pain. That night his condition worsened and he could not sleep. Mother called my grandfather Salim, and my uncles

Jamil and Yousef. The neighbors also came to spend the night with my father. Before dawn they sent my uncle Jamil to Al-Mashta to bring the doctor. I don't remember where I was but I think I was asleep. My mother says that my uncle returned an hour later and told them that the doctor had refused to come with him unless he gave him three lira in advance. My mother gave him the money and he went back to Al-Mashta. Suddenly my father felt better. He got up, washed his face and talked with my grandfather and my Uncle Yousef about several matters.

The doctor came and examined my father and joked with him. He concluded that he had pneumonia and gave him an injection. He told my mother how to care for him and then left to visit one of our distinguished neighbors. The visitors also left and my father went back to bed. My mother went to prepare the compress for him according to the doctor's instruction while I remained alone with him. This is all I remember, but my mother told me that my father must have lost consciousness as soon as the doctor gave him that accursed injection. She later counted the names of the doctor's other victims in our village and the neighboring areas.

I remember that my father motioned to me to come sit next to him. I approached him in fear. I saw his sun-bronzed face becoming increasingly pale. The clouds outside returned to encircle the earth and to smother it. Their dark shadows entered the house next to my father and me. The air didn't move, and it seemed to me there were many thick clouds crouched on my father's chest but no rain. I sat next to him while my mother was outside preparing the compress for him. He didn't talk to me and I didn't know what to say to him.

He stretched out his hand to hold mine. It was hot and shaking. He tried to smile, but his smile was unusually cold, pale, and broken. I was afraid and I didn't know what to say, drowning in deep silence. The dark shadows of the clouds lay waiting on the walls and almost concealed the corners.

My father's hand reached out and took mine. He took my

hand to his lips and kissed it. He pulled me to him and leaned his face against mine. He laughed when he felt me trying to wiggle my face away from him.

His hands rose suddenly toward the ceiling and fell down slowly. He gnashed his teeth, and I stared at him, terrified. In his eyes I saw a big change. He must have seen death face to face. I couldn't move. I called my mother in a strangled voice. My father gnashed his teeth again. Then he died.

It seems to me there is a thin, invisible thread between extreme sadness and joy. Sometimes I think that death was both sadness and joy for the children in our village. It happened so often, to every family. Four of my brothers and sisters had already died. Death was one of our games.

When a man died in the village, we children dropped everything and went to the cemetery. We watched all the faces and expressions and listened to the hymns and climbed the trees or stared in between people's legs to the casket as it was lowered into the grave and showered with dirt and rocks. After the mourners dispersed we picked the acorns from the huge oak trees. We used to take those special acorns and play with them, making up games of chance.

That fearful day after my father died, I went to play with my friends Munif and Salim. Their mothers passed by our game on their way to our house to console my mother. My eyes met the eyes of Munif's mother and she stared at me strangely. She said to Salim's mother, "Is this the son of the deceased? The boy is playing. He doesn't know the meaning of death."

Salim's mother answered. "He is only a child, the poor thing," she said.

I lowered my head, embarrassed and ashamed, and rushed toward our house. I got lost in the crowd of mourners inside. They had laid my father in a wooden casket and made the necessary arrangements to take him to the cemetery, having decided to bury him on the same day, only a few hours after his death. Out of mercy for my mother and us children, his friends carried him to the cemetery where he would forever lie by the large oak trees.

Burying him only a few hours after his death did not ease my mother's grieving. Her sadness deepened and her grief stayed with her the rest of her long life. On the day he died she shouted while women held onto her, "They took you away from me, my beloved. They took you away from me. Return him to me. His body is still warm. You buried him while his body was still warm." Quietly she sang to him, "You vanished beneath the earth like a grain of wheat. Who will give me rivers of tears so I can cry?"

The next day, it was said that a man from the neighboring Al-Mahairey village passed through the cemetery the evening my father was buried. He heard moaning from inside my father's grave and ran away in fear. One of the neighbors told my mother about this rumor and she fainted. Since then, using what little I know of scientific principles, I have been trying to convince her that the rumor could not have been true. I have tried in vain. She still thinks that my father passed away because of the shot the physician gave him, and that the people who buried him only a few hours after his death were brutes.

Many years later she would say angrily and bitterly, "In this life I only feel sorry for your father. May God take that doctor's life. If it weren't for the shot he gave him, your father wouldn't have died. He got up from his bed, washed his face and talked with us as if nothing was wrong with him. He talked with his father and with his cousin Yousef about his trip to Al-Mashtaya, Marmarita, and Hab Namra. When the doctor gave him the injection he lost consciousness. That doctor killed many patients. May God make his way difficult. People in our village, my son, are inhuman. They buried your father while his body was still warm. How did his father, brothers, and cousins allow this? They took him away from me against my will. He died at noon. They made his casket, dug his grave, and buried him in the afternoon. I wish they hadn't buried him until the following day. That man from Al-Mahairey heard him moaning, but he ran away instead of calling the people of the village. May God make life difficult for those barbarians."

After my father's death, my mother struggled in vain to make a living in the village, and was finally forced to go to Beirut. She found work as a baker and also worked as a seasonal harvester in a distant area which the people of the village called the East. When she established herself and found a place to live she sent for us. I was about ten years old, my sister was eight and my brother six, when my uncle Jamil loaded some of our things on his best mule and we walked behind him on rough, narrow roads toward the town of Safita. Umm Yousef, also a widow working in Beirut, accompanied us. We climbed mountains and hills and descended into valleys near and through villages and landmarks we had only heard of. Every time we crossed a river or a brook, I took off my clothes and dipped into the water. I put my clothes back on without even drying myself and continued walking. We rested on hilltops in the shadows of trees by ancient shrines, especially when it was necessary to pull out the thorns from our bare feet. We slept in the shadow of Safita's tower, and the following morning we took the bus from Safita to Tripoli. There were more chickens on the bus than there were passengers; they were tied together by the dozen. I jumped up from my seat when I saw a passenger climb onto the bus with a baby goat that had white spots on its forehead. At first glance, I thought it was the baby goat I had raised and sold to the butcher just a few days before our departure but it wasn't. And of course the goat did not recognize me.

In Tripoli, I remember being amazed at the crowds of people, carts, horses, donkeys, dogs, sweets, vegetables, fruits, trash, and dust. Was this the city I had heard so much about? I was relieved when we rode a horse cart up a hill and the streets widened and the shops grew larger. The trees were planted in rows like guards receiving a great leader. My attention was drawn to the pastry shops but I knew that I was not supposed to want candy, as my younger brother did, because we did not have any money. In spite of my hunger, I didn't ask Umm Yousef to buy us anything. I knew she was no richer than my mother. But she must have realized what was going through my mind because she went into a store and bought us a little bit of candy. From the hill we took a larger, newer, and cleaner bus into Beirut. I don't remember anything else except for the hills rising out of the sea, the waves breaking on the rocks, and the Ra's al-Shaq'a Tunnel. That's because I remember the Senegalese soldiers who stopped the bus at the entrance of the tunnel. It was the first time I had ever seen a black man. They took us out of the bus and asked for our identification cards, something I hadn't heard of before. Umm Yousef explained that we were too young to have I.D. cards. They insisted, threatening to send us back to where we come from.

Umm Yousef managed to convince the Senegalese soldiers to allow us to continue to Beirut. We arrived there late on autumn evening in 1942 and this city was to become my second home. World War II was in progress, the hidden struggle had already begun between the darkness and the dim lamps that were painted dark blue to deter air strikes. For Beirut was involved in the war, whether it wanted to be or not. The bus driver set us down in a small alley that branched off Al-Burj Square towards the east. I heard whisperings that we were in the middle of the red light district but I did not exactly understand what that meant. I found it strange, however, to see women shamelessly showing their legs.

We had to go to Al-Hamra Street in Ras Beirut so we walked behind Umm Yousef, towards the train station. My sister wore wooden clogs which made a lot of noise on those silent, dark, tiled streets. Jokingly, I told her to take off her clogs so she wouldn't wake up the city and get us taken to prison by the guards. She quickly took them off, putting the clogs in a small bundle she was carrying on her head. We still remind her of this and laugh together. We were surprised to see the train approach, since it was not what we expected. We rushed at it like the others did, climbing in without hesitation. We entered its belly like Jonah entered the belly of the whale. But this whale had windows. I contemplated its glass windows which were painted dark blue and I thought about how colorful the city was. When I walked around the next morning I realized that the city was not particularly colorful. I wonder why that first impression has remained with me.

To this day, my mother insists that my father was the sacrifice for her life, that he died instead of her so that we would not be orphans. My mother used to say, "The orphan who loses his father is no orphan." She meant that the mother would not remarry after the death of her husband, but instead, would devote her life completely to her children and then to her grandchildren. And my mother has done exactly that.

*(Translated by Bassam Frangieh)*

# Kathryn K. Abdul-Baki

# *GHOST SONGS*
## chapter one

Thirty is a dangerous age for women in my family. My mother died at thirty. So did my grandmother--from a chill, they say, caught one morning from not wearing her scarf to the cemetery. It had never seemed conceivable, before, that I could outlive them. This past spring, when I turned thirty, I felt particularly vulnerable, frail, as though a mere breath would blow me away. I needed solidity. And, although I had been trying to deny it for the past month, I knew that I needed Ameer.

It was a spring morning in 1989 in the Ghor Valley on the shores of the Dead Sea--a morning drizzled with sunlight and fecund with the promise of warm days ahead. I sat in a bus in the parking lot of the crowded Jordan customs area waiting for clearance to leave for the Allenby Bridge. Several miles ahead lay the Jordan River and beyond that, my destination: balmy, fertile Jericho.

Branches of ivory-blossomed almond trees had stirred like angels' hair in the breeze as the taxi carried me down through the hills from my home in Jordan's capital, 'Amman. Ravines sliced the high hills--the mountains of Moab--which sheathed in a patchwork of lime, yellow, and russet growth. The slopes were like folds of velvet, enveloping us against the cool morning. Yet once we had reached the Ghor valley, some eight-hundred-feet below sea level, the chill had given way to warmth, the farms turning a lush jade skirting the blue of the Dead Sea.

Behind me, now, the rows of vegetables and banana trees were speckled with the fuschia scarves and black robes of the village women tilling them. Ahead of me was the stretch of dusty, neglected border land which would become no-man's-land at the Allenby Bridge.

I sat a few rows behind the driver's seat, trying not to think of Israeli customs across the bridge or the sad reason for this unplanned trip. I tried to focus, instead, on what my eyes could readily see--the mountains beyond the river, their mauve tips buried in a nest of clouds. On clear days, when I drove down from 'Amman for a swim in the Dead Sea, I could usually discern the Mount of Olives in that looming range, even Grandfather's red-roofed house at the top.

It was still early, but the heat had already seeped into the old bus which was beginning to fill with village women carrying bundles and fretting children, trendy young women in short skirts and make-up, men in business suits or Arab headdress reassuring everyone that it would all soon be over.

"*Kazoz*, Cola, orange!" A boy with cold drinks and a tray of candy climbed into the bus and strolled down the aisle, popping off the tops of the bottles for the sweating passengers the way the vendors did during intermission at the cinema.

An elderly, village woman with blue tattoos on her chin followed him, hauling up a wooden cage filled with hens. She struggled down the aisle, then settled herself in the empty seat beside me, dropping her cage on the floor next to her. Her eyes quickly appraised the passengers, for an instant resting on me before they shifted to something outside the window. Her long, velvet *thob*, in contrast to her face, was vibrant with orange and pink flowers embroidered at the bodice and down the sides. Across her forehead, beneath her white headdress, lay a row of gold coins. I pictured her in customs, arguing with the Israeli soldiers on the tax she would have to pay on her gold.

From the corner of my eye, I could see her studying me. Blond hair and light skin were not that uncommon among Arabs in these parts but my looks, I knew, were somewhat extreme. For my mother had done the unthinkable for a Muslim woman thirty one years ago when she married an American journalist who had been a Jerusalem correspondent for *Time* magazine. *Stephen Larsen.* Her marriage had doomed us both--I to forever being 'foreign' among my own people, she to heartbreak when my father abandoned us and returned to America when I was three.

But Stephen Larsen was only part of the reason for my looks. An even earlier strain of foreign genes had been bestowed upon our Tirani clan by my mother's great-grandfather, an Albanian soldier who had come to Palestine in the last century as an Ottoman recruit. Albanian Muslims had been conscripted in large numbers by the Ottoman Turks who had ruled the Near East for centuries, and countless Arab families claimed these European forebears who had been sent to Arab lands. Our family name, *Tirani*, had evolved from the Albanian city of Tirana that our ancestor had left behind. Several of his descendants--our family patriarch, Sheikh Hussein, as well as great-grandchildren like Ameer and myself--had inherited the Albanian's light hair and blue eyes. Yet, I was the only Tirani who actually looked foreign. Today, on a bus filled with Arabs about to cross the Allenby bridge, I stood out.

A Jordanian soldier climbed aboard the bus and demanded to see passports. When he reached our seat, he checked the old woman's next to me, pushing her caged hens further against her seat with his boot. Then, he glanced at mine.

"Salma?" he said, shifting his gaze from me to the American passport.

"Yes," I replied, in Arabic.

201

"You are going to Jerusalem?" he said in English.

I nodded.

He stared at me, looking skeptical, hesitating a moment before returning my passport and moving to the next passenger.

Finally, the soldier and young drink vendor left and the bus driver returned and leaped up to his seat. With a jolt of his arm he started the engine and throttled the bus out of the customs lot toward the road that cut across the parched land before us.

The earth outside the window formed yellow-white plateaus in the shapes of craters and corals of an ocean floor, the ridges like the coarse covering of a clam's shell, as if only yesterday this had all been under water. The soil would be softer and mellower across the river in the West Bank. Yet, this rugged Jordanian plain had its own rough purity that somehow reminded me of the children at the handicapped school in 'Amman where I taught.

The listlessness of being in transition brought an uncanny calm over us. To cross this windswept no-man's-land was to be temporarily invisible, as if one might be swallowed up by the dry earth without anyone ever knowing. I knew this stretch by heart: Biblical battlefields of Canaanites, Philistines, Israelites, Romans, Muslim armies from Arabia, Crusaders, Ottomans. Their ghostly presence was as real to me as the flint chips and potsherds they had left behind. In ways more real--certainly more bearable--than the evidence of more recent history sharply intruding ahead in the form of the shell-pocked remains of a Jordanian-army barracks that had been destroyed during the 1967 war.

I thought of the disbelief in the soldier's eyes as he had looked at my passport. Why, indeed, would a foreign woman put herself through this border crossing unless it was absolutely necessary? Unless the pull of what was on the other side far outweighed the distressing humiliation of getting there?

The Bridge. We were only too aware of its significance. Named after the British general Allenby who had defeated the

Turko-German forces in 1917, it linked the two banks of the Jordan river whose scant waters divided this land into the 'East' and 'West' Banks. The river had once nominally divided the area of Palestine on the West Bank from Trans-Jordan on the East. But with the creation of Israel in 1948 out of more than half of what had been Palestine, Jordan had been given Jerusalem and the West Bank Palestinian towns to govern along with its own East Bank so that the Allenby Bridge had simply connected Jordan's two territories. But twenty years later in 1967, Israel captured Jerusalem and the West Bank lands and the river became the new border separating this expanded Israel and its newly occupied West Bank, from Jordan. During the war, droves of refugees from the fighting had fled across the river to Jordan, pursued by the enemy army and napalming aircraft. Days later they were still scattered about these dry plains like confused birds unable to decide whether to return home to a new alien ruler or remain in exile in Jordan. Finally the new borders had become official, sealing out those who had left. Since then, this plain had gained the significance of being a no-man's-land, traversed only by these buses ferrying Arab passengers and a few tourists between the warring states of Jordan and Israel.

At times, the very Jordan River the bridge crossed over seemed elusive, as if the water itself were shifting, setting up new boundaries and erasing old ones depending on wars and politics. To Palestinians living in Jordan, it was the vital lifeline that connected us to our past, to a family or home across the river. Yet as the official border, it was also a barrier that shut us away from those same things.

Sometimes, although it was a barrier that had been imposed upon us, it was one that I, myself, had kept up between me and my family. During the past month, especially, it had buffered me against having to take a decision I was not yet ready to.

Although it was only a short ride to the bridge, the

anticipation of what lay across the river always made the bus ride an eternity. To journey from 'Amman to Jericho, where Israeli soldiers conducted exhaustive passport, luggage, and body searches, and then ascend up the West Bank hills to Jerusalem, was to sink into the abyss of the soul and rise again, as if just granted a new life.

I had barely slept the night before, wanting the day to come and be over with, dreading the Israeli customs check which had become even more severe since the *Intifada* uprising had begun nearly three years ago. Now, drowsy from having waken up at dawn, I leaned against the window and shut my eyes to the lulling, jolting ride.

My thoughts raced ahead of the bus, out of control, to what I feared the future might hold. A few days earlier, I had received word that Sheikh Hussein Tirani, our family's last surviving patriarch in Jerusalem, had suffered a heart attack. Since there was no telephone communication between Israel and Jordan, a friend of the family who had crossed the bridge from the West Bank had brought me the news along with my Aunt Badriya's instructions to go to Jerusalem at once. Sheikh Hussein, apparently, had asked to see me.

I had made a point to see the Sheikh several times when I was last in Jerusalem. A year ago, a stroke had paralyzed the Sheikh's right side. Ever since, he had seemed to grow less and less aware of his surroundings, as if he had lost interest in those around him. For the first time, the possibility of his death had been mentioned in the family. My aunt and I were particularly close to him, for besides being my grandmother's first cousin, he had also been her first husband. Although their marriage had not lasted past the wedding night, the Sheikh had always seemed partial to my mother and aunt, my grandmother's two daughters from her later marriage to my grandfather. He had acted especially protective of my aunt and me after Grandfather's death, as if he were personally responsible for our wellbeing.

News of this latest illness had shaken me. More than anything, I wanted him to recover, at least enough to be propped up in the sitting room to smoke his *nargila*, or to sit on the veranda and gaze at the flowers in the garden.

My aunt's message had been blunt, although she usually tried to spare me traumatic news, as if the death of my mother from diabetes when I was ten was all the hardship she expected me ever to bear. Her message had also been vague--she had obviously not wanted to disclose the details to her friend--but it sounded like the Sheikh had requested to see me over a matter involving a bequest by him to me.

The thought that Sheikh Hussein had bequeathed me something puzzled me. As the granddaughter of his cousin, I was not entitled under Islamic *Sharia* to inherit from his estate unless he chose to grant it to me during his lifetime. His three children--his oldest son Yousef, his daughter, Nahla, and his younger son, Ameer--would inherit the citrus farms and properties that he had amassed over the years. In the past, in his typical, explosive generosity, Sheikh Hussein had parceled off several of his properties as gifts to various Tirani relatives. During the time it had taken me to obtain official permission from Jordan to cross the bridge to Jerusalem, I had worried that the Sheikh might have taken a notion to present me with such a gift. With all my heart, I now hoped that this was not the case. The last thing I wanted was the enmity of his family, especially Nahla, my least likable cousin.

But there was another reason for my wish to avoid any family discord. On my last visit to Jerusalem, Ameer, the Sheikh's younger son, had asked me to marry him.

*Ameer.* For years he had seemed far removed from my daily life, yet on the bus, now, I saw him as clearly as I had imagined him every day this past month that I had been away: his slim, lanky body moving with coltish energy, belying the fact that he was over forty; the careless way his brown hair brushed away from his forehead and temples; his blue-gray eyes. His mouth that could break into an easy cat's grin one second, so that it might have been the smile of the young Sheikh in some timeworn photograph, and as quickly purse to a distracted, pensive frown--the trademark Tirani scowl. But the most intriguing quality about Ameer was a certain larger-than-life air he possessed, an almost surreal quality infusing his glances and movements. In that way he was most like his father. For until recently, Sheikh Hussein had retained the aura of one who could overcome anything. It was this trait, perhaps, that was most attractive about both men, although neither seemed particularly aware of it--the distinct, palpable sense that they were invincible.

All at once, a ripple of tension shot through the bus. I opened my eyes. Beyond the parched plain racing past my window was the sight that always made me catch my breath--Jericho!

The faces of the other passengers registered the same excitement and longing as I felt. It was always like this, a plummet into silence, whenever we first glimpsed the West Bank and Jericho, the morning sun shining down onto its green iridescence.

We came to the last Arab checkpoint.

Once more, a Jordanian soldier climbed into the bus. This one sipped from a glass of hot tea as he inspected our passports. Before getting off the bus, he reminded the driver to bring him back some item from the "other" side of the Bridge, careful not to say "Israel" which was a forbidden word since Jordan and Israel were officially at war with one another.

Now the bus proceeded to cross the narrow Allenby bridge. But before we reached the end, we were stopped again. At the top of a tall pole before us there appeared a white flag with a six-pointed, blue star in the center--the first sign that we were entering Israel.

The bus hovered above the river, its passengers stifled in anticipation. Below us, the rain-swollen Jordan flowed lazily toward the Dead Sea.

This time, it was a bearded Israeli soldier in khaki fatigues who boarded the bus, gathered our passports, and took them to a small room on the bridge. Several young Israeli soldiers sat on stools, their machine guns sprawled across their knees. They looked tanned and fit as boys back from some beach holiday. Familiar with the routine of the border crossing, they seemed oblivious to the anxiety raging through the bus as they casually traded insults with the Arab driver as if he were an old friend.

"Send me your sister," one of the Israelis called out.

"Send me your *mother!* " our driver growled back in Hebrew.

Finally, the bearded soldier brought back our passports and we were waved forward.

"*Your mother!*" our driver repeated to the soldiers, this time in Arabic, a disdainful grin sweeping across his face as the bus lurched forward and off the bridge.

Before us now, a mountain of sandbags and more white flags floating blue stars announced our arrival into Israel.

The same despair tore into me as the first time I had arrived at this spot after 1967. Before that, we had simply driven across the bridge from 'Amman, stopping in Jericho only for a cold drink before continuing on to Jerusalem and the Mount of Olives. After the war, crossing to Jericho meant entering a country that Jordan was at war with, a land that was no longer ours.

As the bus pulled up to a vast, gray building surrounded by pyramids of sandbags. Israeli soldiers in helmets watched us from behind mounted machine guns on the rooftop.

As if on cue, the bus passengers began to surge forward, streaming into the aisle, grabbing belongings and children in a frenzy to get off the bus and into the long line for customs inside the gray inspection shelter. The old woman next to me clutched her chicken coop and fought her way to the front of the bus as I followed her.

Some Arab Jericho boys, hired by the Israelis as laborers at the bridge, unloaded our baggage. I retrieved my blue suitcase and, after hesitating a moment, walked up to an Israeli soldier who was silently watching the commotion. I showed him my passport.

"American?" the soldier asked. His rifle swung toward me.

"Yes, American." *American.* I had never singled myself out for special treatment before. Normally, I insisted on going through the grueling Arab customs like everyone else. My American passport, like my father's genes, had been involuntarily bestowed upon me and although I kept the passport for practical reasons, I had long since discarded my father's American name. But I had to get through customs as soon as possible this morning, for the Sheikh. For this purpose, I was American.

The soldier jerked his head in the opposite direction from the Arab inspection station, grunting for me to leave my suitcase on the side.

As I began to follow him, I saw the tattooed village woman with the hens still standing near the front of the bus, looking lost among the moving throng. I wanted to ask the soldier to wait while I gave the woman directions, but he had already started toward the smaller, foreigners' shelter. I hurried after him, hoping that he could help me finish quickly. When I glanced back, the old woman had hoisted the noisy cage to her head and was striding toward the Arab shelter behind the other passengers, her velvet gown licking the dirt.

Several people who appeared to be tourists were entering the smaller shelter ahead of me. I walked behind them through the metal-detector at the door. A female soldier who looked like a high school student took my passport. She read the name aloud, emphasizing the Arab pronunciation. Then she took me aside and ushered me into a cubicle where she told me to unbutton my jacket and blouse. With a hand-held device, she scanned my chest, arms, and legs. She rummaged through my purse. Then she led me back out to the main room to wait for my suitcase. The other tourists were chatting with the soldiers and I caught a few words of German as I stared at the walls covered with colorful posters of Jericho, Yaffa, The Dome of the Rock mosque, the Wailing Wall, the fortress of 'Acca, Haifa. Formerly Arab towns and villages now being billed as Israeli attractions.

When the baggage was finally brought in from outside, a tall soldier walked over to a metal counter and signaled for us to bring our suitcases for inspection. I brought mine to the counter. "May I go, first?" I said. "It's an emergency."

The soldier glanced at me, then at the stack of passports on the counter. He had braces on his teeth and seemed as young as the girl who had searched me. Obliging, he flipped through the passports and pulled out a dark blue one as though he were performing a card trick.

"Yours?" he asked in English.

"Yes."

He scrutinized the picture, then looked up at me. "You are *Salma*? "

"Yes."

I could see his eyes change. Although he stared directly at me, I felt I had suddenly become invisible to him.

He glanced from me to the passport photograph and the name printed below it, his eyebrows raised, quizzically, a knot of contempt forming. Then he tapped on the suitcase. I opened it and stepped back, watching as he slowly moved his hands across my clothing, almost daintily lifting the layers without scattering the contents onto the table as was routinely done to Arabs. He peered into a bottle of shampoo and inspected a tube of toothpaste. Then, he examined my high-heeled shoes and replaced them, without cracking open a single heel as had been done the last time I crossed. Instead of sending me to a room to be strip-searched, he seemed satisfied and tapped the suitcase

209

again.

I closed it, not believing it was all over so quickly. I lowered my suitcase to the ground and started towards the door.

"Wait a minute!" It was a woman's voice.

I turned, my feet pivoting soundlessly as though on ice.

A blond female soldier I had not seen before was coming toward me. She was older than the others, and frowned as she held out a ripped piece of paper with a name and telephone number scribbled on it in Arabic. "Yours?" she demanded.

I felt my clothes tighten against my skin as if they feared being ripped off me. I stared at the name and telephone number of my aunt's friend who had brought me her message. I had written them down in case I needed them but had forgotten to throw away the paper. It must have dropped out of my purse when the soldier had searched me in the cubicle.

I looked at this blond soldier. Once again the blood rose to my cheeks. My breaths became uneven. Unsure whether or not she knew, I calculated the risks of lying. An imposter. Then, I remembered the Sheikh and my need to hurry. "I don't know what it is," I said, quickly. "I don't read Arabic."

We stared at each other a moment longer, then, without waiting for permission, I carried my suitcase out of the shelter and into the Jericho sunlight.

Through the open windows near the ceiling of the main customs shelter came the muffled voices of the Arab passengers still waiting for their papers to be checked, for the luggage and body searches that often took the entire day. Over a child's irritable cry, a voice on a loudspeaker blared out the names of those next in line.

The soldier who had guided me from the bus to the shelter was now standing in the sun near a row of taxis, eating a sandwich. He nodded at me. I nodded back. Then he smiled. He was handsome, I now saw, with gentle eyes and tawny skin.

My euphoria at being through customs suddenly eased into a seductive happiness. Had I been in some other place, had I even been a real tourist like the Germans with me in customs, I might have been pleased by the attention, allowed myself to be flattered by this soldier's smile. I might have smiled back, charmed by the boyish grin, may even have imagined his bronze arm around me, allowed him to welcome me to his country.

Instead, in this place and time, I looked straight past him, succumbing to the primitive, hostile feelings erupting in me. I wondered if he suspected that I was not a tourist, that I begrudged his ease in welcoming me to this place that I had once been able to consider my own. Could he guess what it felt like to Arabs to have this border erected, to see East Jerusalem occupied, to visit West Jerusalem for the first time since 1948 where Israelis now harvested Arab fields and lived in the stone homes that Arabs had fled twenty years earlier? Did he know how it felt to suddenly become nobody?

When one of the Jericho porters, a little boy, offered to carry my suitcase to a waiting taxi I did not object. As I passed near the soldier, I tipped the porter and thanked him in Arabic, distinctly loud enough for the soldier to hear.

# Daniel Moore (Abdalhayy)

# THE BLIND BEEKEEPER

*for Musa Muhyiddeen*

1

I'd like to make a movie entitled
  "The Blind Beekeeper." Alphonse,
or it could be Henry, blinded by sparks from a
forge when a teenager on his family farm
circa 1943, walks like a man on the moon
(funny how the phrase "man in the moon"
    predated the historical event probably by
        centuries) toward his white
wooden bee sanctuaries,

he's wearing no protective suit or headdress,
knows the mental workings of bees,
  can call them individually by
    name, they swarm onto him, if
      that's the right term, they
cover his torso, stripped as he is to the waist,
his face wreathed in smiles,

and he does the dance of the bee with
bees all over him, like a bee pin cushion,

this man against a green field on a
   sunny Kansas afternoon, the
     camera rises in a
 spectacular crane shot of Henry
   shrinking smaller and
    smaller, black with
bees, calling each one by name, his

voice on the sound track, each time he
repeats a new name, there's an increased
  buzz response, the music of the
soundtrack is a single violin note,

the sun's beating down, suddenly there's a
flash of light

and in the place of Henry and his bees
there's a large jar of honey, almost white,
as if from Paradise, glowing like a
   pot of gold.

All of this could take place before the
  credits.

Now the story begins.


2

We are taken into the bee's world.
Zarzz (all the bees have names starting with
   "Z") has progressive ideas,
he's been to France, feels independent,
  wants to revolutionize the bees

lives, thinks about
breaking out of the routine and
   starting his own hive, saves up
pollen secretly in some abandoned
   hexagons in a nearby field,
is in love with Zuzz, wants to
make her his queen.

Zarzz, although commendable on
one level for being a
   bee who wants to make a difference,
doesn't appreciate the divine pattern involved
in being a bee. That there's only
   so far you can go before you
betray beedom, or, potentially tragic in this case,
build, not so much castles in the air, as
hives in hell. But his
   intentions start out as good.

He's in love, he has some thoughts on
improving the lot of bees, but his
   radical ideas might ruin this
hive forever!

Enter the blind beekeeper. He wants to
   learn the higher metaphysics of
bees, to touch with the
   knowledge of his heart the
geometric perfection of the bee, its
almost symbolically ritualistic sets of
   patterns, building patterns, dance
patterns, whose results are
deep medicine for man, prophetically
   ordained, and
the continuation of the species. The

flash he experienced that
  blinded him he wants to
reproduce in the realm of spiritual
  illumination.

Meanwhile Zarzz and Zuzz leave the
  hive in search of
    greener pastures. They pack up their
legs with pollen, and head out after
sunset. But bees don't
  fly after dark. They get lost.
They fly into foreign fields. They get
 cold, which is
   fatal for the
    flying mechanism of bees, who
have to keep themselves warm by whirring their
wings. Their story gets quite sad, actually,
and Zarzz suddenly realizes he may have
  doomed both their lives to
   extinction. Being a
thoughtful bee, he is wracked with
guilt and worry, and
starts to pray, for bees are believers,
  as attested to by the beginning of that
word, and have a

beeline to the Divine Reality Who
gave them their wisdom.

3

Zarzz: Zee zuzz za za-za-za
  zarzi zuzzo zab zuzzo
   zizz za za-za zarzo zoo.

Zuzz: Zarzi zaz zaz zo-zo-zo-zo-zo
  ziz zar zuzzo zizz zo zo za-za
    zazizzo zazizzo.

Zarzz: Zazo zizo zizz?

Zuzz: Zazo zinzinzup zardo-do zinzanzo
  zar zar.

Zarzz: Zee Zuzz, za zwa zi za zo.


4

But the beekeeper is also in love, and he
  also wants to build hexagons of
    perfection and a palace of
      pure sweetness.
Her name is Rosa, a poor girl from a
  foreign country, and Henry is
her strength and she is his eyes.

But here is the strange part: as Henry
works with the bees, and talks to
  them in their language,
he starts seeing them, visually
seeing each one of them. When he's away from their
hive he's blind, but when he faces the
hive he's an alchemist achieving pure gold.

He comes to the hive in the morning.
The hive is in an uproar. He sees them in
clusters talking about Zarzz and Zuzz.
The queen is laying her eggs. The

nurses are taking them to the nursery.
At the center of the hive everything is

  going on as normal. But out in the
streets the bees are literally abuzz.
*"What will we do? What have they*
  *gone and done? Where could they*
*have gone? How can we get them back?"*

The blind beekeeper looks into the hive
and sees all this. But suddenly he has
double sight. He sees Zarzz and Zuzz
nearly frozen to death, trying to
sun themselves enough to fly. They are
in a field a few miles away
  bounded by meadow flowers.

There's no time to lose! The beekeeper
calls to the bees. Their round shiny
  multiple eyes all turn to him.
He dances. He dances the dance of
  the map to the field they're in.
He turns in circles to indicate miles. He faces
  in their direction. He tilts
  his arms to show the longitude and
    latitude of their
      position.

Now he calls each one by name to
  go to them, to bring them back: "Go
Zuza, Zee, Zan, Zy,
  Zarzo, Zeeza, Zanzan, Zink,
go Zeno, Zardoz, Zo, Zooey,
  Zap, Zeeper, Zazoo, Zip,
go Zeezee, Zantham, Zoetrope, Zany,

Zeke, Zap, Zazz, Zoe,
Zanzinzo, Zoonzinzan, Zeezay, Zope,
go Zaza, Zipe! They buzz their response!
Go Zak, z-z-z-z, Zook, z-z-z-z,
    Zipper, z-z-z-z, Zay!

They lift from the hive like an ecstatic
    cloud, they buzz like chainsaws
and off they zoom. The blind
    beekeeper smiles and waves them
        on. Does the story end happily?

They all burst into song!


5

Zarzz and Zuzz come back to the hive.
Everyone's glad they're still alive.

The queen makes Zarzz her intimate vizier.
Zuzz marries Zarzz and gets busier and busier.

The blind beekeeper makes lots of money
selling their extraordinary honey

and marries Rosa in a flash of light
so utterly intense he regains his sight.

# Evelyn Shakir

# REMEMBER
# VAUGHN MONROE?

Well, not to brag, but him and my cousin Belle used to be on speaking terms. That's after the war, when Vaughn had his own radio show and was hitting it big with numbers you never hear any more, like "Racin' With the Moon" or "Ghost Riders in the Sky." Nobody, I mean *nobody,* ever sang like Vaughn, in that deep voice, making you pay attention, just like he was somebody's papa.

To me, though, Vaughn's best was "Ballerina" because I like a song that's more like a story. Okay, this story had a sad ending, I'll give you that. But sad can make a person sit and think and that's how you smarten up. That was and is my opinion. Belle's, too, and she'd know, rubbing elbows with Vaughn like she did.

Belle made Vaughn's acquaintance in the first place when she hired on to waitress at the *Meadows.* That was his own restaurant and bar, right here in Framingham. Folks used to wonder "why Framingham?" The answer is Vaughn came from around here, and he was true blue--that's a well known fact.

The *Meadows* is long gone now, of course, but back then it was a pretty sight to see, sitting on a hill, lit up white like a Christmas tree, and a big neon sign flashing Vaughn's name down on Route 9. Not bragging exactly, just signaling folks: here's one of your own, made good.

Myself, I stepped foot inside just once—if you're minus a *steady* to show you a good time, you're out of luck. Or a hubbie, which I never had, neither. But, hey, what don't come round wasn't meant to be—that's how I look at it. Naturally when you're young, you have your hopes. But you better start out on the right foot or it's no use. And anything you want, the big thing is you got to be lucky, like having naturally curly hair or being thin, or like chumming with a celebrity. Myself, I stitched kimonos in a factory for thirty years and made forelady, so I did okay and I'm not complaining. But you can see for yourself, it don't hold a candle to waltzing in and out of the Meadows like you own the place.

As I remember, Belle went in at five to work her shift, and mind you, she got to dress up nice, with a black velvet band in her hair and a black ribbon round her throat. She even got to call Vaughn "Vaughn," right to his face, so that was something too. One time she showed me a glass ashtray with his name signed in purple, so deep it wouldn't scratch out. You had to know Vaughn personally to have an ashtray like that.

Belle was the type always dreaming about show business and being like the next Rita Hayworth--except Rita was too beautiful--so maybe Ginger Rogers, if only Belle could dance and drop some weight. It was a long shot. Still, you had to give her credit for wanting to better herself. At home, I remember, she used to put the victrola on and take a bow, like she had paying customers lined up on the sofa instead of just her sisters and me peeking in the door. You should of seen her then, tossing her curls and shimmying round the room while we're laughing and clapping and Vaughn is singing "Ballerina."

Like I say, that song was the weepiest. All about some gal who makes a big mistake 'cause she wants to dance on her toes and go round the world and be famous and have everyone love her instead of marrying her boyfriend and being happy. But whenever she's dancing on stage, she can't keep her mind off this empty seat in the second row she's always saving for him, so right away you can tell she's sorry and she knows she made this big mistake. See what I mean? You can learn a lot about life from a song, and what not to do.

Anyways, Belle liked to prance. Lucky for her, the parlor in her house was big enough, it made a good stage. But the kitchen was close quarters. When I was in there, I was always squeezing by somebody, b-hind to b-hind, or getting flattened against the icebox if I forgot and stepped in Belle's way.

Don't get me wrong, Belle wasn't what you call obese. But she was big boned, just like me, and had my big paws, which I truly hate, except she didn't try to hide them. Anyways, she was a lot for Mitch to get his arms around. Mitch was her sister Emmie's husband, and one Thanksgiving, after a few beers, he's all over Belle in the foot of space twixt the kitchen table and the sink. I don't notice nothing's going on til "Hey, Buster!" and she gives him a good shove. "It don't bother me," Emmie says. Yeah, she's there too. She's laughing and Mitch is laughing. "Help yourself," she says to Belle, "I'd *like* a rest!"

It came to me that Mitch must of touched Belle somewheres he had no business to be. She wasn't cute as Emmie but she had an enormous big chest. I guess, when you're lucky, you're lucky. But I didn't care to picture Mitch and Emmie or any in my family doing you-know-what. And then for her to let on or kind of hint about it in front of people, and suppose her papa walked in that minute to get himself a glass of water--well, maybe he was gone to his reward by then, but that don't change thing--Emmie should of known better.

Understand, our family was all working class, but we were a good family. We knew all about right and wrong and "Shame, shame!" I think it was because our parents came from across and hadn't latched on as yet to American ways. And they were real careful with daughters, especially Belle's mom and dad. Back when the gals were in school, the poor kids couldn't stay after for Glee Club or even extra help. And in gym class they had to wear long pants 'cause uncle and auntie didn't want them in bloomers showing off their legs. Uncle wrote a note to the principal to tell him, and Evelyn had to carry it to the office. She cried and said she wouldn't, but uncle said she had to or he'd go in himself.

And do you figure those gals could maybe take in the Saturday matinee at the Rialto? Uh uh, that was risky, too. Suppose some fellow sat down beside them, and suppose he started talking to one of them--in the dark, don't forget--and suppose she happened to answer back. One thing leads to another. Nope, uncle and auntie weren't taking any chances. Go to school, do your homework, that's it. And "help out."

Now I don't just mean darn stockings and iron pillowcases like we all did. I mean, *before breakfast* they'd be out weeding this humongous garden that the family ate out of all winter. Auntie canned corn and beets and beans and peaches and pickles and grape leaves and three different kinds of jelly--and that's just to give you an idea. After the gardening, they'd wash the back stairs every day (which was overdoing it) from up the attic bedroom right down to the cellar. *Plus* they all had to crochet for at least one whole complete hour a day. Don't ask me what they were making! I don't think it mattered. Uncle and auntie just figured they wouldn't get married if they couldn't crochet.

Well, the joke was on them 'cause they had a hard job getting rid of those gals. And it's not because they weren't pretty, they were pretty enough. But they didn't know how to catch a husband, and that's the long and the short of it. With Emmie, it was easy. One day Mitch's grandma put her fur piece around her neck and rode the commuter cars from Boston to Framingham because a little Arab birdie whispered in her ear that this family from Zahle--that's her hometown in Lebanon--they had a pack of "brides" available.

When Auntie Mai heard company on the porch, she did like always and whipped off her apron. Then she put on a smile, opened the door, and sang out the usual *"Ahlan wa sahlan,"* which is just a fancy Arabic way of saying "Welcome." Then the two of them sat down like old school chums and started chatting about this and that but not the main thing. (Belle was eavesdropping from the kitchen and she made a good story of it later.) When they'd been gabbing long enough, auntie showed off the merchandise, making the gals parade into the living room, meek as lambs, carrying trays of Turkish coffee and giant pistachios and home-made macaroons and Fannie Farmer chocolates. The old lady says, "Bless your hands" four times--to Evelyn and Yvonne and Antoinette and Belle--but when she sees Emmie bringing in the grapes, she says, "That's the one." Which, of course, didn't sit right with the others because Emmie was only fifteen and had no business to be first.

But naturally they had no say. So Emmie got married and moved in with Mitch's family, old-country style. Then from morning til night, it's, "Emmie, bring me a glass of water," and "Emmie, come brush my hair," and "Emmie, don't roll the grapeleaves so tight." 'Til Emmie was mama to three sons--which made her somebody--and she began letting the in-laws get up and wait on themselves, and they began falling all over each other telling what a good cook she was.

After what happened to Emmie, I let the world know I wouldn't stand for anyone pulling that "arranged" stuff on me. And Belle said the same, and so did her sisters. I guess they were waiting, like I was waiting, for a blue-eyed boy to romance me and promise to spend his life making sure I was happy. And it would be just between me and him and *no one else*. *American* style.

You'd think the *Meadows* would of been a good place for Belle to meet her dreamboat, but if he showed, it must of been on her night off. The only fellow she came home talking about was Vaughan, and she wasn't in his league, irregardless of the fact that he liked her to call him Vaughan. But to think of all those customers going in and out of the *Meadows*, and Belle still coming up empty. Even me, without Belle's ches I could of done better.

So time went by without much happening til one Christmas I'm at Belle's house, and Arthur shows up with a fruit cake in a tin. I don't know where she picked Arthur up, but he was the puniest thing I ever laid eyes on, with little-boy hands and feet, and nothing to say for himself neither. So after a while, even though he's company, we just talk around him like he's not there. Even Belle.

And all the time I'm watching auntie (like I said, uncle--rest his soul--had passed on) and guessing what's going on in her head. I figure she's noticing that Belle's not getting any younger--she was upwards of thirty and already growing a little moustache. (Hairiness is the curse of our family! Men *and* women, but it don't matter so much in a man.)

Problem is he was Irish. Italian or Greek or even Jewish would leastways have been a little better. Them people were like us, the old timers were always saying. They had feelings and loved their families and knew about honor. But the Irish were almost as cold as the English. Of course, Arab would have been best of all, except from the day Uncle Assad came down with TB, no more folks from Zahle came calling to check out the brides.

Me, I looked at it differently. The last person I'd ever want to marry is some Arab. But I wouldn't want to marry Arthur either. His no-color hair gave me the creeps. That's why, after I saw him at the house a couple more times, I maybe spoke out of line.

"Belle," I says, "no offense, but what do you see in him?"

"A gal's gotta think about her future," "she tells me.

Which set me to thinking would I ever get married. Mama and papa could of been wondering too, but they never said boo. To tell you the truth, I think the folks liked having me home, and not just for my salary neither. I was always good company.

Belle and me, we used to gab a lot on the horn, but after

that Christmas she didn't hardly ever ring up. Could be she was mad at what I said about Arthur, or could just be she was spending every minute with him. Somehow I didn't have the heart to call neither. Not that I was jealous, because there were lots of fellows I could of had if all I wanted was a pair of pants. But I knew what I was after.

I'll be honest. Up til I was twenty-one, I never went on a date. My folks wouldn't let me. After that, I went ahead and went out anyways, four or five times I guess. But I didn't like the way fellows were right away wanting to touch me on the knee or poke my breast or suck on my mouth. I couldn't see they had the right. Or maybe I didn't have the normal feelings a gal's supposed to have.

On Saturday night I'd get to thinking about that and about what Belle and Arthur might be doing together. I tried to picture them wrapped 'round each other, and I'd fix their arms this way and that, trying to make it come out romantic. Then I'd try turning Belle into me, and Arthur into this light-complected fellow I used to see buying Lucky Strikes at Josie's Variety. In my mind, I'd let him kiss me all soft and sweet and I'd give him just the right words to say to make me feel special and like nothing could ever hurt me with him there to look out for me and know what I was thinking and wanting without me ever even having to tell him. Jeez, that was tiring work! And if I didn't concentrate real hard, he'd begin saying the wrong things or repeating himself so's it got boring and, worst of all, he'd start turning back into Arthur. But it's Belle I'm telling you about. One Saturday after my birthday--so that was April--she gives me a call. "How bad are they?" she says. In our family, everybody knows your business. Just like I knew Aunt Mai wasn't at the Lebanese church luncheon 'cause she had a migraine, Belle knew I wasn't there 'cause I had cramps. Except I was faking it. I was getting too old to tag after mama and papa and watch the gals I went to school with showing off their husbands and babies. I know you're thinking I could maybe

227

meet someone nice there, but I already told you how I feel about Arab fellows. I wanted a blondie with smooth arms and chest and no disgusting hairs sticking out of his nostrils. Belle felt the same and maybe that's why she said a long time ago her church-going days were over.

"I'm feeling Okay," I says.

"Well, come on over then and let's go shopping," she says.

"For what?" I says.

"Oh," she says, "garter belt and heels and other stuff I gotta have. You come over!"

"Whattaya need me for?" I says.

So then she tells me that Auntie Mai is laid out on the sofa with a cold rag on her forehead, whimpering like a puppy, and complaining to *Allah* that Belle's killing her, the way she's always hurrying off to the stores and must be spending money like water, and auntie's asking *Allah* please to put Belle back in her right mind.

"She's the one driving me crazy," says Belle, "she still thinks you can buy a nice dress for five dollars! But if you go with me, it's okay 'cause she says, thank *Allah, you* got sense.

That was a dig--in my family, they all think I'm tight-- but I let it pass 'cause it's entertainment to me, looking around in the stores, even if I am careful about spending the few dollars I have. Of course, the folks would find out like they always do everything, but my cramps could of gotten better, and anyways it wasn't like I was running out to do shame.

When I get to Belle's house, Aunt Mai is still on the sofa, but she's quieted down.

"How are you feeling, auntie?" I says, bending over and giving her a peck on the cheek.

"Thank Allah, no worse, *ya auntie.*" See, "auntie" is what Arab aunts call their nieces--their nephews, too--when they want to show they love them. Uncles call them "uncle," and mothers call their kids "mama," and fathers call their kids "papa," and so on. It sounds backwards, I guess, but if you grow up with it, it's natural and gives you a warm feeling.

Auntie grabs hold of my hands and rolls her eyes in Belle's direction. Then she whispers—but loud enough for Belle to hear—"take care of her, *ya auntie*. She's *majnooni."* For a minute, I pictured Belle behind bars in a nut house.

"Don't worry, auntie. Belle's smarter'n me," I says. "And uglier, too," I whisper on our way out. She don't take the bait, just makes a beeline for my car like she can't wait to get at Shoppers' World, which was the first shopping mall in all of Massachusetts and something for Framingham to be proud of. Of course, the thing *really* put Framingham on the map is these doctors who been testing the same folks for years, trying to find out what brings on heart trouble. I always said I could tell them something about that--if you get my drift--even though, myself, I'm of a cheerful disposition. It's because I got the gift of seeing into people's feelings.

For instance, I could tell that Belle didn't care that much about the shopping, she was just aching for some girl talk. "So how's Arthur?" I says, to get her started.

"What?" she says. Well, I wasn't born yesterday. I figure she's in love and dying for me to say his name again. But I don't feel like playing that game. So I'm waiting for her to talk, and she's waiting for me, and it's getting pretty quiet in that car. Which makes me antsy, so I give in.

"You still seeing that Arthur?" I says.

"Yeah," she says.

So I says, "You two serious or what?"

"I dunno," she says, "maybe." Then she says, "Can you keep a secret?"

"Well, sure," I says, and I wait for her to come out with it. But she takes her time. I figure I'll help her along so I says, "Are you engaged, Belle?" But she don't say nothing, just smiles a little. Then it comes to me out of the blue, and before I know what I'm saying, it's out of my mouth--"Are you *married,*

Belle?" That makes her laugh out loud like she's real happy. And I'm starting to scream and carry on (and trying to stay on the road at the same time) til she sobers up and says, "Of course not!" But she don't sound like she means it, not exactly. Now I'm getting exasperated.

"Quit kidding around, Belle," I says, "what's the secret?"

"Promise you won't tell," she says.

"I told you I won't," I says.

"OK," she says, "don't get mad." Then she waits, like she's thinking it over again. This time I don't say a thing. I figure if she tells me, she tells me, and if she don't, well that's A-OK, too. By now we're pulling into Shoppers World and I'm nosing into a parking space.

"This close enough to the stores?" I says.

That's when she blurts it out--"Me and Arthur, we're eloping!" So I sit there a minute, picturing the two of them climbing down a ladder and suddenly it don't make no sense at all.

"Why, Belle?" I says, after I'm out of the car. "Why can't you have a regular wedding?"

"Because mama don't like him," she says. "At first, she wouldn't even let me and him go alone for an ice cream soda. She made Evelyn and Antoinette tag along, so he had to pay for everyone. That wasn't right, was it? And then after a while mama said I should let him know not to come around at all. It was just on account of silly stuff, like one time she offered him some ba'lawa she baked, and he says thanks and takes a piece right away instead of hanging back and waiting for her to insist."

"That's the way Americans do," I says.

"Uh huh. And then she noticed he's always waiting for *her* to say hello to *him...*"

"That's bad," I says.

"Yeah," she says, "instead of him showing respect by coming up to her first thing and asking how she's feeling."

230

"Well," I put in, "auntie *is* a lot older than him."

"I know," says Belle. "So mama says that's all bad breeding, which means a bad family we wouldn't want to get mixed up with. You know how the old timers are. But she can't fool me. If he was *ibn arab,* she'd overlook a few things."

"Or if he wasn't so puny," I thinks to myself. "So when are you gonna do it?" I asks Belle.

"Soon," she says. "Pretty soon. We got some planning to do first."

By now we're right outside Jordan Marsh and who should show up but--you guessed it--Arthur! Well, I'm not stupid, I see this was no accident. When Arthur sees me, he's surprised, but he gives me a big smile and asks how am I. Then he looks at Belle real serious and says, "Belle." Just like that. "Belle." Nothing else. And I can see he's been worrying where is she, so he must love her all right. She starts explaining why she's late and why I'm there and so on, but he says, "Never mind, let's go," and Belle says to me, "Meet you back here in a couple hours, okay?" And before I can open my mouth, they're running off somewhere, and I notice he don't look so small any more.

"Well, la dee da," I says to myself. "Thanks a lot for dumping me here." On the other hand, it was fun to be in on things. "But I gotta think about this," I says to myself, so I goes into Bickford's for a cup of coffee and I begin turning over in my head the Arab girls I ever heard of that run off to get married, beginning with old Mrs. Haddad's pretty daughter, Helen, the one who's a little slow. She went off with her second cousin. Then there's the youngest Khouri girl, her fellow was another Khouri, but no relation, and she told her mama ahead of time but not her papa. In our own family was crazy cousin Selma who fell in love with this pastry maker just off the the boat from Damascus.

Anyways, it always turns out the same. At first, the gal's folks cry and carry on like it's the end of the world, but sooner or later they say okay, it's the will of *Allah* and we gotta accept it. What else can they do? They don't even know to think about annulment, and divorce is a no-no. And let's say the gal and fellow run off and forget to get married, that gal is damaged goods (even if she didn't do nothing bad), so naturally no one else will take her. And the boy's folks have to go along, too, because it would be a big disgrace on them if their son don't stick to the girl now and be a good husband.

So that was all right. After I worked it out, I still had time to kill so I looked 'round the kitchen department at Jordan's in case they had a sale on something that would do for a wedding present. I seen some new-fangled things Belle would like, a steam iron and one of those pressure cookers, but I'm the type I like to sleep on it overnight before I rush into anything.

Belle and Arthur met me right on time, but other days they kept me waiting, sometimes a whole hour. Yeah, we went through the same rigamarole a few other Saturdays, and weeks I couldn't do it, they must of managed on their own. But I was getting nervous having to pretend to my folks and to auntie Mai. I kept saying, "When are you gonna take off?" And Belle kept saying, "Don't you understand? We gotta plan things right. Arthur knows what he's doing."

"OK," I says one day, "but you got a head, too."

"Hey," she comes back at me, "don't be such a kid!"

"Kid!" I says, beginning to get steamed.

"Don't be mad," she says, "You're a good kid. You ain't a woman yet. A woman knows things. A woman knows when you're in love, you're as good as married anyways in your heart, so having a priest say a few words, it don't much matter if it's this week or next."

Well, that didn't sound like Belle, it didn't sound like nobody I ever heard, I mean outside of the movies or True Confessions. Right away this picture pops into my head. There's Belle and Arthur sitting on a midnight blue, velveteen sofa facing a stone fireplace--like you see in Good Housekeeping--with logs crackling orange and pink, and the

232

two of them holding hands and whispering, "I love you, darling." "I love you, sweetheart."

Just then Belle grabs my hand. "Listen," she says. Then she makes me swear all over again I wouldn't give her away, which naturally I wouldn't, but the whole thing was weighing on my mind still and I was wishing that she'd tell Yvonne, too, or Antoinette or any of her sisters, but she kept saying no, the whole bunch was thick as thieves with their mama and she couldn't trust any one of them.

The last time I drove Belle to meet Arthur, she was early coming back to the car and I see her eyes look red. "Anything wrong?" I says.

"No," she says, trying to smile, "just a lovers' quarrel."

"Well, there's kleenex in there," I says, meaning the glove compartment, "and you better comb your hair and put on some lipstick before you get home." I don't say nothing 'bout her lip bleeding a little from where she must of been biting on it.

She does like I tell her, and then she says, "Me and Arthur are about ready to take off. We should of done it a long time ago. Soon as we're married, everything will be all right."

"I know that," I says.

"Yeah," she says, "one more week and we're off. Arthur has a friend in New York."

So all that week I'm on pins and needles, waiting for it to happen and imagining what the family will say and reminding myself that no matter what, mum's the word, 'cause my line has gotta be that I never knew nothing was cooking. Leastways, til everybody is friends again. By the end of the week, I can't stand the suspense no more, so early Saturday morning I rings up Belle, and Auntie Mai answers. She says Belle can't come to the phone 'cause she's sick to her stomach. Now Auntie never fibbed to me in her life, but I'm suspicious. "I wouldn't be surprised Belle's gone," I thinks to myself, "and auntie's covering up." Pretty soon my own tummy starts doing the dipsy doodle, I'm getting so nervous and worrying maybe I did wrong to keep Belle's secret.

Another day goes by, and I'm on the phone to auntie's again. This time Belle picks up, which I'm not expecting.

"You're there!" I says.

"Uh huh," she says and that's all, so I figure she can't talk.

"Belle," I says in a whisper, "just say the day, like 'tomorrow' or 'Wednesday.' They won't catch on."

"Mama's calling me, I gotta go," she says and hangs up.

Next thing I know, my mama is telling me Belle's gone to spend a few days with auntie's cousin Florence in Maine. (The one who's married to a rich doctor, but that's another story.) I wanta say, "You can tell me the truth, mama. Hey, I knew about it before any of you!" But I don't say a word. I'm feeling ashamed. And I'm just wishing it was the old days, with Belle spinning round like Vaughn's ballerina, and us gals clapping and carrying on til auntie told us to hush.

Another week and guess what! Belle's back home. I seen her there with my own eyes. But no Arthur, just this rocker looking empty where he used to sit. Belle looks kinda pale and don't say much to nobody, and don't look at me at all. But just when I'm leaving, she gives me the high sign so I meets her out in back under the quince tree, where there's an old wooden table and benches. "I changed my mind," she says, and all the time she's kicking at the rotten fruit in the grass. "I got other things to do, I'm not the marrying kind."

"Oh," I says, feeling like a jerk and picturing--I don't know why but I'm picturing the jars of quince jelly setting on a shelf in auntie's kitchen. "But what about Arthur?" I says.

"His heart is broke, of course. He never cared for no one the way he cares for me. And he never will. Even if he gets married, he never will love her the same. And she'll know it, too, 'cause when he's dying and she's standing over him, he'll look up but he won't even see her, and the last word on his lips will be 'Belle.'"

"Oh, Belle," I says, feeling it's too, too sad-just like a

story-and-wanting to make everything right again.

"It's okay," she says, looking up at me, all cheerful. "I got me a new job with the phone company, I'm gonna be a long distance operator and say hello to people in Europe and China! That's almost as good as traveling 'round the world!"

"What a great job!" I says, forgetting about poor Arthur and thinking to myself, "That Belle always was the lucky one."

---

\*   Certain circumstances in this story are drawn from life, but the main action and the major characters are entirely fictitious.

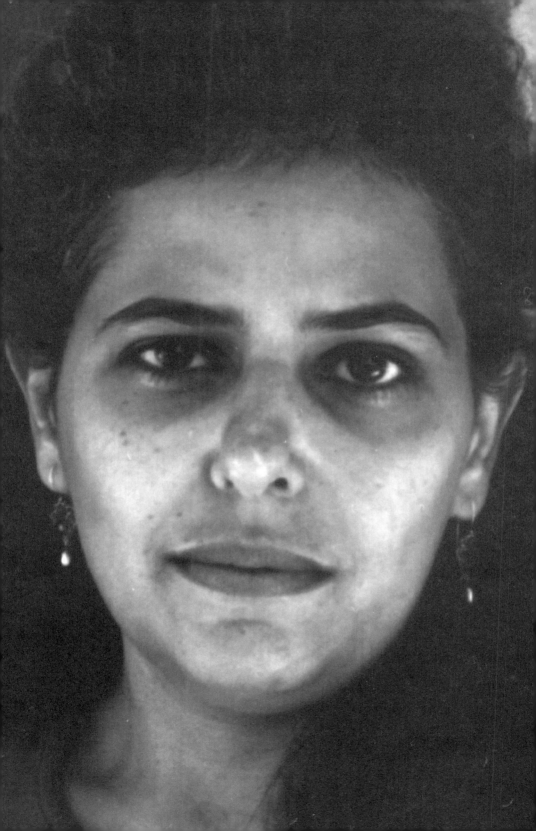

# Pauline Kaldas

# TWO POEMS

FRAUDULENT ACTS

to be walking on the corniche
nostalgia bordered by sticky smog of polluted air
to hail a cab, negotiate a fare
        hold the silent facade      of being Egyptian
who impersonates
    walking through a Nubian village
people guess: "he's Egyptian you're Foreigner"
the waiter in Felfela taking me for a European woman

But once in Siwa a young man recognizes I am Coptic
"it was your eyes"
the first time I imagine my religion
        shadowed on my features
          like a palm tree carries
          its ripened yellow dates
and Maggie tells me Copts have big round eyes, small chins
I search out faces    to decipher the lines that draw us
at the spring fed pond near desert edge,
where soon an Italian company will build a luxury hotel
advertising the healing waters of Siwa,

a young boy assures "Copts are bad and must die"
                                        taken to where

*there was a woman who found herself drowning in the water*
*while carrying her child. desperate because the child had not*
*been baptized and death was near, she said in the name of the*
*father and son and baptized the child herself in the sea's water.*
*after she was rescued, she went to the church, but every time*
*the priest lowered her child to the basin, the water dried up.*
*three times this happened until the priest asked her if this child*
*had ever been baptized before. the woman confessed and told*
*him what had happened. and the priest said, God has accepted*
*your baptism.*
                having carried
                this story against so many doubts

"So you'll have to wear a veil"
a breath to inhale to explain
overlooking heads: anyone with uncovered hair now suspect
likely to be Coptic
taken for what     at the airport's glass enclosures
aren't you Egyptian why the passport stamped Tourist

# FROM A DISTANCE BORN
*for Céline*

1
From a distance born
into snow wind
hazy sky moon drive to the hospital
for thirty-six hours
                    your head a keen piercing
turning low inside me

                    my body resists your entrance
clear dawn light
a display of rectangles
        the hospital building at right angles

each contraction spread thin like fish skin stretches over *tabla*
    to push you out only a pretense
into a round of unutterable consonants

2
From your father's hand pressed tight into mine
dark musk smell
                    mixture of incense, coconut traced to
Aswan market street, dusk light
burlap bags rolled open: sassafras, hibiscus,
smell of peanuts roasted in sand
    a breath walking on the wind

a man sits at the marina's edge,
            his arm a seesaw on the *rababa*
                    music strung through water and sand
        catapults
                    to a plateau of sounds

3
What can I give you here
I have been able to hold nothing
each year, I return to the moment of departure
a careening convulsion of fear
   shifting earth planes break apart to
isolation
  a loss of chatter  uncles  aunts  cousins  grandparents
unable to utter
  letters in Arabic script to spellout
  home like an iceberg dissolving

the doctor's arrival with forceps
your father's voice, a command exerting you out into

On my body
  I lay my hand over you

4
The second night
  still awkwardly balanced
          in my cradle hold
closed eyelids quiver with your mouth's movement
for a long time   you eat

ten minutes later, the nurse returns
    your face a reddened demand:  hungry
                    crying
out of my own desire for sleep I hold you
eyes intent on my face   dark
as if the night of our labor is still in them
  merging into black   I can't trace their circles
you turn away from my breast
only your eyes reach my face like a hung note
straining its pitch

at last you take two sips
then fall firmly asleep
having confirmed that crying will always lead
                           to this place
you claim me for your own.

# Paula Haydar

# PICTURE US

I saw a photograph of us
sitting in a mountainside cafe.
Do you remember that day we spent
on our long journey to The Cedars?
That restaurant.
That old man.
How he unlocked the doors just
for us and welcomed us in to where
I had never been
and always been.

I can hear the music in the background
winding out of the jukebox he oiled
with arak. "It cures all--
the sting of the razor, the smell on your hands
after fish for dinner..."
Fayrouz's voice churns
in you the days of a village boyhood.
I can see you there on the mountainside,
breathing mountain air,
mischief in your smile.

It is summer and you are a boy

hunting birds and turning stones,
eyes as bright as the snow as it melts
from the Cedars beneath the summer sky.
Your hair is black as kohl,
your body olive brown,
your cheeks red as the rooftops of Hasroun,
red as the pomegranates your mother
in full burning youth
plucked from the cliffs of Hasroun.

You skip down into the valley
with the drive of migratory birds.
You dodge the thorned stinkweed thistles
stopping at times to smack the ripe ones
splashing the sticky juice
onto your brown leather shoes.
You wipe the sweat that drips from your brow
like arak trickling from the still.
Your legs throb,
your eyes search the ground.

You wipe the arak and rest a while
searching the ground for something to capture:
a snail, a scorpion, a wild snapdragon,
something to examine, to show off.
With the spunk of youth,
you spring to your feet.
And as you resume your childhood journey
someone pulls at you from behind.
You turn around and there I am:

A young girl from your village
and I ask,
"Can I come along?"

# Hayan Charara

# CAMP DEARBORN
## and other poems

HAMZA AWEIWI,
A SHOE SALESMAN IN HEBRON

The taps have not been running
since July seventeen,
his wedding day.
Now it's twenty-nine days
without clean water.

He has tanks on the roof.
Some days he manages to shave,
or his wife prepares the tea kettle.
But he knows the price of water.
It's holy, hard to come by.

Outside his shop, fat and bald,
an electrician with seven children
admits he does not wash his clothes.
A young girl, a yellow ribbon
in her hair, is laughing.
She knows grown men
should not smell that way.

He yanks a nail from a shoe
that needs to be resoled.
He knows he doesn't need to fix them
to walk far enough where people live differently.
There, boys are washing cars,
housewives water lawns.

He seems troubled, hesitant,
looking for something in the distance.
But a cluster of trees
blocks the view.
He still daydreams
about taking long showers,
or even two a day.
But it's almost noon,
the temperature unbearable.
And the shoes are piling up.

## THE PREGNANCY

I swore I'd never forget
that afternoon: the fractured light
of midsummer lingering
on slanted rooftops,
the pressure of your hand in mine,
the exact fare of the cab ride
to Woodside. I remember
the phone call the night before,
the great distance between us,
the unnerving noise
of a car alarm outside,
neighbors milling around the street,

the yellow and orange sunset
eerily welling up above the trees.
I said I'd always remember
that sterile clinic—
the first listing in the Yellow Pages—
where the nurse told us
not to be ashamed,
how I licked my fingers
and counted out $300.
But these say nothing
of human sadness.

I wiped your forehead
with a cool washcloth
and when you were asleep,
cradled your face in my palms.
That afternoon I saw living and dying
in everything: the slight downpour
that trickled off the fire escapes
into the muddy earth,
maple leaves hanging
like drooped flags,
my mother always and forever
in the photograph.
I saw it in your pained smile,
how you woke on a narrow bed
wanting to glimpse the future,
to make the treachery of tomorrow
vanish. I tried not to think
of what we'd done,
not to go over the hurts
we call the past.
I said I did not want to forget:
a boy and girl,
our innocence unwavering.

But that was a long time ago.
There was so much death then
and ours was murderous.


## CAMP DEARBORN

The bathrooms had no toilets.
The lakes were man-made
and in September, five days
after Labor Day, they were drained,
the muddy floors sprouting
mufflers, broken bottles
and eight-track tapes.
There were vandalized trailers
and police patrolling the fishing dock
used condoms behind the cafeteria,
bird shit everywhere.
The camp was not even
in Dearborn.

Some of us lived there all summer.
We smoked pot and cigarettes,
lit matches to torch garbage cans
heaped with paper plates
or hid in the stalls and watched girls
hold their breath under the showers
to see their breasts swell.

Near the waste dump
a dam plunged the river,
the water thudding off the rafters.
We climbed barbed wire fences
and disappeared over the edge,
bobbing up in the stream,

levitating our hands in praise
of gravity.
When the *Herald*
reported a boy from Milford
drowned at the bottom of the dam—
his neck crooked, his stomach
bloated—they staked a sign
that read: Keep Out-Danger.

That summer we visited the dam
every Sunday, bragging
about how many times
we went over, about the seaweed
that nearly kept us under.
We imagined the sight
of the mother's face staring at the casket
the father who stood outside
the funeral parlor, and cried.
We knew something bad had happened,
we knew a sign would not keep
boys from dying.
We stood in line, hesitant,
until someone shouted "pussy"
or "chicken-shit"
and we knew what we had to do.

249

# Sekeena Shaben

# TWO POEMS

### twentieth ode

i'm taking a cab
down to the bowery
only because
there's a street there that lays open
yellow lines directing
action down long corridors of retreat
changes shifting
this is the part of geography's speech
i don't understand
brodsky patiently sitting at my bedside
how his mexico
collapses even the hardest heart
bogus scrawled on my bedroom door
revolution etched by my mirror

i sit on my fire escape
this is an early morning serenade
to the christian mission on the corner
to hassam at the grocery
to the drug dealer i spot across the street
i'm being seduced

by the dirty fingernails
and syringes on my doorstep
romanced by catcalls and four letter words

"i want to touch you
i want to be your friend"
slow hand dipping low
red hair cuts me down the center
i want to rearrange the letters in your name
remembered how once we sat in the grass
scared of weather and words
then remembered
it wasn't you at all

it's only noon here
and already a lifetime has passed by
brodsky wasn't god's spy
don't think he was ever that certain
of a task
his words like pillows to rest on
a window open to the plight of countries
i'll never understand

**april 5/97**

in music on howl on telephone
in black and white on second hand book
on your passing
the drift you may be feeling
the opening or closing of a fist

but a closed fist is not
how i held you

remember the length of the wall
remember the surge of sunlight
in your innocuous boulder room

what is it
with the holding of this memory
clinging to the edges
tied restlessly to a rapid overflowing western creek
you
the lower east side evangelist you
the berkeley 1955 pilgrim you
forever fixed here
in a mercer street workroom
a room of work for love
not money
(the pipes banging corner loft
not my home
but mine for a while)

i think i said a toast for you
it wasn't the right thing to do
better to leave you alone there
where you are being chanted a thousand times

# Saladin Ahmed

# GRAVITY
## and other poems

POEM FOR COUNTEE CULLEN

Remembering him
Remembering
The jungle
I remember
remembering
The desert
Neither of us
Has ever been there
For both of us
It is home
Where he found
Echoes of tribal rhythms
And the celluloid chatter
Of Tarzan fauna
In unfiltered 20-hit packs
Of Harlem
And
Screechy gray parrots
In Brownstone
Rainstorms
I find Bedouin

Cattle drums
In cavernous
Hip-Hop clubs
And sift
Camel hairs
Out of
Oil puddle
Rainbows


UMAR: AN AFFIRMATION TWO HOURS LATER

They say "You Can't Kill The Truth," but
America respects dead artists

Rigor mortis of the muse sells records
Stagnant poems fill swamp-water
journals of same old same
old avant-garde
Another poem about streets at 3 a.m.
Another poem about heroin and masturbation
Another poem about John Coltrane

Crackpipe addiction to
canonized revolution
burns in our lungs, screaming
"New Ways!"
"New Ways!

Find New Ways to cram
chewing gum wads of perspective, of
knowledge into the spaces in
brain matter left burnt and empty by
post-modern,
post-cold war,

post-feminist,
post-militant apathy

Find new ways to polish
blue steel bullets of sincerity,
open fire indiscriminately,
leaving 'em lying in the street like a gangsta rapper
capped up by truth instead of
illusion

We have seen hacked up
corpses of 16 year old girl revolutionaries
We have seen people supposedly
in love with The Art
whose arms around our shoulders
leave a smeary trail of bullshit
We have seen voices that threatened sincerity
suck down buckshot cough drops,
drown in free market cyanide,
consumed by cancer of the cantbeatemjoinem

But still, optimism

Optimism shining out of eyes not sealed with sleep dust of
naivete, optimism not stoned on fumes of
idealistic foolishness, optimism certainly not fat off the
artery hardening meat of sold out

Optimism that tastes like the
creator's master plan
Optimism with energy that
cuts like the razor of youth
Optimism with patience that
guides
like the roadmap of age

Two facts ring out like the
splat
of corporate white male skulls
cracked against liberty bell:

America respects dead artists
but sometimes you really
can't kill The Truth


GRAVITY

Call this thang Calvinism
de la Corazón.

Yes, let's not fool ourselves; what we are
talking about here is no less than

Allah's fingerprint on earth, the
faintly smeared ridges and whirls that are

Divine Might made manifest.
To be honest we are

talking about trying to
define the sun, trying to

spell it S-*U*-*N* as each
roman letter is consumed

in yellow flames of inadequacy,
trying to discuss 'helium composition'

and 'celestial orbits' as crackling
solar flares catch in our throats

See, the truth is we are
talking about a force

which one rarely notices,
which one takes for granted,

until one is plummeting parachuteless towards
a smiling, craggy landscape 40,000 feet below.

A force which brings Easter-egg hued planets
hurtling out of celluloid orbit,

smashing together in fiery.
screaming sci-fi oblivion.

A magnet over metal shavings that drags brain
cells unerringly toward the conclusion

that despite the chic of the jaded, despite
our collectively morphinated sense of wonder,

despite muthafuckas buying up
cynicism like it was goin' outta style,

some things are still worth our awe,
some things are worth blood and ink,

some things are still worth falling for

# Mohja Kahf

# READ
## and other poems

MY BODY IS NOT YOUR BATTLEGROUND

My body is not your battleground
My breasts are neither wells nor mountains,
neither Badr nor Uhud
My breasts do not want to lead revolutions
nor to become prisoners of war
My breasts seek amnesty; release them
so I can glory in their milktipped fullness,
so I can offer them to my sweet love
without your flags and banners on them

My body is not your battleground
My hair is neither sacred nor cheap,
neither the cause of your disarray
nor the path to your liberation
My hair will not bring progress and clean water
if it flies unbraided in the breeze
It will not save us from our attackers
if it is wrapped and shielded from the sun
Untangle your hands from my hair
so I can comb and delight in it,
so I can honor and annoint it,

so I can spill it over the chest of my sweet love

My body is not your battleground
My private garden is not your tillage
My thighs are not highway lanes to your Golden City
My belly is not the store of your bushels of wheat
My womb is not the cradle of your soldiers,
not the ship of your journey to the homeland
Leave me to discover the lakes
that glisten in my green forests
and to understand the power of their waters
Leave me to fill or not fill my chalice
with the wine or honey of my sweet love
Is it your skin that will tear
when the head of the new world emerges?

My body is not your battleground
How dare you put your hand
where I have not given permission
Has God, then, given you permission
to put your hand there?
My body is not your battleground
Withdraw from the eastern fronts and the western
Withdraw these armaments and this siege
so that I may prepare the earth
for the new age of lilac and clover,
so that I may celebrate this spring
the pageant of beauty with my sweet love

MORE THAN ONE WAY TO BREAK A FAST

Your lips are dark, my love,
and fleshy, like a date
And night is honeyslow
in coming, long to wait—

I have fasted, darling,
daylong all Ramadan—
but your mouth—so sweet,
so near—the hours long!

Grant but one taste—one kiss!
You know what good reward
feeders of festers gain
from our clement Lord—

See how the fruits are ripe
and ready, O servant of God—
Kiss me—it's time, it's time!
And let us earn reward

263

READ!

By the birds,
by the birds
you release in me

By the skies
you open
in my breasts
and my arms

By the forests,
by the dark
of the forests
you grow in me

By the fish
you send streaming
through my green sea

By the moons
of your eyes'
black gleam
on the lakes
of my eyes

By your hands
when they brush
like the wings
of angels over me

By your body
like river
waters running clean
over pebbles on the bed

of the earth in me

You and I
We are stars
We are signs

We are God's
poetry

# Walid Bitar

# THREE POEMS

PERFECT GALLOWS

Often, I pick up
the receiver, and dial
6, 7 numbers—
the more the memorizer,
neither right nor wrong.
These numbers conspire—
in no time they're ringing,
then they're a voice.
Now a ghost can't wait
for the death of what it was;
it doesn't exist
until after the death.
But the voice I dial,
my ghost's, is somehow
ahead of itself:
"hello?" it says,
as if it doesn't know
who's calling.
I hear what I need to,
its timbre, volume, tone.
Then I hang the phone.

But left to myself,
my balance is thrown:
"it's as if," 1 say
to my 2 profiles,
"I sit on a fence,
and you push me over
both of its sides
simultaneously,
like bougainvillea,
like the past and the future."
The present, like some chord
in me, must be on strike.


SALTIMBANQUE

She comes after the fact—
she's fact's younger twin,
set, like a clock to be 10 minutes late,
which frees her from gravity:
when she dives, she freezes
in mid air—
call her *fly-stopped*—
not a motion, a position—
10 minutes later,
she drops—her splash,
like a camera angle,
is inaudible—
the water she displaces
is for eyes, not ears.
And the races whose genes
pass through her like ships
in the night have no idea this
(or anything else)
ever takes place.

The angel knows,
though he takes no place—
he's juxta*something,*
not position.
Smile, move his lips,
he can't—
they have no position
from which to move.
It's not a question of airports
from which to fly,
but planes—*one plane*—
in which to appear.
At times it seems clear:
*there is no angel,*
no witness to her act.
But she double-checks:
she shadow fences—
there's a resistance—
she hears *sounds* of it—
*swishes* in the air.
They balance, these sounds,
in one ear and the other,
as if sounds were pounds,
ears scales
she keeps trying to tip,
turning round and around,
swashbuckling:
anything to find
a position in which
her right ear is weighed
down more than the left,
or the left ear down
more than the right.
Even if she succeeds,
she won't be any closer

to her ultimate goal,
her people's before her,
back for generations:
for one ear to hear
angelic sounds
10 minutes before
the other ear does—
one ear on time,
like a fact—the other
late, chip off the old block.


## THE MENACED VENTRILOQUIST

He skips, he scratches,
like a needle on a record—
my voice (basso),
*his* r.p.m.s—
our tag team hits
play from Borneo to Ghent...
But like the square root
of 2, he's impossible
to identify precisely.
Sometimes we wrestle
in marble (*I* sculpt it).
Sometimes he slaps me—
I turn—he turns—
the other cheek...
I turn it faster;
I *am* the one slapped.
I slap him back;
he has turned the other cheek
before being slapped,
this man who describes me
like 400 rabbits

describe a drunkard.
But his words escape me
into embassies of air,
asylums no one
can follow them into.
I let his eyes judge,
even though I'm unsure
if they're squinting, or italicized.
If squinting, he's responsible.
But if italicized,
who could have written down his eyes?
I myself
have cat-o'-nines for pen.
To friend and foe alike I say:
to whip is human
to be whipped divine.

# Dunya Mikhail

# FIVE MINUTES

In five minutes
The world will end
The owner of the nearby store
Has already put a" Closed " sign
And gone out
As if he knows
there is no time for work
There are other stores
                    open
Their owners are still busy
But the world will end after...
A bunch of happy guys
   are passing the street quickly
A dog follows them
Leading an old woman
The traffic light is red
The bus driver is adjusting his mirror slightly
There are still some scenes
To passed through the mirror
He is pulling out now
The traffic light is green
It will continue to change
Even after five minutes !

A young man is looking
At his watch
Waiting for the bus
In the park
A couple is passing by the statues
And smiling under the sun
The statues are carefree
Looking firmly into nothing
A tourist is wandering curiously
And taking photos
For what will be absent shortly
In the white hospital there
Women are giving birth to new babies
                                    too late
Maybe they will leave the world
Without names
In one unit
Some babies will be left
In incubators
                forever
While the mouse in the lab
Will finally get rid
Of the big eye
Watching it
All the time
The test was not difficult
But the time ended
Before the answers were filled in
It doesn't matter anymore
Whether you know them
                        or not
Smell the rose and go on
It knows
The world will end in minutes
The blue shirt behind the facade

Seems very beautiful on the manikin
One of two girls
Pointed at it.
They went through the revolving door
To be swallowed up by the high building
On the wall
There are glittering advertisements
    Big sale now
    A new medicine for facial lines
    Modern houses on Mars at low low prices
    We have healthy cigarettes and other things
But the world will end
Inside his fenced room
Inside the fenced palace
Inside the fenced city
The tyrant was biting an apple
And watching himself on TV
I can't believe that he will leave the throne
In five minutes
Here is another prisoner for life
The attorney applies for appeal
But the world ...
Passengers roamed through the departure lounge
Others came out of the arrival door
A girl is putting her bag down
And waving her hand
It is not me
Somebody is waving to her
From behind the glass
It is not you
I don't know if they met
Or the time ...
That undergraduate student
Prefers to travel by train
It doesn't make a big difference

at this moment
He has agreed with his friend
To go on a picnic
I don't know whether the picnic
Ended before the end of the world
Or the world ended before the picnic!
As for me, I was writing a letter
I don't think it was finished in five minutes.

# Hasan Newash

# THE SCREAM 98

Thoughtful Mr. President not to strike in Ramadan
Pound the Collider, knock him hard a few days before
Let the uni-power guns, from the land of the free
Rain at midnight, but before Ramadan
On the Baghdad corral!
They may celebrate their Eid in mass graves
In Bosnia, a shredded country too, of the right timing
Of whose wondrous blows, as you come
And zip away into a smile
While she waits until your next address
From the oval office?
The UN parolee today, you call a criminal
Gassed Halabja's Kurds in '88
While a president stood in silence
Then gassed Nowruz of Arabestan
Aloof, the president, still was silent
"Degrade his ability to produce weapons of mass destruction"

The President declares in '98. To global consensus
Waves a finger, bites a cigar, and the Cruise again,
Desert Fox of his time, falls on Sumer
As the sanctions of nine annums collapse
Her into famine, while gold is shimmering,

Spills along the Tigris, turns imperative
Bilharzia a daily drink in the city of Basra
Nine-year sanctions virus-taint her drinking water
Is not a weapon of mass destruction
As she sleeps on depleted uranium bed
Prolifies her rate of child leukemia
And sends the Maryland veterans home to whither
And twist on Bethesda's steps in lies
Of the Gulf Syndrome

Vampire flares tonight are falling
As the palace television beams
The hottest news: His Majesty meets
With Party officials adopting measures
To shield the Royal Family of Quam'aan
From a new aggression
Next frame a hospital ward
Soumayya's lugging her three year old Marwan's
Limp body bleeding from a bandaged head wound
Bellows, waving her other arm
"Why do you do this to our people?"
Saad Er-rasafi, a seven year old, died
Today at 8:03 of malnutrition
Tylenol has been out at Al-Rasheed Clinic
For eight days. Hisham Samerraii, a two year old
Salwa Sa'ibee, a nine year old, died of a brain tumor
At 9:00 am. Salwa's life could not be saved
Sanctions allow no drugs for chemotherapy

Who is the enemy, the talk show host
"The President is wrong, don't just bomb
Level the whole country off?"
Who is the enemy, Mr. Joe Hill
As the nightly news trumpets the Enterprise
Proud Navy men who sign their feelings

On the two-ton bullets before they load:
"Merry Christmas," another: "Here is a Ramadan present"
Another, pointedly: "Die you maggots?"
Who are we fighting, Mr. Joe Hill
And whose side are you on, today
As the killer in Jerusalem is now a minister
While Kathy is a Voice in the Wilderness
Facing prison and fine for taking toys
And Tylenol to children of Babylon?

Impeach postponement, today
Impeach Ramadan
Of silence and pray not to God in Mecca
The Emir has sold Him an option on Wall Street
And His son, His son's body I saw auctioned
In Wye River for the airport in Gaza
*Walum yalid walum youlad*
*Walum yakon lahu kofwan ahad*
In my face: "You're nothing"
Scream the hollyhocks
Lavender, white, and blue to cripple
My already sluggish pace
As Jihad in Sabra is weeping
For Kosovo
Today impeach my silence
Now, I take on the mob

# Penny Johnson

# THE LESSONS OF LEILA

A poster of two young lovers on a sunset beach was enscrolled with the word "Forever." I once asked Leila if she had ever been to the beaches near Tel Aviv, an hour's drive away from Ramallah, or to any of the other Israeli beaches on the snaky Mediterranean coast. She said she hadn't been herself, but she had heard about the beaches from some Palestinian girls from Jerusalem, whose parents used to take them once in a while before the Uprising. They sounded nice.

Boutique Jamal in downtown Ramallah was stacked with the drippy objects that Leila thought were so adorable: fuzzy trolls bearing messages, pigs wearing sunglasses and posters of babies and kittens separately and in tandem. Whether girls naturally oozed coy sentiment or whether it was induced to mask their uncomfortable animal natures was a question to ponder.

I stared at a heart-shaped box which declared that love was eternal and thought Leila might like it for her thirteenth birthday. She was drawn to lofty principles. I had known her now for only six months, but she had assumed a disproportionate role in my life. Leila had been responsible for my first arrest and currently she was in charge of my political education. Yesterday, for example, she took me to visit her aunt in Amari refugee camp.

Even though the camp is on the main road into Ramallah, I didn't know exactly where it was until the beginning of the Uprising. When I came to the West Bank, I thought refugee camps would stand out like grainy black and white newsreels amid the Kodak colors of everyday life. But Amari was just an ordinary bunch of run-down houses jumbled into a valley on whose heights perched the villas of the Ramallah middle class, inconveniently enduring the edges of the curfews, teargas and army patrols directed against their neighbors.

It took us ten minutes to walk from the center of town to the entrance of the camp. Entrance is perhaps the wrong word, since two rows of cement-filled barrels blocked the road into Amari, courtesy of the Israeli Defense Forces. In the first months of the Uprising, soldiers put up the first row. Then, as legend has it, the Prime Minister chose the entrance to announce to the press that the army had things well in hand. A barrage of rocks and chunks of cement hurled from behind the barrels led the the army to hastily erect another line of defense.

Leila's aunt Randa turned out to be eighteen-years old, an activist in one of the leftist factions. We only saw her for five minutes before some other young women came to pull her away to a meeting. I was relieved to see her go; she had begun to lecture me on U.S. policy, a subject for which I felt a growing repugnance. Being an American in the Middle East is like being caught in a tape loop, subject to lectures repetitious with truth or to unanswerable questions people ask after the evening news. I am genuinely puzzled when asked whether Bush is more foolish than Reagan, a subject that has come up more than once. Certain interjections do not demand a reply. Yesterday, I met a middle aged lady whose car tires had just been shot by settlers who didn't like her version of a U-turn. As she told me her story, she raised her hand like a prophet and declaimed "Bush, America! Bush, America!"

Um Abed, Randa's mother, had a lined face and a weary body which suggested old age until I looked directly in her eyes, just as she was telling us about a neighbor's tumor that was as big as a baby. She was probably younger than my forty heavy years, although the line dividing her youth and middle age must have been drawn for her much earlier. Um Abed turned on the television and insisted that we stay and eat *frike* soup, thick and grainy, doused with lemon and served with knobby *taboon* bread. I left feeling satisfied, but Leila insisted we must come back and talk to Randa: "She knows everything about politics. Everything. She always leads the women's demonstrations."

The sound of a shot outside the stationary store reminded me I should hurry; more shots might bring all the metal shutters of the shops down for the day and I wouldn't have a present for tomorrow's party. Leila was excited about becoming a teenager but I wasn't sure why. When she came to invite me to her party, I had tried to tease her about boys but she only looked puzzled.

My own thirteenth birthday had been on a sticky August Midwestern day. I was worried about underarm stains on my new yellow dress; my mother produced dress shields, items which made me feel queasy, like her fat blue box of Kotex. I spent my party wishing I had different friends. All girls, we sullenly ate  chocolate cake and vanilla ice cream while discussing the physical peculiarities of our teachers. I was sure other thirteen year old girls had more daring topics.

I finally chose a cheap plastic radio for Leila, pink with purple flower decals, and bought a Julio Iglesias tape against my better judgment.

"Do you have batteries?" I asked George, who reached behind the counter to produce an obscure brand I had been sold before, guaranteed to last for exactly two and a half cassettes. George studied at the University where I taught, and was political. He usually knew what's going on.

"What's happening today? I heard shooting."

"The army killed an old man in Amari this morning," George replied. "The camp's under curfew, but the kids from

Kaddoura are burning tires and throwing stones over by the post office."

I asked the age of the man who died. Certain ages struck me as sadder than others; I don't know why. Children were obvious, but why a 50-year-old woman was so much sadder than a 26-year-old man baffled me. The man in Amari was 72, and repaired shoes, probably the mournful shoes of the poor. His death seemed no sadder than others. When the first student at the University was killed several years ago, I had grieved, perhaps falsely, and even started a poem. Now I pocketed my change and hoped I would be able to get to the grocery store. The three days of mourning would mean all the shops were closed. Maybe Leila would cancel her birthday party.

❏

Leila stood at the window and watched the boys running up the alley after setting a tire on fire. She felt she was with them, her heart pounding, running fast down the narrow alley between the Birzeit and Nablus roads. But she couldn't go out and join the boys by herself; they would stare at her and maybe tell their families, who would certainly tell her father. Maybe she should go downstairs and look for her girlfriends: in a group, girls could roam the streets, chanting and putting up barricades. Sometimes, they even had their own demonstrations, inspired, and sometimes prompted, by the boys. Leila saw Walid dart behind the corner; his hightop sneakers and tight jeans looked new and she wondered if his relatives in Detroit had sent him money.

Leila opened her top drawer and looked at her treasures: a bead bracelet in the color of the Palestinian flag, three rubber bullets picked up near her school, a picture of Tom Cruise in smeared newsprint, and a picture of Radi, the boy from the next street who was killed last year. She had carefully peeled the poster off the telephone pole to which it had been glued, but a jagged tear cut off the top of Radi's head. She though he was very beautiful, his smile soft and sweet and his eyes understanding. Sometimes she imagined having his baby; she would give him a revolutionary name, a name that would make Radi proud.

From the window, she saw the foreign woman walking heavily down the street, the plastic bags of vegetables twisting around her fingers. She liked to go over to Annie's house and drink sweet tea and listen to Annie's music tapes. Sometimes Annie talked too much and her questions bothered Leila.

❑

I looked at the stained porcelain of my sink basin, the latest in a long line of yellowing sinks. This particular sink I had tried to conquer, recklessly pouring the thick green bleach until the whole house smelled like a laundry. Now I was resigned.

The afternoon hemmed me in as usual; in the morning, when the shops and the University's temporary offices were open, I sped around like a cartoon character, buying the newspaper, getting supplies, and doing a limited amount of work teaching my English class in the bedroom of an echoing apartment rented by the University after the army closed the campus. A class in mechanical engineering was in the kitchen, and various squeaks and scratches broke into my explanation of Emma Woodhouse's moral failings as the engineering students maneuvered mysterious pieces of equipment smuggled from the closed University labs.

At noon, everything stopped and the adrenalin drained away, leaving a mild restlessness. I wandered through my rooms, looking for something to do. If only I had something to tend: a child, a lover, a cat. I tried to write in a diary, but the paragraphs melted like ice cubes on the page.

Leila rang my bell as the light had narrowed into a band across my bedspread. I didn't feel like company, but I thought Leila might see me come out of the house later and feel bad.

Leila greeted me politely. She tended to be well-mannered at the beginning and end of our conversations and ruthless in the middle: hectoring me for my faults in politics, social convention, and especially, in the Arabic language. "You have to try," she would counsel fiercely, "you have to study every day." When I pointed out that her tendency to mock me when I made mistakes was not particularly helpful, she looked even sterner. Leila was an advocate of the punitive school of education.

I answered Leila first in Arabic, saying I was fine, praise be to God. Then I added in English: "I'm really tired and bored." I said it again in Arabic, in case Leila didn't understand. Then I asked Leila how she was.

She said she was fine, praise be to God, but then she added: "but I'm sad today about the martyr in Amari."

Leila started to cry, and I patted her head, noticing for the first time that her shiny black hair had streaks of midnight blue. I was ashamed that Leila's emotions operated on a more public-spirited level than mine and I struggled to ask the right questions: in Leila's version, the dead man was 68-years-old and worked in the biscuit factory. I went to make tea and open some of the factory's dry chocolate wafers for Leila, who seemed to be nourished by sugar.

"Tomorrow is the funeral," Leila said when I returned with the steaming tea. "If you want to go, we can get into Amari early tomorrow morning by the back way and go with my aunt. All the women will march together."

A rush of blood made my head tingle unpleasantly. I knew exactly when I had stopped being brave: the date was Mayday 1971 during a demonstration held under the bold slogan "If the government doesn't stop the war, we'll stop the government." Weary after a night bus ride from Albany, but intent on following the instructions for my affinity group, I stepped into the street at 6:15 A.M. to block the morning commuter traffic across the M Street Bridge. A few minutes later, two policemen grabbed me by my long, straight hair and began to beat me, without much method but zestfully. They told me to get out of town. I was surprised, then indignant, then afraid. My immunity was over.

"It's important for all the people to see that foreigners care about the Palestinians," Leila informed me sternly, making me feel like I embodied that elusive concept, the international community.

I didn't feel up to the role. I was far too self-conscious, for one thing. And I had planned major errands: ordering a gas barrel for the stove usually consumed a day's energy. I even worried my period might start, although it was several days away. Lately, I had also been prone to anxiety that it wouldn't come, signaling early menopause.

I looked at Leila and nodded.

"I'll pass by tomorrow at 6:30," Leila said firmly and drank the rest of her tea quickly. "I've got to go home now and help my mother with making pickles." Leila was often engaged in massive household tasks that took days on end: she made jam and goat cheese and stuffed all varieties of vegetables in time-consuming rituals that reminded me of my grandmother on her Illinois farm surrounded by Bell jars.

I nodded my head again, and went off to look in my closet for something to wear that was dark enough for mourning, warm enough for a rainy Ramallah day, and respectable enough to stop soldiers from shooting me.

❏

Leila's stomach fluttered as she suddenly woke up to the first luminous fingers of dawn. She hoped Annie wouldn't embarrass her in the camp; maybe she shouldn't have invited her to come today. The sounds of the morning nudged her out of bed: the smell of coffee laced with cardamom, Radio Monte Carlo, her mother humming to the Marlboro commercials. Last night, she had carefully ironed her jeans and best pink shirt with the blood-red skyline of Los Angeles outlined on the back, along with her father's shirt and her mother's white headdress, which always gave her trouble. Ironing was her favorite household task. She moved the heavy iron in swift, sure movements around buttons and pockets.

"Morning, *immi*," she said, trying not to look at her mother's slippers. They had once been her eldest brother's and the stained green plaid fabric and the tufts of yellowing lambswool of the lining always looked dirty, although Leila's mother was always washing them and hanging them on the line. When Leila nagged her mother to throw them away, her mother only replied that they were warm and she liked them. Leila however, was sure that her mother liked to snuggle her feet into the slippers of her favorite child, now a hotel clerk in Abu Dhabi.

"It's early for you, Leila. Did you forget there's no school today?"

"I'm going with the foreign woman to visit Randa. We want to go to the martyr's funeral."

Leila's mother turned away to the stove, making a sad, fluttering gesture with her hands. She wanted to keep Leila home, safe with her schoolbooks and her neatly-ironed clothes hung in a row. When she was a girl, her grandmother had told her not to make friends with girls from the camps, and she had obeyed. Now, she usually excused herself when Leila visited Um Abed. The camp was too crowded and she felt uneasy walking its narrow alleys, as if suddenly the houses might cave in and bury her. In any case, Um Abed was only a distant relation, the youngest sister of her least popular uncle, a timid, uncertain man, hired finally to sit in someone else's shop and sell bits of electrical wire and an occasional light bulb. The family hadn't grieved much when he died of diabetes and discontent.

Anyway, the death of the martyr seemed remote. She didn't know him and he had been old. The relentless deaths of the young men were the ones that moved her. With each new martyr, she wept and then felt a surge of relief that her son was safely away in the Gulf. But now Leila had started to worry her.

287

She remembered herself at Leila's age; listening to the radio during the Suez invasion, she had sworn she was ready to die to defend the Arab homeland.

"Be careful," she said and moved heavily to the counter to take down a jar of white cheese she had made last spring for Leila to take to Um Abed. "Don't let those godless soldiers kill you. And come back early; your birthday cake will be waiting."

Leila tore off a small piece of bread and slathered it with pink jam. The thought of death was like being buried inside the jam, suffocated by a substance without air or life.

❑

I woke up with the queasy feeling I usually associate with entering an international airline terminal. Events were moving a little too quickly. I hoped a couple of cups of coffee and a nourishing breakfast would increase my enthusiasm, but the refrigerator shelves offered only two sad, cold pieces of bread and half a carton of crusted yogurt, its damp paper top forlornly flapping into itself. I thought of American breakfast specials with ham or bacon, Egg McMuffins or elegant Cambridge café-bakeries, places where morning spelled plenitude, whether of grace or grease. My morning seemed sour and scary. Even the coffee was a disturbing color. The doorbell rang and I found myself smiling.

❑

Leila was surprised by how easy it was to get into the camp. A curfew had sounded to her like a big, dark bag that could be clamped around the camp and its people. But she and Annie slipped from the back road down the hill and into a series of doorways and courtyards until they reached Um Abed's. Annie had chattered about morning birds and told Leila a story about a robin at her mother's house in Illinois who was so fat he couldn't fly. Under Annie's direction, Leila had learned to spell Illinois correctly, but she imagined it like the Los Angeles skyline only without an ocean.

In Um Abed's house, Leila ate a second breakfast,

ravenously consuming an egg fried in olive oil and dotted with dark red sumac, even though at home she had refused to eat eggs for the 1st year, saying it was too much like eating a baby. Her stomach felt a little strange afterwards, and she poured another cup of strong tea laced with sugar. Annie ate her egg with zeal and continued to eat morsels of bread with *labaneh* and *zaatar* while Randa asked her about the latest American peace plan. Leila listened carefully to her answers; Annie was doing well but Leila was still nervous that she would make a joke nobody would understand.

When Randa offered Annie a cigarette, Annie's grimace struck Leila as rude. She loved the way Randa smoked, the cigarette emphasizing her thin, restless hands and her words that came quickly from deep in her throat, pushing and prodding the laziness and selfishness of the world.

Outside the window, the streets were still deserted but the morning air vibrated with piercing whistles as the boys signalled to each other. The funeral march was about to start in a few minutes. Leila smoothed her hair and redid one of her barettes. Um Abed had stayed up all night sewing a flag for Randa to carry. Leila planned to stay near Randa, hoping Randa would ask her to hold the flag. Her mind flickered over a scene of Randa, wounded and bleeding, passing the precious flag to Leila, who lifted it high into the wind.

❑

When Randa said it was time to go to the funeral, I was sure it was too early. I felt comfortable eating breakfast with Um Abed, even Randa's incessant questions were easier to answer, punctuated by doses of warm family food. Randa seemed less awesome, more like one of my students, or like myself lecturing my mother on tiger cages, or even like my younger sister, persistently asking me about the relation of orifices and babies. I was ready to retreat to the kitchen, doing the dishes with Um Abed, discussing why so many American women were unmarried, a topic that seemed suddenly rich with mystery.

Randa had already risen and opened the door to the street. "Let's go," said Leila impatiently. "It's time."

"Where are we going,?" I asked, suddenly aware that I didn't even have my instructions. This was worse than Mayday.

"To the martyr's house and then to the cemetery." Leila was already in the doorway, her eyes fixed on Randa and her hands urging me to hurry.

Outside in the street, littered with plastic bags and soda cans, I linked my arm with Leila, wanting to keep her close to me. Our bare arms touched; Leila felt warm and solid. There were two types of adolescent girls, I had observed: one swelled to fill her growing body, pushing at the flesh until it pulsed and glowed. The other shrunk inside herself, too small for her skin. I had been the latter type; Leila, blessedly, was the former. The feeling of flesh was comforting. Other women joined us from nearby houses, too many women, women singing and making a high, keening noise. I was in a march and I knew what happened to marchers. I nudged Leila to stop for a while to allow me to collect myself, but she pulled away and moved forward until she was a little ahead of everybody else. For a moment, I stood still, and the women swirled around me.

Leila beckoned from a doorway and I scampered to her, so relieved to find shelter I was close to giggling. A little too late, I realized it was the house of the old man who had died and I tried to look somber and composed.

❑

Leila led Annie to the inner room where the wife and daughters of the martyr were sitting in mourning. Annie shook hands in the wrong order, holding onto one of the daughter's hands a long time, embarrassed at her own tears.

Leila walked up to the wife of the martyr and congratulated her on her husband's courage and sacrifice. She said she would always remember him. The woman glanced up briefly but didn't reply. She was looking past Leila to where

Annie was standing, still close to the daughter, still grieving.

"Who's the foreign woman?"

"An American, teaching at the university."

"Let her come here. I want to ask her something."

Leila summoned Annie, hoping Annie would rise to the occasion. The woman pulled a rumpled piece of paper from inside her dress and smoothed it out on the small table cluttered with cups of coffee.

"For God's sake, help me, a poor old woman," the woman said to Annie, her eyes finally filled with tears. "Help me with these people."

Annie looked at the piece of paper and recognized a long and intricate U.S. government form in triplet.

"Social Security," said the woman in her first and perhaps only English words. Annie took out her pen and began to work.

❑

The house of the martyr was just beginning to feel as familiar as Um Abed's breakfast table when Leila once again told me it was time to leave. The chants outside suddenly swelled, lapping at the door, murmuring a meaning I couldn't quite get. I was sure I had gone far enough: through the dawn streets to the curfewed camp, contributing my opinion on Americans and peace, breakfasting on comfort, afraid, so afraid, in the streets, and now here in a house of death circumventing American bureaucracy. I had fulfilled my contract. Leila would be upset, but after all, I was free to decide what I wanted.

"Leila" I said firmly, the adult to the child, "I'm going to walk back to Um Abed's house. It's not necessary for me to go to the cemetery; I've paid my condolences to the family."

"Fine," Leila said with an indifference I remembered myself displaying whenever my mother announced her plans. "I'll find Randa and see you later." She shook the hands of the mourning family in reverse order and opened the door. As she swung out of the door, the letters on the back of her shirt pulsed like an aorta: "Welcome to L.A." Life was draining out of the room, leaving me with the leaf-withered woman and her rattling forms.

"Wait for me, Leila." I stood up hastily, but the old woman stopped me; I promised to go with her to the American Consulate when the curfew was over. As I stepped out of the door, a plastic bag twisted around my foot and I stooped to throw it away. When I looked up, Leila was far ahead with the crowd, her pink and red shirt staining the darker mass with its dawn colors.

I wasn't sure how to get back to Um Abed's. I was too shy to go back in the closed door, present my condolences again and shake all the hands, like a summer re-run. My best move was to go in the opposite direction of the crowd. I turned and began to walk, my head down, not wanting to see or to be seen.

"Go to your houses," boomed an army loudspeaker from where in a guttural Arabic. "Curfew. Go to your houses, people of Amari."

It sounded like a good idea but I heard people shouting No. "Disperse or we will open fire."

I started to walk faster, as though the voice was aimed at me, wanting to scatter me into my abstract parts: foreigner, lady teacher, awkwardly-aged single person, failed utopian, all severed and distinct. I heard an army jeep roar and stop; soldiers were now between me and the crowd that bore Leila away. I didn't know whether to feel relieved.

Then I turned and saw the demonstration coming towards me like a mirage. I looked for Leila's pink shirt before I realized it was a different crowd. My assumption that a demonstration followed a coherent structure like an anti-nuclear march on Washington did not apply to refugee camps. Movement sparked movement like points of light; there were no monitors or arm bands.

I was still staring as the demonstration moved forward. The mass of people shimmered like demonstrations on television; I had always thought it was a special lens that reduced people to waves of light. People were unnaturally close together. Everything was there: flags, tattered banners, shouts of "Allahu Akbar" and "Palestine is Arab." I wasn't convinced I was in the picture, until, behind the screen, behind me, jeeps rumbled forward.

I looked for a doorway, or an alley, but the alley near me was a dead end. A soldier behind me lifted his rifle and I ran straight into the crowd.

"Watch out, come here, you're fine, don't worry," Voices came from several direction and my arms were marked with hands like ribbons around a Maypole. I was in the middle of the demonstration. Several young men looked amused.

"Don't worry. The soldiers usually shoot over our heads for a while," a young guy in an Oregon State T-shirt said encouragingly. I was only saved from unabashed hysteria by the urge to be accepted. The survival value of the herd instinct suddenly became apparent.

I didn't see the soldiers fire, but suddenly everyone was running backwards, but together, like Balanchine's dancers stepping back in order to leap forward. "It's only rubber bullets and tear gas," said the same guy, now holding my hand, as he pulled me around a corner and down a narrow street. We stopped behind a garbage dumpster which was comfortingly large. I hoped it was stuffed full of bullet-stopping garbage, thick, soiled paper diapers, perhaps, or the heads and hoofs of sheep that I always found so disconcerting when discarded on the sidewalk outside Ramallah butcher shops.

I was suddenly embarrassed that he was still holding my hand. The usual binary questions clicked through my mind: was his leg pressed deliberately against mine? was he breathing hard through physical effort or desire? was he looking at my breasts or past them, watching the street? was the look in his eyes seductive or weary? And always, the question of the lone woman turning down a deserted street, hearing steps behind her, walking through deepening shadows: who will help me here?

"We're OK. The soldiers went the other way," said Oregon State and dropped my hand. "Are you alright?"

I blushed and we began to introduce ourselves. His name was Omar and he was visiting for the summer. He didn't go to Oregon State; he worked in his uncle's liquor store in San Francisco and dated a girl named Betty. I used to live in San Francisco, when cocaine and underground politics were still perfectly balanced, and I was surprised girls named Betty lived there.

We mapped ourselves through the geography of San Francisco: he aspired to the Marina and I loved the Mission. For me, San Francisco had been an uneasy haven during the chilly Nixon years, all of us making it on food stamps and pills, street paranoia and hope on the record player, the talk still of George Jackson and the Weather Underground. For Omar, the city was a bank account, a girl and a promise. I had often sat, impatient and bored, while two Palestinians laboriously traced their family identities until they had woven an interconnected web; now I saw how this exchange chipped away at the hostile, alien world.

By the time I brought up the subject of burritos, Omar wasn't listening. There was shouting in the next street. Omar gave out a high whistle and I shrunk into the shadows. He shook my hand before he ran off, zigzagging down the narrow street, stooping to pick up a stone.

"Be careful," I said to his departing back. The garbage dumpster seemed lonely now and the distant sound of voices drew me a few steps down the street. Curiosity was suddenly stronger than fear. I wanted to see what was going on, without being seen, so, like a spider, I scurried from doorway to doorway. A couple of times, the acrid smell of tear gas clenched my stomach and blurred my eyes, so that the dusty walls of the houses seemed to sparkle. A group of women holding flowers turned the corner ahead of me and I joined them. A large woman with flashing eyes gave me a weary smile and took my arm. I was marching.

The cemetery was huddled in a corner of the camp. Grave stones, were jumbled together in the dry, rocky soil. It was surprisingly quiet. I stepped over a few graves, where rusty tin cans held a few carnations, all sprayed vivid colors like cheap sportswear. The women stood by the martyr's grave, which bore wreaths from popular organizations, many with the colors of the flag. A picture of the martyr stared at the mourners. It had been taken perhaps at a wedding or the birth of his first son; he smiled widely, a vigorous young man with one gold tooth and brilliantined hair. Away from the grave by the fence, Leila sat with her head in her hands. She was curled up like a snail.

"Hi, Leila. Are you alright?"

Leila looked up. Her face was mottled like the streaky shadows in a grape arbor. "Annie, something terrible has happened."

I had been waiting for these words all day. I knew I couldn't escape them.

"Annie, I'm bleeding."

I crouched down beside Leila. "Where Leila, tell me where." I tried to sound calm but my head rang with newspaper headlines.

"It came on my birthday," Leila mumbled sadly. "I started bleeding on my birthday. I don't know what to do."

I began to stroke Leila's hair and I finally knew what to say. "Never mind, never mind," I repeated. "It happens to everyone. There's nothing wrong. It means you're not a little girl."

"I can't get up," Leila whispered fiercely. "I'm bleeding. Everyone will see."

It had happened to me in math class when I was fifteen. My chair felt sticky and I waited for the bell to ring, doomed and desperate. I was ashamed to ask any of my friends to help. I

295

let all the other kids leave before I crept out, my white plastic purse plastered to the back of my skirt. The girls' bathroom was like the Holy Grail, as desirable as it was unreachable.

"I'll walk behind you, Leila. Don't worry. Nobody will notice; they're all busy with the funeral and the soldiers."

Leila tried to smile at me. I could never have smiled; Leila was much braver. "OK, I'm ready," she said, cautiously standing up. I spread my skirt and Leila slid into its shadows. We walked out of the cemetery like a clumsy four-legged beast, two women in a horse costume distracting the crowd before the main attraction.

When we got to Um Abed's house, Leila rested against me for a minute before she disappeared into Um Abed's bedroom for her initiation. Outside, Randa still moved purposefully in the vibrating air, and the camp was once more under curfew.

# Salah El-Moncef

# A TREE WITH A DREAM

We were putting our school things into our bags with the mechanical sullenness of yet another cold school morning when Ahmed started calling.

"Amina, Amina, come see what I've got for you!"

As far as Amina was concerned, whatever he's got for her was worth opening the window, cracking the blinds, and flooding the room with the crisp cold of the January morning.

("For God's sake, Amina, can't you wait till we're out in the *garden*, with our *coats* on?")

But not Amina. Ever since she had lost her leg on that paddle boat in the Louisiana Bayou, she developed a bizarre addiction to Ahmed's monstrosities. Actually, always seemed to me there was more to their relationship than just the mechanical bond of addictive need--something more consistent, almost systematically principled, a sort of unspoken pact sealed in tender agreement. Fuelled by her irresistible charm, Ahmed's fantasy was constantly rollercoasting on an inflationary curve, a strange drive that would make the records of Wall Street look like the grocery bills of a Buddhist monastery. He would sit for hours under the red ant-and termite infested pomegranate trees, pondering over something new he would have for Amina, while his tea bubbled away on its ashen embers, evaporating into hellish pitch. There, amidst the intoxicating fumes of terminal

297

caramel and carbonized weed, Ahmed's ecstatic labor yielded the most gruesome conceptions: things that never failed to light Amina's onyx eyes with a spark of malicious joy.

With a mixture of hedonistic appetite and experimental rigor, she helped him put a scarab on stilts by taping its legs to evenly cut straws. Then they sat and contemplated the dance of the scarab, its overwhelmed motor system choking with the drunkenness of unaccustomed heights. They put a lettuce leaf at the end of a strip of mica thickly daubed with superglue and watched a slug inch toward the goal with increasing slowness till it lay completely flat and still in its fatal ripples of solidified jelly. They observed it for days slumping into the stupors of dehydration and famine. Some Sunday afternoons you found them munching red ant pralines under the pomegranate trees. One day in advance Ahmed put a wok under the pomegranate trees and poured honey into it. By Sunday afternoon there was thick lines of industrious, anal ants heading systematically to perdition. Then Amina came and watched Ahmed start the fire. He picked up the wok, left hand on his hip, and tipped it with a dramatic flourish for her to see. Holding the wok over the fire, he threw in a bar of butter to break the mass of honey. As soon as the mixture started sizzling, he started stirring with a wooden spatula, till it broke up into amorphous clumps of red ants prematurely fossilized in half-charred candy.

Those were some of the ways my sister started relating to the living world after she lost her leg to that Cajun alligator. It was on the summer before I started going to high school. I remember Mother crying on the phone when I came in. She was talking to Grandmother, who lived in Alexandria, Egypt.

"He said he can't make a strong case against the state. All the experts he consulted told him it had *never* happened before. They never attack unless they feel threatened--plus, he said the guard *saw* her lean over and poke it with a stick. [Pause. Sobs] He said he'll see to it that the state takes care of the expenses the policy doesn't cover. I told him I will *not* have her [pause. More sobs] carry anything synthetic in her body and be barren for the rest of her life."

Later that evening, she told us more about this American attorney, Mr. James Ehrlich. She said he couldn't understand how she was going to act against her daughter's will and disfigure her for the rest of her life, forcing on her an outrageous stick instead of a state of the art prosthesis. When it was obvious that all his scientific-esthetic arguments were wasted on her, when he realized there was no way he could convince her that there was no link whatsoever between synthetic material and the fertility of her daughter--that, as a matter of fact, the best way to make sure the young woman got *inseminated* in the first place was to supplement her fertility with the decent likeness of a leg--he let Amina talk to her. With tears in her eyes, Mother told us how our mutilated sister cried and moaned and begged her to let her have a more credible version of her vanished limb. First, she didn't even know how to *discuss* it with her. But as the painful conversation dragged on, as she felt her resolve waver under the weight of our sister's tortured entreaties, she *ordered* her to arm herself with the memory of her ancestress and namesake Amina Bayram, who had to wear the painted egg of a swallow for a left eye and was still so beautiful she managed to win the heart of a Mongol prince. Now the attorney was back on the phone, telling Mother that since she decided to go for wood, he would suggest something from South Carolina, his native state. A very distinguished type of wood. It was so tough the legendary Andrew Jackson, a man who lived constantly in the eye of a hurricane, was nicknamed after it. And, by the way, while she was talking to Amina he made a few calls. A museum in New York could get an artist from San Francisco to carve and paint Amina's leg. We would split 50% of all exhibit and reproduction rights with the artist; the other 50 would go to the museum. When/If she outgrew the leg, though, she would have to "donate" it to the museum. She told him she would check with the family first. She'd call him back tomorrow. Then she called Grandmother, who was thoroughly scandalized that she would even *think* of settling for hickory. No matter how presidential it was, a hickory leg could *never* equal the bludgeon of her ancestor, the great Barbarossa II of Algiers! As to the carvings of this artist, they couldn't compare with what the wild hand of *History* had carved, painted, and bas-reliefed into a bludgeon that had faced the furious claws of polar bears, the copper padlocks of thrice-bewitched Indonesian coffers, the hermetic skulls of ambitious Dutchmen-flying, sailing, and otherwise transported.... With such a leg Amina would conquer the New York museum *and* the Smithsonian! She was going to send her brother to New Orleans right away, with the future leg.

The day after, uncle Yunes called Father. The director of the orthopedics division said he was washing his hands of the whole thing. Now he could perfectly understand how the attorney could handle all this craziness--otherwise how could he *be* an attorney; but what he was asking *him* to do was not only an affront to his humanity, it was also professionally devastating. Considering the gravity of the situation, however, the board of trustees would consider renting him clinical space, surgical equipment, and paramedical staff--provided he took care of hiring the services of an orthopedist with a valid license issued or approved by the National Medical Association. Just a moment ago, Mr. Ehrlich had his secretary contact the major TV networks to see if they could broadcast an emergency ad/announcement. Since CNN had covered Amina's story, they agreed to run the ad. He'd let us know as soon as they found somebody.

When Father was done briefing us, Muhammad switched to CNN. Hours later, I was struggling to keep up with the "grown ups." Coffee, chocolate, candy--nothing could keep me awake. In the morning Mother woke me for breakfast. Uncle Yunes and Mr. Ehrlich had found a doctor. Amina's doctor was a Navaho American who told uncle Yunes that he believed in a certain spiritual continuity between the human body and the organic realm in general--although he didn't really say if he believed in the relation between chronic barrenness and the partial synthetization of the body. Anyway, she was now assured once and for all. Thank God, now she knew her poor little child was in good hands. She'd be back with us as soon as she was done with rehabilitation.

As it turned out, rehabilitation started rather vigorously for Amina--at least by uncle Yunes' standards. Later, he told Mother how impressed he was by the first signs of her recovery. Shortly after the operation, when he asked her what she wished for a convalescence present, she told him she had heard in the news that the guards finally found the alligator. He had slowly choked to death on a fragment of her femur. She wanted to have him for a suitcase. Although he knew he couldn't refuse the sacred wish of a convalescent, secretly he had to admit that his little niece's was a rather odd (not to mention embarrassing) convalescence present. You know how it is, Miriam, had she asked for it in Egypt, it would have been a *totally* different matter. But in a country where people are religiously fussy about their zoological patrimony.... Much to his delight, when he could finally get himself to *confess* Amina's wish to the Navaho doctor, the latter answered his concerns with the acquired eloquence of Anglo-Saxon lawyers. Amina's wish was not only a legitimate consumer *right* in a Free Country, his brother, an herbal pharmacist, would gladly help her *exert* that right. Except for gutting the alligator and using his brain for the tanning, his brother was capable of preserving him in as natural a state as possible--thanks to an express-embalming technique he had learned in a colloquium of Native American pharmacologists at Chichén Itzá, in Yucatan. But when the three of them went to claim the suitcase-to-be, the Park officials told them they'd have to wait a few hours before they could buy it at auction. For hours he had to battle all sorts of potential owners: peculiar collectioners of the Hitchcockian-bachelor type, blood-thirsty sensationalists of the X-rated type, traumatized Vietnam war veterans, angelic environmentalists. Finally, he managed to save the alligator from his last opponent, the sales manager of a particularly aggressive company specializing in the manufacture of sado-masochistic paraphernalia. While America's private consciousness was still high on the media hype, they were trying to market the first-rate fetishistic value of Amina's accident by processing the animal into luxury scourges, whips, handcuffs, anklets, and amulets-each item coming with a picturesque narrative presenting the historical background of the artefact.

As long as she was in New Orleans Amina's accident was, in a way, an abstract *event*. It was only when she came back that I started *living* the full extent of her pain and the profound change that came with it. Every night she woke up in a swelter, holding her leg and screaming. One night, as we stood motionless around her bed, we saw Father cry for the first time. He was sitting on the edge of the bed with his hand on her head, his face blank, his chin dripping with tears. That was when she asked Mother to let her sleep in my room. It took her many days before she could manage her nightmares. For many times I woke up with a start and found her sitting in bed, her hands clutching her leg, her face distorted with agony. Those were the most painful moments for me--when I saw her mutilated, disfigured, slipping away from me with only the frail light of a lamp and the vague contours of a rug between us. And the stubborn stillness of the night still ringing with her scream. Then one night, when I couldn't choke my fear any longer, I went to her and buried my face in her hair--as much to hug her and soothe her as to be hugged and soothed by her. Choking on my own tears, my chest still pounding, I held on to her firmly--as if to keep her from drifting. With an eloquence born of despair, I told her that together we could chase away the horrors inhabiting the night, together we could people the darkness with fistfuls of star dust and talk the hours of despair into broad daylight--if only she would open up and tell me.

Since that night, we would lie together in bed, hand in hand. She told me how as soon as she went to sleep her leg started *getting* all kinds of things--like people who get stuff in their eyes all the time, you know. She just couldn't help it. All day long she kept thinking of it for hours, telling herself that it was just a piece of dead wood. Every night, she would go on and on reminding herself that she was sleeping under a roof, that her leg was really nothing more than a piece of *dead* wood lying on a mattress, tucked safely under a blanket. But the nightmares came every night, and every night she found herself somewhere outdoors. When her leg was green it was snails. She could *feel* them sliding up her leg ever so slowly. The tickle was unbearable. In the middle of the dreams she kept telling herself she had to shake them off. But she just *couldn't* get her leg to come off the ground. It was as if it had roots. When her leg was cracked and dry it was termites. She felt them *everywhere* drilling their way into the scabby cracks, then into the muscles and the bones. It was like thousands and thousands of long, hot needles driven in at the same time.... As her voice started drifting into a sleepy drone, I lay there holding her hand in the stillness. I had developed a special sensitivity to her dreams in my sleep. With the first twitches I would sit up and shake her.

One night, after I woke her, she lay on her back, smiling. It was the first time I had seen her smile since she came back from New Orleans.

"I was wearing a gas mask and there was a *huge* can of pesticide next to me. So I started fumigating the hell out of them. It felt so *good*. You should've seen the bastards. They were all over the place. Dead--perfectly *dead*."

Amina leaned back on the sill, window wide open and blinds flapping back and forth. Ahmed had called out to her.

"He said this time it's really-- "

"God, Amina, how about closing that window *first*!"

When I leaned over to hook the blinds, he was still looking up, his weathered tuft of canary feathers like a dissolving wisp of sulphur smoke stealing between the endless creases of his stark white turban.

After breakfast, we found him waiting for us in the courtyard. Amina was hard at his heels, her wooden leg stomping with a thud when it went between the cobbles.

"See there?" Ahmad pointed in the direction of the peach tree. All I could see was the pitch fork standing upside down like a candelabra next to the tree. Amina must have seen it first, because she went hopping along even when Ahmed stood back. I came closer too, and there *it* was, hanging at the end of a silver branch propped on the prongs of the pitch fork. Ahmed stood close by.

"I saw it this morning. I thought, first thing let's prop that branch on a pitch fork. Then I stepped out of the mulch and recited the prayer of thanksgiving right here on the dirt. But what I still can't figure out is how on earth the branch didn't snap with the night frost and all. This thing is *bigger* than a mango!"

As he rattled on we stood there completely still, our eyes riveted on this twist in the order of things, this winter chimera, this unbelievable peach of January. There was something about it both crippling and enchanting as it hung among the maroon twigs speckled with scabby spots where the leaves came off in the fall. Its fuzz was so bristly in the crisp cold it shone like a translucent film of silver haze over the burgundy blush. Like a sleepwalker, Amina stepped up to the pitch fork, holding onto the handle, her leg sinking into the mulch and wet dirt. She too had a deep flush I had never seen so intense on her amber skin. She leaned over the fruit, her face coming close, her nostrils twitching.

"By God this peach is mine. I swear it's all mine. " Saying it she sounded both wistful and resolute, as if she were whispering a tender, secret vow to someone hiding close by.

304

"Of *course* it is!" said Ahmed. "Go tell Mrs Miriam, now. Tell her the peach tree's had a dream."

"What?" I was awake at last, suddenly wanting to know what all this was about.

"Yes, sir. Trees dream all the time. But, with luck, a *good* dream happens only once in a thousand years."

That day we didn't go to school. All day long Father and Mother were on the phone. Being the farmers daughter she was, Mother wanted to call aunt Najia first--before she went on air. She wanted "our tree" to get an announcement in "The Voice of Nature," aunt Najia's program. At once aunt Najia decided to reschedule everything she had prepared for this morning. Through the earpiece you could hear the frantic buzz of her voice. She thought the best way to rearrange the program was to make it sound like a casual spur-of-the-moment call. Aunt Najia would run it as a spontaneous interview where Mother would basically try to sound casually entertaining, anecdotal. Yes, entertaining, casual, and anecdotal are the words. Keep this in mind: most of the listeners are farmers, taxi drivers, and janitors. Nothing factual, dryly formal--or informative, for that matter. Just keep feeding them all that folksy stuff.

I positioned myself on the staircase, at what I thought was the middle point between my room and the living room. I sat there with my face stuck in the balustrade, watching Mother all tensed up on the couch while aunt Najia's velvet voice cooed through the open door upstairs. Everybody else was sitting around Mother.

"This morning I received a *very* special call from a *very* special listener. It was my sister who wanted to share a *fabulous* event with me--something that happened right in her garden. When she told me the whole story I was simply *dumb*-founded. I said, you know, Miriam--you *have* to share this with our listeners. You can*not* avoid it. Well, after some hesitation, she agreed and that was that. So I decided to reschedule today's

305

program and let my sister tell you about this *unique* story. She'll
be calling us right after this. Stay tuned for the story of the
year--sorry, the story of the *millennium*!"

After the song and the commercials, Mother called in. She
did most of the talking, aunt Najia directing her occasionally
with a few questions. She started talking about the dreamlife of
trees. She said Grandfather used to tell many stories about the
beliefs of Berber peasants. One day in winter, when he was
inspecting the orchard with Ahmed, the Berber supervisor, he
saw a midgety almond on a twig. That was when Ahmed told
him about the dreams of trees. He said the tree had had a bad
dream--a dream that had yielded an abortive fruit. If you saw
the abortive fruit and didn't nip it off immediately, you could
see a great deal of misfortune for not easing the misery of the
tree. And indeed the tree had good reason to feel miserable.
Because it was the first in many of its kind and line to have a
chance to do boundless good. Somewhere in the bowels of the
earth, it seems, it was written that at the close of one thousand
years in the life of a particular line of fruit tree it befell only *one*
tree to bear the dream of good luck and prosperity. Toward that
goal, all the trees in the line would sacrifice their summer yield
and go barren and leafless for an entire year, so that the chosen
tree could keep all their sap and juices for itself to nurse its
dream in the dead of winter. For all this sacrifice, nursing the
winter dream is no easy matter, because somewhere in the
bowels of the earth it is also written that, in order for the dream
of the chosen tree to come to full fruition, it had to clash with
the bad dreams of 999 descendants of other lines. Even the most
exhaustive family tree analysis could not predict with *the
faintest degree of probability* the time or place of such a rare
fruit. Legend had it that for many years Ramses II spent
sleepless, frustrated nights with a top secret committee of
Berber sages hopelessly trying to find out if any felicitous
dream was due on his land during his lifetime. If Ramses II
troubled his sleep about a good dream for so many years, it was

306

certainly worth his trouble, because whoever was lucky enough to spot the winter fruit in their orchard would see bonanza crops burst around them within a radius of 999 kilometers from the 1-kilometer epicenter of the dream. The epicenter, a real agricultural orgy zone, was fated to bubble with indeterminate fertility for one thousand years. The first person to touch the fruit would trigger an irreversible process of instantaneous growth, perennial foliation, and chronic fruitfulness all through the epicenter. Anything planted or sowed would grow almost immediately to vertiginous proportions, yielding again minutes after it was harvested or picked--on and on, relentlessly, for one thousand years, as long as there were pickers and harvesters. It was slightly different with the remaining 999 kilometer radius, where you could only grow the crops and trees of the area. And those were only the *direct* effects of the dream. The *side*-effects would fan out from those who ate or touched the fruit, those who came into primary contact with them in *any* way whatsoever, and those who directly or indirectly came into contact with the latter, down to 1000 persons. This group of individuals was called the "secondary carriers." They could spread the side-effects of the dream through a line of 999 tertiary cariers, each of whom would carry the side-effects to 999 people non-negotiable. From the eaters of the winter fruit a spectrum of good luck and prosperity would spread like a happy plague--the more they traveled and came into contact with other people, the more good luck and prosperity would spread around them: terminal cancers unexplainably terminated, doomed bridges suspending the fatal call of gravitation for a few crucial seconds, sagging shares rising to undreamt of heights.... And those were just a few of the happenings she could think of--things that any infected person could cause without even *trying*. Obviously, the people who came into contact with the peach in a primary, secondary primary, and even millenary primary way could do much more than that...

As Mother went on listing the countless gradations and

nuances of good luck and prosperity which came with the millenary infection, I saw Father stand up, almost jump past her, and fly up the stairs past me. What he should have predicted when Mother was rehearsing with aunt Najia had finally dawned on him! I heard him speaking on the hotline phone.

"This is the Minister of Defense. I'd like to speak to General Nadhir."

When he got through to General Nadhir he gave him his code name and asked him to send a company, a communication team, and a switchboard.

Mother was still on the phone, talking to Grandmother this time, when we heard Amina cry out. For a split second we stood dead still. From very far, it seemed, I could hear Mother's sharp, excited voice drop to a hoarse drawl.

"I'll call you later, Mother. All right? I'll call you later."

Then the twelve of us ran out to the garden to see all the trees in the orchard covered with leaves, their branches sagging with clusters of fruit. Amina stood next to a sapling.

"It's growing, it's growing! " she shouted. She had nipped a twig off a quince tree and was watching it grow by the second.

Father was the first to come to his senses. Now he knew that it was all true, that he had not called General Nadher in vain, that his daughter was really the blessed carrier of a millenary plague of good luck and prosperity. Slowly, he walked up to her as the tree rose in the sallow January light, its first burgeons shining in their silver fuzz like minuscule buttons of satin. He knelt down before her and, with a trembling voice, asked her to touch his head. As soon as we got over the excitement of hugging, and kissing, and mutual touching, Father called the officer in charge of security. He had him place four guards around the tree.

The calling frenzy started even before the switchboard was installed. While Father was making invitation calls upstairs (the President, some family members, friends and colleagues),

Mother wanted to make sure *her* family flew in as soon as possible. She called aunt Fatma in Ankara, knowing that if she called her first she would spare herself many other calls. Aunt Fatma's husband had his own jet. They were going to pick up Grandmother and uncle Yunes on their way. Then it was London. She could join uncle Ali in his office. Then it was uncle Salem in Scotland and uncle Omar in Malaga. With those calls, she knew the "family that matters" wouldn't miss the event. I had never seen her talk with so much excitement. When she was done with the last call she said Grandmother was so enthusiastic she swore she would bring with her the lock of Josephine Bonaparte's hair. (It was a deathbed gift--or a plea for secrecy, she never knew--from her grandfather, Admiral Murad Bayram, as he lay hopelessly besieged by the deadly swelters of Sudanese malaria.) We would burn it in the living room and with its smoke confound the global Evil Eye, which would soon be fully focused on our house.

Meanwhile, a commotion of apocalyptic proportions was raging outside. The troops, who, by now, had fully encircled our mansion, were pushing and threatening the onlookers who wanted to venture too close to the palisade. The news was spreading so fast. Amina and I grabbed Father's binoculars and ran to one of the balconies. Amina was the first to spot Mr. Ben Jaffar. She pointed in his direction and I zoomed in on him. He was still in his pajamas, and I saw a cellular phone in the pocket of his dressing-gown. He was busy checking a shrub with tiny clusters of what looked like small, tough dates. I had never seen a coffee shrub before, and it was only when I saw him crush the berries that I understood. Mr. Ben Jaffar was the biggest coffee importer in the country. Then he dialed a number and, wedging the phone between his shoulder and his cheekbone, he went on talking and picking the berries, which were replaced by new ones almost instantaneously. I gave the binoculars to Amina and went to the other end of the balcony. Beyond the thick circle of soldiers and armored cars I could see the crowd rushing with hysterical restlessness from one spot to another. As soon as a twig started growing there would be a roar of jubilation, the crowd would rush and form a huge circle, cheering, and then climaxing into chaotic tumult when the tree sprang up in their midst. All the streets were now choking in green. Then someone came up with a crazy idea. When they ran out of dirt surface they started throwing seeds and sticking green twigs into the deeper cracks of the bitumen. That's when the soldiers started getting very nervous. The situation was getting rapidly out of hand, and so far they had no orders except to protect our mansion. I saw an officer run through the gate. General Nadhir was inside. Then, shortly after he came out, I. heard the evacuation order on the megaphones.

But the crowd was thoroughly intoxicated by the wonders of its creative drive, the new gushes of green now bursting in the middle of the bitumen, cracking the cobbled alleys and the driveways, overturning cars and palisades. It wasn't before they started moving on the trees with the tanks and firing rounds in the air that the soldiers could get the area cleared out. When the neighborhood was quiet again we heard the drone of a helicopter. It was the President.

It wasn't the only helicopter to have flown over our neighborhood that day. Most networks were covering the story. After lunch, Najib and Sami brought the TV down to the game room (the communication team took over the TV room and the living area was already crowded with Father's guests) and we watched the news. The reports were already overwhelming. Almost every major TV network had its special show with its special guests: food industry experts, political analysts, military strategists, stock exchange wizards, top executives of major airlines, E. U. ministers of agriculture, botanical geneticists. They were all speculating on the global impact of the event. All refuted vehemently the objectivity of this Ali Babaesque act of charlatanism--a piece of mediatic vaudeville mounted by the

Tunisian government to boost a sagging tourist industry and speed up ratification of the free trade agreement still under consideration in Brussels. Still, despite worldwide agreement to deny the reality of our peach, despite all nervous attempts to downplay the knock-on effects of the event through the frantic use of what a French propagandologist called "media counter-events"--despite all this, the President and the members of his Cabinet kept constantly going back and forth between the living room and the TV room to confirm to the mighty men and women of this world that this peach story was truly a lie. One by one or in groups, our government officials rushed into the TV room, ttold the same story, and came back with a new one.

In the meantime, Mother's family were arriving grouplet by grouplet, escorted by the Presidential Guards. Much to our surprise, Grandmother and her group, who didn't have to rely on commercial flights, were the last to arrive. She said she had virtually turned the house upside down and still couldn't find the lock. The only place left was the chest down in the cellar. When Hikmat and Fatma started worrying about its being late and all that, she told the servants to take the chest to the airport and load it into the jet! Now we had to find the lock, burn it in the living room, and then she would proceed to the slicing of the peach. Father had two servants bring the chest from the truck. It was the sarcophagus of an unidentified Pharaoh princess--a convalescence present from the Head of the Cairo Institute of Egyptology.

While the peach waited on a silver plate in the dining hall, we stood there in the living room for what seemed like endless minutes, watching the children as they rummaged through the dusty chest. ("Let *them* look for it, Miriam. Don't you know their hands are guided by the angels? If they don't find it nobody will.") It was Amina who found it in a small scallop-shaped mother-of-pearl box. Grandmother ordered the lock dipped in rose water and brought along with an incense burner. With religious pomp Ahmed brought the lock and the

311

incense burner on a tray of burnished copper. It was now late in the evening and the events of the day were reeling in my head like pictures whirling in the wind. When Grandmother ordered us on our knees, I suddenly felt a painful longing to lie down and let myself drift in the dark fuzz of sleep. Kneeling there among this unbelievable congregation of an occasion, this human concoction born of faith and hard-headedness, the truth burst on me that one day I could wake up in a dark and lonely room with the unbearable burden of time lying on my soul like Grandmother's gaping chest. I looked up. Grandmother lifted the carved lid of the incense burner, threw in the lock, and spun it around three times. While the smell of charred bone filled the air of the living room, her voice cracked the stillness like a whip.

"God preserve us from the evil of those who tie the knots, the tracers of patterns in the sand! And now, to the dining hall!"

But Grandmother couldn't start slicing the peach yet. The Secretary General of the United Nations wanted to speak to Father.

When he came back with a transcription of the phone call, we were all standing around the dining hall table. Today, the Security Council had met in an emergency session. They had unanimously voted in favor of declaring Tunisia a "No-Access Zone." Financial experts were predicting the worst. All the major stock markets were already bubbling with the riotous fever of this peach of discord. In a matter of hours Tunisia had become the thumping nerve of a global hysteria. For the first time in history stock markets the world over were running around the clock. Literally every single minute in the life of this blasted peach had witnessed the birth of the wildest fantasies. Sharkish real estate wizards were rigging a virtual sale of huge tracts of Tunisian desert to wealthy Americans in quest of eternal youth. Unscrupulous speculators were destabilizing stock market indices, announcing all kinds of airy deals and dirt-cheap shipments, ranging from popped-on-the-cob corn to ready-to-go coffee roasted and flavored in the pod. Maoist nostalgics, vegetarian gurus, antimilitaristic save-the-whalers, and the Indian Association of Active and Dormant Fakirs had formed an across-borders coalition and were fanning the dying flame of protest in the hearts of sixty-eighters long converted to yuppyism and the new world order. Now they were hailing the advent of the *agri*cultural Revolution. In Worms, Germany, an underground coalition of millenarists and historical materialists had come out of the closet--"the times" being "ripe," as they put it announcing the historical, economic, and spiritual necessity of a Lufthansa-sponsored mass pilgrimage to the "Land of Rebirth." All these crazy collective whims were creating the wildest air traffic patterns in the history of commercial and military aviation. On account of free competition and the dictates of supply and demand, the flights that weren't directed to our part of the world had suffered nauseating slumps into the bottomless pockets of devaluation.

He *must* realize, the Secretary General went on, that if this situation goes on unchecked, it would automatically lead to a devaluation of the concept of wealth in general and, in the long run, the very concept of peaceful cohabitation between the social classes in the Free World. If this debacle was not monitored by a multinational force, the situation could truly degenerate into what some countries were already calling the "Green *Blitzkrieg*." And, as a matter of fact, he was calling to tell him precisely about *that*. Indeed, considering the irrefutable fact that this peach business was taking a rather sour turn, the Security Council had also voted an emergency resolution putting the peach under U.N. control and, by the same token, banning whatever forms of sensory contact with the said peach, be they realized through instruments of observation; conventional and non-conventional methods of ingestion, transfusion, and cutaneous assimilation; olfactory consumption in artificially or naturally distilled form, including spontaneous evaporation. Consequently, and in view of the said resolution, he should expect a multinational force to begin evacuating the area located within the troubled one thousand kilometer radius--namely, the Protected Zone designated by the said declaration.

But Father, who by now knew more about the unimpeachable edicts of fate than the Secretary General himself, told him he could identify with his dilemma only too well having spent all his life hunting down the hysterical rhetoric of false political prophets, the chimerical hopes of mock-green revolutions, and the bloody promises of genuine-red ones. Still, the world could not evade the sad irony of this terrible truth: whether this peach thing was a deplorably happy incident or a happily deplorable one, it all depended on where you happened to be when the Green Lottery started cranking its numbers. What's more, as with all things chancy, the peach had now picked up a momentum of its own, and there was nothing he could do about that. That said, he had yet to inform him of the saddest of all ironies. His call had come too late. We had already eaten the peach. It seemed that this tragic event had already been inscribed in the womb of time, and that nothing on earth could ever erase it.

# Joe Geha

# *BACK IN THE BLACK*
## excerpt

These are two excerpts from a novel-in-progress which is tentatively titled
Back in the Black.
Background: The narrator, Sam, came to America from Lebanon when he
was a young child. He's in his early twenties in 1976, which is the novel's
present time. The War in Lebanon is almost a year old.

*In the first excerpt, Sam's Uncle Taffy has gone into a coma from
anesthesia during dental work. A hospital vigil ensues, involving the entire
extended family, and it lasts for many days. One Sunday everyone is
gathered before supper to watch a 60 Minutes broadcast devoted to this
new war in Lebanon. Sam recalls a trip he and his cousin Eddie had made
to Beirut the summer before the troubles began, when Eddie was trying to
set up an export business; upon first coming to America, Sam had had
trouble adjusting; later, on that trip back, he realized he didn't exactly
belong in the old country anymore either. As they watch the television
footage, different family members see places they've been, wounded
children who resemble their own children and grandchildren.*

*Suddenly, a call from the doctor: Taffy has awakened. Sam and Eddie
hurry to the hospital, taking three of the family matriarchs with them.*

*Yallah, yallah!* the old women urged me on from the back
seat—in English, step on it!—my mother and Aunt Afifie. But
not Aunt Nejla, and she should have been urging me on. Taffy
was her husband, after all. But she sat quietly in back between
them, patient, too sweet to say anything about my driving. It
had been Eddie's idea for me to take the wheel. That way I
could drop everybody off at the door; then, while I went around
to park the car in the ramp, Eddie and Aunt Nejla and the others

315

could already be on their way up to the ICU. It made sense: if things went bad, Mama and Afifie would be right there to comfort Nejla.

"Go for it!" Eddie said as a light ahead turned yellow. "Go, go, gogogo—yeah!" He'd been sitting forward, one hand propped on the dash as if ready to leap out at any minute. Now he began tapping his dash as if ready to leap out at any minute. Now he began tapping his fingers against the dashboard in a galloping, hurry-up rhythm, *pa-TA-ta-rum, pa-TA-ta-rum,* his pinky ring flashing even in this dim light.

"Would you knock that off?" I said. "Please? I'm getting you there as fast as I can."

Eddie's reply was simply to turn his face toward me and drum faster.

"I don't want to be a wet blanket, but...," I said, and waited.

To show that he wasn't impressed, Eddie finished with a flourish—*pa-ta- TA-TA-RUM!*—before asking, "But what?"

"What we just saw on tv. That bomb went off just down the street from the American embassy. It's starting to look like a war, Eddie. You think something like that isn't going to cause a hitch for you and your import- export business?"

"War!" Eddie waved away the very idea. "Ah, that stuff's not going to last."

War? The women in back were silent with listening.

"How do you know? It's been on the news more and more for almost a year now."

"The news, they build it up themselves. They got to talk about something."

"And it looks like it's getting worse."

"It's not in our blood."

"What's that supposed to mean?"

"We're business people. Look at Beirut. It's all international banking. Look at our history. We're merchants. All the way back to the Bible times and before."

I thought I heard a grunt of approval from the back seat.

316

"So?"

"Business people don't let things go that bad for that long. It's bad for business. You watch, soon as business starts hurting they'll step in and put a stop to it. You watch."

"We are beaceful beobles!" Aunt Afifie in the backseat couldn't resist putting her two cents in.

"That's right, Auntie," Eddie said. His voice was like honey. "We are peaceful people."

But now my mother piped up, repeating in Arabic that most truly we are a peaceful people, and therefore we can hold our heads up to anybody.

"I suppose so, Ma," I said, and heard the honey in my own voice.

After a moment, and with Aunt Nejla between them uttering small Arabic sounds of agreement to encourage them, the two of them began a running commentary: "We are lawful people. We are honorable. Why? Because it is not in us to do the shooting and the blowing up. It is in other peoples."

Who, for instance?

"The Irish, they are on the news every day!"

"I don't know, Ma," I said. "I think we're starting to catch up to the Irish. Remember that song of Papa's, that song the people of Zahle all sing, about dying from the mouth of the rifle?"

Contradicted, my mother fell into an angry silence. So Aunt Afifie spoke up for her. "That song is from the old days," she said. "Before you got born, *habibi*. Before I got born, too."

"But it's what they told me, our cousins in Zahleh, last summer when I visited the old country. They said Papa liked to sit in the vineyard and sing it."

Mama had had enough. She spoke up now in English. "You fadder he don' sink no sonk!" *if you've refused to understand till now*, her using English said, *you cannot refuse to understand this*. "An' us, we don' do da killins needer! *Khallas*!" The end! Shut up and drive.

*Us?* I thought. *Us, who?* Never mind. Just shut up and drive. The traffic lights on Monroe Street were synchronized. I found a constant speed and began making them one after the other.

Us? Long ago I had decided that there was no such thing as an us. Those Sunday afternoons listening to my Uncle Yousef go on about this small country at the great crossroads of East and West, invaded repeatedly over thousands of years, by anybody and everybody, from Egyptians to Macedonians to Mongols to Turks to European Crusaders.

"Us?" A teenager with opinions, I couldn't help but interrupt. "We're lucky hummus and tabouli survived!"

Laughing, Yousef hastened to add, "Australians, too, and the French Senegalese," before going on to how the people of this small country used to be natural sailors and merchants, travelers; how they founded Carthage, Marseilles, Malta and colonies beyond the Mediterranean; how they circled Africa and even touched, Yousef firmly asserted, "the coast of New England, U.S.A."

Us? After that kind of mixing over thousands of years, how could there be an us?

The old women were still carrying on as I pulled under the hospital's canopied entry to drop them and Eddie off. Then I drove on in silence, following the arrows to the parking ramp.

*Us who?* I used to think. But going back to Beirut had changed all that for me, a single evening's elevator ride. Everyone in the city lived in buildings much like the one I was staying in, balconied apartments stacked high around the central shaft of an elevator. Ascending in the slow cage elevator, a person could hear everything in the building, and smell everything, too. It was suppertime, and the shaft was fragrant with roast lamb, garlic and onion, cinnamon, the unmistakable aroma of toasted pine nuts. Just like the aromas of my growing up—but then the noise too seemed so familiar, the accumulation of voices funneling up that shaft: familiar dinnertime shouting, snaps and retorts and the yammering

318

laughter of a nervous people. Is that what we are then, I thought suddenly, a nervous people? My father had been called that, my father who'd been excused for being an old man, a sick man, finally a *welad baqdouq,* a rascal, who slammed dishes on the floor, who would not let things be but sniped and cursed and said vicious things until Mama was in tears. I had heard these very same noises in my own house at dinnertime, rising voices echoing up the shaft surrounding me, a pleading wife on this floor, a screaming wife on the next floor, giving back as good as she was getting, the old familiar curses of blood clot and blindness and choking in confusion. And all of it in the same Arabic dialect I had grown up with, the same after all these years, family after family up the slow ascent. Some of the voices were only talking—I knew that—light, affectionate talk amplified by the building's hollow, but even the talkers, even the laughers, seemed to have that dangerous urgency to out-of-breathness ready to blow up into shouting. Somewhere below my feet I heard something explode sloppily against a wall. A food-laden dish; I recognized the sound.

Not all of us are like that, I reminded myself, and with the very thinking of such a thought—that there were others like Aunt Sophia and the Yakoubs who sat to quiet dinners and gave you Arabic blessings instead of these curses I was hearing now; others not rascals, but decent people, and kindhearted and patient and more than welcoming, famously hospitable—with the very thinking of it I began to realize that, yes, there is an us. There had to be or else I would not have recognized it. And I had recognized it again today, more than a year later, watching those television children propped in death against a wall, their dark eyes like the dark eyes of my nephews and nieces, of myself in the old photographs, the whorled curls of their hair like my own hair, the same golden skin, those little teeth that should be smiling. There *is* an us.

319

*This second excerpt takes place during that same trip back to the old country.*

I didn't belong here, and everyone seemed to know it. Cab drivers could tell I was an American. So could barmen and waiters and ticket takers at the museums. Knowing the language wasn't enough in a foreign country. Understanding one another, I decided, was a stretch, a gulf to be leaped. I found myself exaggerating everything I did—handshakes and smiles, all the day-to-day gestures of request and gratitude—in my attempts to blind-guess the idiom of these people.

"Guess the idiot?" Eddie was puzzled.

"The *idiom.* The way things are done. They way people say things."

"Where?"

"Wherever. In any language."

"Sammy, you and me, we're talking English here and *I* don't understand what you're saying."

"Okay, do people talking English say 'Last night I *watched* tv,'" or 'Last night I watched *the* tv'?"

"What is this? You know."

"Right. And we say last night I listened to *the* radio, not last night I listened *to radio.* I mean, only a foreign guy would talk like that, right?

"Yeah." Then Eddie made the sound that showed he was hearing something new here, "Hunh."

"Do you know why we say one and not the other?"

Eddie shook his head.

"There is no reason. We just do. There's nothing in the rule books. The way we talk, that's what an idiom is. And you can know all the English you want, but if you don't know the idiom, you're going to sound like a foreigner."

"Well," Eddie thought a moment. "But so what? You *are* a foreigner here."

"I guess I'm finding that out," I said. "I tried the Riviera beach the other day. Natives aren't allowed to swim there. They told me I have to show proof I'm an American just to get in. They wanted me to go back and get my passport and show them."

"Then do it. Hey, if you're a foreigner anyway, why not take advantage of it?"

❑

Why not indeed? The beach was like stepping into an old Technicolor movie that had been retouched with a heavy hand: too-blue sky, too white sand, the stripes of the canvas beach chairs almost painful in their contrasting brilliance. I sat in a slung canvas chair, knees up, sipping a drink.

The beach was crowded, mostly couples of varying ages, but there were a few families with children. In the babble around me, I heard mostly French and some German, but no Arabic at all. And for that matter no English either. Every few minutes an airliner rumbled in low from the west, its following shadow like a quick dark slap across the surf. I figured that the Beirut Chamber of Commerce, or whatever they called it here, must have charted this route to the airport. A week ago, I had arrived in one of those planes, my own face along with those of my fellow passengers pressed to the windows to glimpse the marvelous beach we were passing over.

And now here I was, on that very beach, gazing up at the descending planes. Lower, sea birds soared, singly or in pairs. Now and then one of them buckled its wings and plummeted, striking the water like a controlled crash. Fishing. The sea must be teeming.

Finishing my drink—the sun was baking me alive—I clumsily got myself out of the chair. It was like climbing out of a sling. The water wasn't as warm as I'd expected, and might take some getting used to. I tried to ignore how I must look standing there at the sea's edge, a grown man, acclimating myself, letting the cool foam engulf my ankles, while all around me little children dashed headlong in and out of the waves. I counted the waves for a pattern. Every fourth wave, I noted, broke hard and white. The water was to my waist now, warm, its saltiness lifting me onto my toes. I counted—two, three, and dove headlong into the fourth.

I felt dragged out by a strong undercurrent, and I let it carry me, trusting the buoyancy of the salt to bring me up. Surfacing, I swam out a hundred feet or so beyond the waves, and found that the water was still only waist high, its clear blue saltiness still lifting my feet. So I bounded in it, splashing into its surface, dove to the sandy bottom and swooped up again, as I'd seen the sea birds do. Finally, I eased into a lazy backstroke, my head bobbing with the action of the water, the voices of children sounding tinny, French and German, then disappearing into a low roar whenever my ears bobbed beneath the surface. I would tell Eddie about this, what it was like, and maybe he'd wished he'd come along, too. Right. Abruptly, I let my feet sink to the sand, and I stood up and trudged back to shore.

I toweled off and climbed back into the slung chair. Situating myself, I looked up and around and there was a woman looking at me. She lay on the sand, about fifteen or twenty feet away, chin propped on two stacked fists. She was one of the prettiest women I'd ever seen in my life, and she was staring directly at me.

At least she appeared to be staring at me. She had on sunglasses, and I couldn't see her eyes. I glanced about, but it seemed there was no where else she could be looking but at the space I was occupying. I waited, and when she did not turn away her gaze, I did what would usually never do: I stared right back at her. After a moment a jot of alertness came to her face, almost a smile, I thought, and I turned away. Her black hair was bobbi-pinned back from her face in a large swoop over each ear. I guessed her to be older than me, but not by much, late twenties or early thirties. Out of the corner of my eye I noticed her shift position. Pretending to doze, I slid my eyes again in her direction. Her bikini was made of a stretchy green material cut European-skimpy so that when she shifted position, hands flat on the sand, pushup style, raising herself up and to one side, she revealed the tanned tops of her breasts. I saw her eyes now, too, above the rims of her sunglasses, and they did indeed seem to be looking up and toward me. They were brown. I closed my eyes.

When I opened them again, sensing footsteps from her direction, I saw that a man was joining her. Of course. I should have noticed from the first that there were things for two people lying about her—two reed beach mats, two paperback books, two empty cocktail glasses spilled over on a wet, sandy tray.

Setting two fresh drinks onto the tray, the man sat down next to her, blocking my view entirely. His haircut was expensive looking, feathered black and gray. He was well-enough built but looked too old for the tight jockstrap of a swimsuit he had on. Certainly too old to be the woman's boyfriend or husband. Maybe he was her father. But when the man reached out and stroked her tanned back in a lingering, clearly unfatherly way, I turned back to let my eyes rest on the seabirds soaring motionless above me. Soon I drifted into a kind of semi-sleep in which I remained aware of the couple on my right if only because, oddly, my right side felt warmer than my left. Realizing I was awake, I let my head roll to the right and I squinted open one eye. The man was lying asleep, apparently, the glass empty next to him in the sand. And there was the woman, peering over his chest, directly at me. Her sunglasses were propped atop her head now. She lay on her stomach, and I could see the two firm green rumps of her behind, the tanned legs bent at the knees and ankle-crossed. Once again, she smiled that almost-smile at me.

What in God's name did she expect me to do? I rolled away. Nothing, that's what she expected, because this was all my imagination anyway. She was staring at the sky, probably at something behind me. Who knew? Who cared?

But still I felt the heat of her gaze. Finally, I climbed out of his slung chair, stood up, planted my feet in the sand and looked straight at her. Her eyelids became heavy. I noticed for the first time that they were shaded with turquoise-colored smears. She turned to lie on her side and seemed to fall instantly asleep. In other words, get lost.

So I started walking, angry now, a determined pace right into the surf. I walked until the waves knocked me off my feet, and then I swam out beyond the surf where I rolled onto my back and floated, rising and falling with the swells.

I stayed that way for what seemed a long while. Then, when I did raise my head and look toward the beach, I didn't see her. I lowered my legs and stood, arms floating out at my sides. Then I did see her, brushing the sand from herself with a towel. The man, their beach bags gathered in his hands, rose from one knee and began trudging off toward the bath houses. The woman didn't follow right away. She draped the towel over one shoulder and stood a moment looking out into the surf and fooling with her hair. Then she did something that caused me to head back in toward the beach. She walked directly over to my canvas chair—I was sure it was mine!—and bent over it a moment, her outthrust behind sweet even from this distance. Then she straightened, and without a backward glance started for the bathhouses.

By this time I was loping ahead, lifting my knees and using my hands to claw at the water. The shore waves caught and threw me forward, as if the sea itself wanted to help. But then the current towed my feet out from under me and I fell flat on my face in the foam.

Of course, she was long gone by the time I reached the slung chair. I looked around for a message of some kind, a note, a sign. I looked on the chair, under the chair, lifted my towel, my little beach bag ... nothing. But when I looked again I found, attached to one end of the chair's canvas sling two bobbi pins.

They hadn't been there before, I was sure of that.

They were placed right where my ear would have rubbed against them when I sat.

But what did they mean? Two. Two o'clock? Meet me at two o'clock? Okay, maybe, but *where?* I pulled my watch out of the beach bag. It was after three o'clock now. Two. Two. Tomorrow at two? That had to be it. Tomorrow at two, the two of us together, next to each other, like these two bobbi pins.

❑

"Two? O'clock?" Eddie acted as if he couldn't believe his ears.

*"Two o'clock?"* We were on the balcony of the apartment, lighting cigars, and Eddie began laughing himself into a coughing spell. "More like two hundred lira!"

"What?" My cigar dangled between my teeth, unlit.

"Aw c'mon, don't tell me you don't need an idiot to get this!"

"You mean idiom."

"I mean idiot. That wasn't the love of your life making eyes at you, Romeo. That was a Beirut *hooker.*"

325

Photo: Tarek Aylouch

# Suheir Hammad

# TWO POEMS

**heifers and heroes**

where the marlboro man where
he at come out
lily belly coward
face me like the man
you supposed to be

where all the cowboys babe
promised were godlike
fearsome and up right
do right citizens

cancer everywhere
the sheriff no
where to be found
the frontier fadin
ash trays full

pimps playas gangstas tumbleweed
to fill up hero space now
but the boots too big
for ghetto smoke

babe would point at the screen
that's a real man in
control of his
cattle king of his castle

I ride
the streets wild lookin
for a good western beat
down country time moonshine
where you at cowboy

i'm lookin for your law
your order your
tobacco calloused staccato to
round up the bad guys
put the fear of god
at least a gun     into folk

you supposed to be here
lassoin this heifer to
safety lookin out for the
republic fightin
hard lovin strong

baba all gruff voice
and nicotine weakness said you
was the manmy skin
leathered waitin for you to show
up show off your skills

been gone too long
pimpin all over     silver
gun metal gold loosies handed
to the poor
like jesus like

solomon like baba

come back cowboy
get off them third world
billboards    marlboro
man you promised my father
you promised me
dead or alive
you'd come back    and heal
these hoof prints
these spur tracks
you left
on my back


## october's daughter

leaves and leaving call october home

her daughter releases
wood smoke from her
skin when she itch
rich in scorpio blood
survived the first flood
each new year marks a
circle around her thick
bark middle

this the month summer and winter
fall into each
other and leave
orange yellow ashes
the vibrancy of death

carry it all
coiled in belly

24 years of belly now
cut on the cusp of
libra her tail tips the scales

tonight i'll sleep naked
remembering my mother's young
body sweating me out of her
two dozen years ago

tonight it is raining in the
tradition of my parents
who wanted a daughter
not a writer

happy birthday poet
who loves you
the way your mama did
under her breast
the way your father did
under his breath

these years got me
tired and old
in the bones
leaves and leaving
have known my
name intimately

i october's daughter
harvest pumpkins to offer
the river eat buttered phoenix
meat to celebrate

it's a new year baby
new cipher for my belly
i got a new name secret
nobody knows
but me

the cold can't call me
leaving won't know
where to find me
october gonna hide me
in her harvest
in her changes

i gather leaves
for the fire watch
the past burn
the ashes turn
the seasons

happy birthday daughter
of the falling
to die and be born again
your legacy

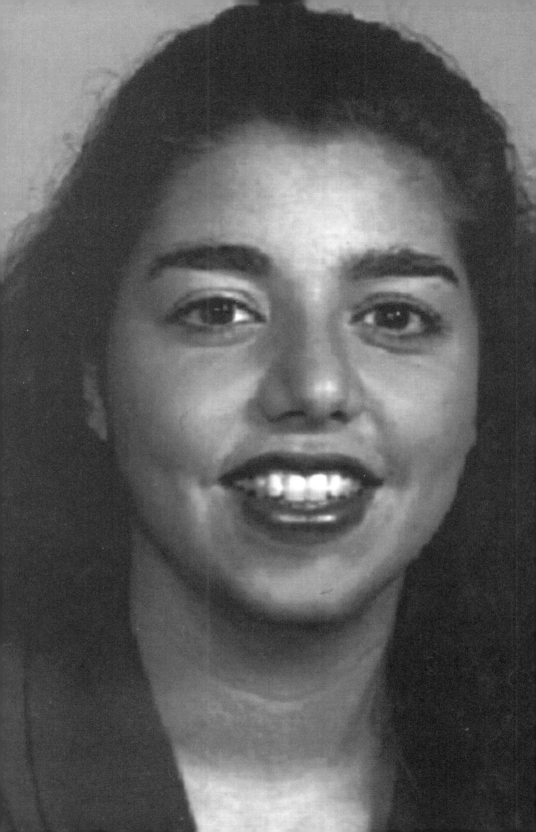

# Mechelle Zarou

# TWO POEMS

THERE IS NO LOVE HERE

no tenderness in grass.
Yellowed blades, overgrown,
sear skin, puncture leaves.
No delicacy in the bark's abrasion
peeling cuticle from nail
so slowly,

like the way they use words,
letting each one pierce,
so you savor the agony.
How your aunts love to prick,
their necks, thorny stems
issuing blood
like their drawling words:
*You look--good.*
*You've—filled out.*
which you think, at first, are a kindness.

But not love.
Not for you.
You know their lips, pulled taut

at corners into forced smile
like the leaf's canopy stretched across stem.
You know they have no love
like an expansive red, red rose.

And why do poets always use flowers
in their love poems?
When has a flower ever given?
Night Shade Iris sunk into mourning,
accusing Bird of Paradise beak,
Sunflower seizing nutrients
so no other life may grow near.

There is no love, here
in nature's mouth
in the words that gather and swell
like the budding blossom,
bursting with the stink of pollen,
the smell that clings,
so heady you think it's sweet.


EVERY POEM A PRAYER

Searching blindly
I sought a rhythm I assumed
I was too young for.
Pulsing tablas never could tell me
what to do with my hands.

Lying on my back on the pew,
when the priest's cries became Arabic rhythms
I alone crossed myself
out of sync

with the congregation,
but the meaningless sound
suggested my hands should seek grace.
My hands have never stopped.
Every poem a prayer.

I see words float above me, entwined
with the incense smoke.
My hands know what to do now,
but my body is gone.

# Nadia Benabid

# RENDITIONS

ODE 124
*after Rumi*

The apple tells one story
that shows two faces
one is yellow, one is red
saffron and roses.

The lovers separated
he took his red share of pride
you were left your yellow share of pain.
Yellow cheeks would not have suited him.
Had you been red and fat
red cheeks would not have suited you.

Look at him now, all flushed, all plumage.
Ignore him, overlook it, do not challenge him.

I am a thorn to my Master's rose
together we unfold deep red.
I sift shadows
in my Master's sunlit world.
He directs the heat of constancy,

I the steady cold.

The heart is born of the body
and man is born of woman
and the heart is king of the body.
Within the heart
there is another heart
crouching, like a horseman in the dust.

The dust is stirring, the dust is dancing.
The horseman stamps his feet, master of the dust.


## GACELA OF THE TERRIFYING PRESENCE
*after Garcia Lorca*

I want water, water -- not the riverbed
and wind, not the course of wind, but wind.

I want night without its eyes
and my heart without its gold.

Let oxen speak to dark and heavy leaves
and worms die deep in deep black earth.

Let teeth shine forth in skulls
and silks drown in warm and yellow dyes.

I can watch the bloodied night
last out its struggle with hot noon suns.

I can resist the green poison of certain sunsets
and the crumbled walls where time is suffering.

But not the light falling clean on your naked body
as it opens like a cactus, black in a bed of reeds.

Let me stay in the black torment of spinning planets,
but do not let me see the cool long shiver of your waist.


THE HUNT
   *after Ibn al-Mu'taz*

The red stained lips of morning
were shot with gold
and the wolfish mane of darkness
had weakened, dim gray.
Even night stars had fallen off, asleep,
when we loosed a fierce and subtle bitch
on a herd of antelope
and wild cows with fear-swelled eyes.
The tail arches scorpion-black,
immaculate as China ink,
bristling like fringe on a woman's dress.
She slinks like wind that never stumbles.
At her side runs a hound,
spotless, white and swift
on the scent of shooting stars.
His ears hang low and blue
as hyacinths.
His nails are drawn like a cobbler's hook
and his flawless eyes blaze like water,
like water in the desert.
He shrinks in and out of dunes like the spotted snake
and sees a herd of antelope leading foals to pasture.
In the flowering field, now no longer a blessed place,
they graze beyond the foothills

in the deep green belly of an emerald snake.
He takes them, fifty in all.
They fall with the ease of a woman's graying hair
and he brings us flesh with blood.

## WITHOUT RHYME OR REASON
*To a lady who refused a gift of melons
and shunned the attentions of an admirer.*

When I sent you melons,
you made a face and said
"melons should be heavy and wrinkled and yellow."

When I said, "so by that token take me,
I am all three."
You scolded me and called me an ugly fool.

## TO A LADY ON SEEING HER BLUSH
## KHALIF AL-MURTADI BILLAH

I grow pale when I see you, Leila.
You see me and are quick to blush.

Were you to ask me, Leila, I would say

a crimson stream departed my heart
to settle in your cheek.

## YEZID TO HIS FATHER MOAWIAH
*on being reproached for drunkenness*

You come again to spike my failings with your anger.
To rant, old man, because I partook of the fluent grape.
To come between my wine and me, old man,
is to clamor in favor of my thirst.

The cup I drained was sweet,
so too is your fury sweet,
and I find myself doubly disposed:

First, I'll drink to please myself,
then I'll drink to displease you.

# THE ZAIRE

Men smoke she-sha on the patio. Red Christmas lights drape across the ceiling. Acrylic paintings hang on the walls. Clouds of incense hoard the air. I walk through the door with Aunt Batta.

A Black Beauty floats around holding a tray of white herbs and a pot of burning incense. She bends down towards Batta's feet. Batta takes off her shoes and wiggles her nyloned toes over the embers. Refreshed, she throws a pound into the women's tray and pushes her my way. The Black Beauty lifts up my arms and waves the pot of incense under my pits. She circles around my face. I pay nothing and catch up with Batta.

Mounds of women. Sweaty. Cellulite thighs and buttocks protrude from loosely flowing galabayas. Basketball breasts deflated by years of child suckling hang low to the ground swinging to the hypnotic beat of the drums. Almond and olive faces grin exposing rotten teeth.

A Lady in Red with Raccoon eyes tokes on a she-sha pipe. Layers of red lipstick coat the mouthpiece. She holds the pipe towards me. I abstain. The Lady in Red stands up and dances to the music. Folds of flesh billow behind her, ripping the seams of her dress. I sit down beside Batta.

Five Sudanese women hold circular drums over a pot of coals. They turn the drums round and round. It hardens the leather. They begin a slow beat. Black Beauty sings. Lady Red tosses a carton of Cleopatra cigarettes across the room. Black Beauty takes out a few packs and stashes them between her breasts. She passes the carton over to the five Sudanese drummers. They puff and beat. Puff and beat. Reheat the drums. Puff and beat. I tap out the rhythm with my foot.

Lady Red, now veiled in white, dances the "Zaire." Forward and back her torso moves, oiling creaky joints. Forward and back. The veil slips over her face. Forward and back. The tempo quickens. Forward and back. Forward and back. Others gather around clapping and howling. Forward and back. Forward and back. Lady Red collapses to the ground in ecstasy. A woman spits rose water in her face. She awakes and drinks from a bowl of rose water.

My Aunt Fia blasts through the door and gives out a roar, "The special drums are not here yet!" Then, the African hip shaker man walks in and Fia grins. With his noise cans the African hip shaker man stomps on the floor. The maid passes candles out to everyone. Women light the candles and the virgin flames burn in unison. The women follow Aunt Fia out the door, past forgotten husbands, past parked cars. They surround Aunt Fia in her long robes. She is being blessed by a medicine man. I light my dead candle.

The pyramid stomach of Fia leads us back indoors. She grabs the white veil and starts to dance. Forward and back. Her buttocks spread like a wide Japanese fan. Forward and back. She cleanses her soul. Forward and back. A trance-like state. Forward and back. The women clap. Forward and back.

Black Beauty carries in two pigeons and places them on Fia's shoulders. The fear stricken pigeons don't fly away. Forward and back. Aunt Fia pulls the pigeons down towards her breasts. Forward and back. Black Beauty slits their throats with a kitchen knife. Blood drips into a bowl she holds underneath Fia's chest. She dips a finger into the bowl and places a dot on Fia's forehead and two others on her eyelids. She paints blood on Fia's arms, legs and neck. Fia parades around the house, proud of her new marks. I stand against a wall in the corner.

Black Beauty brings in a black plastic doll. Fia stuffs candy into its mouth. She pushes lollipops into its ears. She throws candy towards the crowd. Fia kisses the doll and places it on the ground before her. She dances around it. Then, Black Beauty brings a vulture into the ring. Feathers tall, the vulture scowls at the doll.

The vulture hides between Fia's legs. Fia pulls at its wings and pretends to fly like a bird. The evil spirit travels into the vulture's body. Black Beauty slits the vulture's throat. Blood spurts into a bowl. The crimson liquid drips. Black Beauty places a bloody hand print on Fia's chest. Then, another on Fia's back. All the women watch as she pours blood over Fia's head and face. Fia's body is now clean. Black beauty stops to smoke a cigarette. I stop outside for some fresh air.

# Hakim Archuletta

# LIKE RAIN

1

Do we feel for the world?

If the world grieves over
our arrogance while we
project ourselves onto it
are we given then the chance
to voice the sadness of the
sea or the pain of the tree?

Do we sing for the world?

Are we the mouth for the
centuries and the groan
and drum for its years of
war and strife and peace?

Are we the eyes for the stone
the storyteller for the plains
the advocate of the races
are we the tears of the cities?

Do we cry for the world?

As we listen to the song of
the flower the wail of
the wind or the melody of
the dawn and the moon

Do they cry for us?


2

Are we moving through the world
or are we standing still
as the world passes by us?

Floating down the Rio Chama
silently surprising the heron
that didn't expect us

Through the desert in Morocco
on a hot and dusty crowded bus
smelling of charcoal chickens and mint

Down the long straight highway
like a line drawn through
the middle of an enormous Mojave bowl

In a window seat high in the air
watching small anonymous towns
and rivers pass in slow motion below

Standing uncertain in the back of a tiny pickup
whining up a steep hill in Damascus
to a cave where Cane is said to have slain Abel

Hours into the night and dark
with no road signs to follow
through the Navajo Nation

Chugging through the snow
on the Donner pass until
the bug would go no more

In an old Citroen on the freeway
in Paris with the pedal to the metal
and old cars passing as if we were still

Hours off course on a freeway from
New York City with an old friend
to Atlantic City instead of Philly

Through thick fog in the middle of the night
in the Central Valley with the radio
and Jewel singing Only Kindness Matters

And my thirteen year old son telling me
he loves it when we're traveling
cross country and in the morning

it's dawn and we're on the road
to some place we've never seen
and never been before.


3


How many songs are left to be sung?
How many pleas still wait with complaint in our
picturesque dictionary of tales

How many pages left to be turned
in our prolonged and fatal journal?
How many more plays
on the stage of stone and rubble

How many more nights and moons
will write upon the blood
of young and old seekers after treasure?
The gold and silver of trail and scent
wrought by a pen of majesty
and scrupulously inscribed
on the hearts of those who weep?

Smoke rushes in with the dust
and sounds of electronic warning signals
They cannot be heard by any animal
water in streams flow deaf to their call

Light from the houses radiates darkness
and a small child with great eyes
stares unmoving
waiting for us
to what? Draw our sword?
Or to sheath it?

How many breaths
how many beats
still to be pounded out
on the drum of continents
how many births how many loves
to be played out in scripts and screenplay?

How much more try is left
to fill the empty spaces of childhood
cries and aches in the muscles of memory?

How many more?
How much more?
How many opportunities are left
How much longer
will we continue
to ask the impossible?


4


It comes like rain
It comes like snow
It comes like milk

It comes like a package
on the flatbed of an old truck
on a winding country road
from far away on a hill

And after our face is sticky with it
licking our fingers and
wiping it on our clothes
After we've made a mess of it
then we say
I should have used a spoon

No!
What comes to us
is like your breath and mine
we both have to breathe in
and breathe out

And I saw in the color of your eyes
and heard in the turn of your voice
and felt in the flow of your tear

everything

We knew everything
everything we wanted to know
and everything we didn't want to know

It came like rain
It came like snow
It came like milk

Celestial and Divine
it falls from heaven

With resistance
there are floods and destruction
With stillness and acceptance
the dead earth is brought to life

It comes like milk
It comes like wine
It comes like honey


5

It's a semi permeable membrane
some things pass out
and some things come in
This one and that one
rub their cheeks up against it

I've seen the children giggle
squealing with pleasure
until I see them heading

351

towards that wall of constraint
and bang up against it

Without constraint
without constraint!
Without a fence
without a wall!

There's an all black flag
there's an all white flag
it flaps and rages in the wind
of a blizzard beyond all blizzards
with stillness at its center

And those who pass through
musicians, poets, lovers, saints
swimming through that membrane
to the other side
dip into and out of it
like otters diving into and out
of their sea

The heart when it falls in love
falls there
and as it falls discrimination goes
Details of this world and the things in it
become hard to hold onto

I stand here in a ragged body
on the shore of a sea
my tongue groping its way
right now into that place

Through you and with you I have
attempted to go there

To the pond of plenty
the dance hall of namelessness
the field of fearlessness
the mirror of formlessness
the battlefield of peace illumined
by the darkness of light
the lies of truth
the particular of everything
the Heaven of earth.

Beirut, AUB, 1947

# Hisham Sharabi

# *EMBERS AND ASHES*
## memoirs of an arab intellectual
## excerpts

### CHAPTER ONE
-1-

We reached the Lydda airport at sunset one very cold day in the middle of December, 1947. The roads were empty except for British armored vehicles. Yusuf Sayigh's Humber was the only civilian car on the road between Jerusalem and Lydda. He was taking his brother Fayiz and me to the airport. We were going off to America to continue our graduate studies in philosophy, Fayiz to Georgetown University and I to the University of Chicago.

We had been in Jerusalem the day before, and had stayed at the Claridge Hotel in Qatamun, managed by a Lebanese friend of ours. In the afternoon, Joseph Salama and I went to the Cinema Rex to see a movie, *Habib al-`Umr* (The Sweetheart of My Life), starring Farid al-Atrash and Samiya Jamal. We were amazed to find the theater full of people and life going on as normal, as if nothing at all was happening in Palestine.

In the little desolate airport, a TWA employee told us that our flight would be delayed until the following morning. Yusuf Sayigh said goodbye to us and went back to Jerusalem, and we spent the night at a small hotel in Lydda. That was my last night in Palestine.

The next morning, we boarded our flight. From the window,

355

I took a long last look at my hometown of Jaffa. I saw it from the seaside as we flew over the ancient harbor. I could clearly see the al-'Ajami neighborhood and the white Orthodox church next to our house. I thought I could make out our house on the top of al-'Araqtanji Hill. A few moments later, Jaffa disappeared from my sight altogether, and I could no longer see anything but the long white shore, and the orange groves that stretched out behind it to the distant horizon.

-2-

I ask myself as I write these words many years later: How could we have left our homeland while a war was going on -- and the Jews were poised to take control of our country? This question never occurred to me at the time, nor did it occur to my friend Fayiz. It never seemed strange to us that Jews of our age group were all in military service, including many young women, nor did we think we should postpone our studies to stay home and fight. There would be enough people to fight on our behalf, we thought. The same people who fought in the 1936 Rebellion would fight for us again. They were peasants who had no need of higher education in the West. Their natural place was on the land. But for us intellectuals, our place was at another level. We fought at the forefront of thought. We were engaged in the bitter and protracted battles of the mind!

-3-

I recall an event that took place around the time I left my country. A strong wave of enthusiasm was sweeping through Arab countries towards the end of 1947, brought on by the UN resolution to partition Palestine. Students at the American University of Beirut demonstrated in the streets demanding to be enlisted as volunteers in the ranks of the Fighters for Palestine (literally the *Army of Deliverance / Jaysh al-Inqadh*). Their request was granted and a large number of them registered at special volunteer centers that had been set up in and around the city.  They were told to assemble at Martyrs' Square the next day to be transported to Homs (in Syria) for military training.   Out of the hundreds of   students who registered, only a very few showed up.

My friend Yusuf Ibish told me about another incident that took place around the same time which involved him and a friend of his.  Yusuf was one of the people whose enthusiasm had been ignited by the impending Partition.  He and this friend decided to join the volunteers, so they went straight to Damascus, since Yusuf's established and highly respected family was well known there. They went directly to the office of Taha Pasha al-Hashimi, Commander-in-Chief of the Army of Deliverance, and requested a meeting with him.  After a short wait, Taha Pasha received them very hospitably and offered them coffee.  But he categorically refused to let them join the volunteers, saying: "My sons, fighting is not for young men with your background.   I advise you to return to your classrooms.  You are sons of respectable families.  You are educated and can serve your homeland best by means of learning and acquiring knowledge, not by means of war and guns. Let others who are more suited for it carry the guns."

-4-

The strange thing about it all was that both Fayiz and I were politically active (we were both members of the Syrian Social Nationalist Party) and had highly developed social consciousnesses.  Yet without any hesitation or feeling of guilt we both left our country at a time of severe trial, as if the whole thing were the most natural thing to do, requiring no further thought or reconsideration.  In my present efforts to explain this behavior--but in no way to justify it--I find I am at a complete loss.  It may be that our education threw dust in our eyes, so that we came to see things from the point of view of abstract thought alone.  At the time, the world presented itself to us as the subject of our speech and thought, not as an arena for the realization of our actions. It was enough for us to love our homeland with all our heart and dream of a great future for the nation, without having any obligation toward it other than deep sincerity.

When the Palestinian shore disappeared from my view, I opened the tray table in front of my seat and began writing the letter which every departing traveler who may never see his homeland again writes—sometimes on paper, sometimes in his heart alone.

Upon our arrival in America, we encountered a blizzard the like of which the country had not seen in a long time. Snow had piled up in New York and Chicago, and all means of transportation were at a standstill. It seemed impossible to get

Hisham Sharabi (right) and Fayiz Sayigh at the AUB, June 1947.

to Chicago from Andrews Air Force Base in Washington where our airplane had landed, and it was already after midnight. But the trains soon resumed their normal schedules, and I left for Chicago, passing through Richmond, Roanoke, and New York. I arrived in Chicago fourteen hours later, traveling hundreds of miles through snow banks piled high on both sides of the tracks.

I took a taxi to the International House on Chicago's South Side near the shore of Lake Michigan where the University is situated, and as soon as I got out of the car, I heard a voice in Arabic saying: "Welcome to Chicago! The city has lit up at your arrival!" I turned to discover the source of the voice and saw Rashid Fakhri standing at the main entrance with a bright smile on his face. We embraced and entered the building, Rashid insisting on carrying my luggage. I took my room keys to go up to my room and Rashid left me on the understanding that we would meet again after I had some rest.

-5-

I entered my room and closed the door. For the first time since I left the airport in Lydda, I was able to think calmly. Here I was in America at last. My dreams had come true. I had arrived at the University of Chicago, and now I was in my private room at the International House. But a feeling of loneliness suddenly overtook me. My heart was about to burst, and my eyes filled with tears. I wanted to go home. I wanted to return to my homeland, to my family, to the Party I had left behind.

A dream realized is like a desire satisfied: it leaves a melancholy void behind it. I decided to return home as soon as possible. I would continue my studies to obtain a Master's degree, nothing more, and go back home within a year--an idea that afforded me a little comfort. I never thought I would spend most of my life in America, and that when I did return to my homeland it would be for only a short and tragic period.

-6-

I woke up early the next day to the sound of crackling heater pipes. I went barefoot to the window and felt the biting cold, but was unable to see anything outside because of the fog and snow. I took a shower and shaved, then went downstairs to the cafeteria for breakfast. It was empty except for a few students. After breakfast, I put on my overcoat and sat in the lounge waiting for Rashid to come and take me to the registration office.

When we stepped outside, an icy wind hit us and I felt colder than I had ever been in my life. We walked to the University in deep snow and it seemed that my head might split in two from the cold. The first thing I noticed when we reached the university campus was its beautiful Gothic architecture and the severe silence that reigned over everything. Piles of snow seemed to absorb all sounds, making them soft and muffled, including the ringing of the bells of the campanile far away. In a sudden memory I was back in Beirut with the bells of College Hall announcing the beginning of morning classes as we hurried, late as always, to our classrooms...

## CHAPTER THREE
-1-

It continued to snow for days after I arrived. People said the winter that year was more severe than usual. As far as I was concerned, it wasn't just a matter of the cold alone. I didn't dare go outside at all, since as soon as I stepped out the door an icy wind blasted against me, my nose turned to ice, and my ears felt like they would freeze and break off.

Ah for my homeland! Its blue sky, its good air and warm sun! In the first few weeks, I never left the International House unless it was absolutely necessary, to go to class or to the library. When the temperature rose a little above zero, I went across Central Park to the Dirty Spoon Café (as we called it) to

360

University of Chicago, Winter 1948.

drink a cup of coffee and eat a piece of apple pie.

In my first semester, the winter semester of 1948, I took four courses, three of them in the Philosophy Department and one in the Department of German Studies. The first course I chose in philosophy was "Aristotle's Philosophy," taught by Richard McKeon, the most famous American philosopher alive in the field of Greek and Latin studies. The second course was "Pragmatic Philosophy" (from Peirce to Dewey) taught by Charles Morris, one of the leading practitioners of pragmatic philosophy in the United States and a professor of philosophy at both the University of Chicago and Harvard. The third course was "Kierkegaard's Philosophy," taught by Jean Wahl, professor of philosophy at the Sorbonne, who was a visiting professor that year at the University of Chicago. Wahl was one of the bastions of the existentialist school in France and the author of *Études Kierkegaardiennes*, which is to this day the principal reference book on Kierkegaard's philosophy and existentialist thought. The course I took in the Department of

German Studies was on the philosophy of Nietzsche, taught by Arnold Bergstraesser, an anti-Nazi German professor who had come to the United States before the Second World War and whose specialty was in the social sciences. A strong friendship arose between Professor Bergstraesser and I which lasted until his death in 1967.

-2-

Professor McKeon held his class in a middle-sized room on the second floor of Swift Hall, a building designated for the Philosophy Department. His was the first class I attended at the University of Chicago. It had about twelve M.A. and Ph.D. students, all Americans except for me. As soon as I sat down, McKeon entered the classroom, went up to the platform and began staring at us through his thick glasses, a faint, slightly mocking smile fluttering on his lips. He then began to count through the papers and arrange the books he had brought with him.

McKeon was of moderate height and, in spite of my initial impression, had a very attractive personality. He had been appointed as the United States representative at UNESCO, which was to hold its first session in Beirut in 1948, for which a special edifice was built. When McKeon left for Beirut, I wrote to some of my friends there informing them of his arrival. They received him warmly, and Fu'ad invited him to the `Ajami Restaurant and introduced him to a number of writers and other people interested in philosophical matters.

After that first lecture, I went to the Philosophy Library in Swift Hall, which was still separate from the central library and occupied a whole floor. I checked out McKeon's works, which were not many, and read them all—at first with a great deal of difficulty, then with increasing comprehension. After only about four or five weeks it was possible for me to follow his lectures and understand them easily. McKeon asked us to take the philosophical text as our only source of study, and cautioned us against using any secondary sources written by commentators and scholars until we had full command of the text itself. To me, this was a radical transformation of my study method, which I used later with my own students when I became a professor myself.

McKeon's methodology had a profound influence on my intellectual orientation. I became more capable of distinguishing between what was subjective and what was objective, and more adept at using methodological analytic tools with increasing care. This orientation was strengthened by a tutorial entitled "Reading of Texts" which I took the following semester with one of the young professors in the Philosophy Department. I met with him once a week and we read Aristotle's *Ethics* and Hobbes's *Leviathan*. The method in the tutorial was that the student read the assigned text by himself, then read it again with his professor sentence by sentence. The professor commented on the reading and analyzed the concepts and categories occurring in the text, until by dialectical method, the student arrived at a full understanding of the text and its "language." In this way, we read ten pages from the book of *Ethics* and no more than fifteen pages from *Leviathan* during the entire semester.

Only a few months passed by until I began to understand the principles of a critical liberal culture, which the American University at Beirut had failed to teach me. I also began to perfect those two most difficult arts: the art of reading and the art of listening.

-3-

Jean Wahl was a short man with a small body shaped like that of Jean Paul Sartre. He wore round, wire-rimmed eyeglasses like the ones Sartre wore, but didn't have Sartre's famous squint. When he sat on his chair in the classroom his feet hardly touched the ground because his legs were so short. Even though he spoke English fluently, his thick accent often made his words incomprehensible. His teaching method was the classical European one based on lecturing and avoiding discussion in the classroom. He would sit at his desk and deliver his lecture until the end of the class hour, without once stopping from his prepared notes or giving an opportunity for anyone to ask questions or exchange ideas.

From Wahl's lectures it became clear to me that what I had studied in Beirut of Kierkegaard's thought and existentialist philosophy was of hardly any worth at all, just as it had been with the study of the philosophy of Aristotle. It became evident to me that the study of Kierkegaard required knowledge of Hegel's philosophy, and my knowledge of Hegel's thought didn't go beyond a few general themes. Our professors in Beirut had never even mentioned Hegel to us, perhaps because they didn't know his philosophy well enough. Professor Wahl used to take a text and examine it word by word. Then he would start to pose questions and proceed to answer them until he reached the conclusions he sought, formulated with clear and precise points. Wahl's lectures soon put an end to the romantic tendency nourished in me by the way we had studied Kierkegaard in Beirut. I became more concerned with primary sources and texts, instead of depending on the explanations and analyses of commentators.

One day I mentioned to Wahl that the Egyptian philosopher, `Abd al-Rahman Badawi, had authored a book on existential philosophy entitled *al-Zaman al-Wujudi* (Existential Time). He expressed interest in it and suggested that I take Badawi's book as the subject of my research paper for that semester. A few weeks later I presented my paper to him, in which I reviewed the principal points of the book and translated a few passages from it. Wahl called me to his office after reading my paper and said: "The book is ordinary. The translated passages and Badawi's ideas seem to be derived mostly from Heidegger's book, *Sein und Zeit* (Being and Time), with nothing new in them."

In the Spring semester, I chose another subject and entitled my paper "The Kierkegaardian Dialectic: Truth and Existence." Going through my papers recently, I found this research paper with Professor Wahl's remarks on it. It seems that he liked it, because on the first page of it he wrote the following: "Your ideas are clear and your style is strong (except for a few paragraphs I pointed out on pages 1 and 2)." He filled the margins with remarks and comments, using three standards to evaluate my analysis of Kierkegaard's philosophy: *Clear*, to denote passages he liked for their precision; *Right*, to express his agreement with my opinion; and Good, to point out passages he considered outstanding. Wahl particularly liked the last part of my paper and wrote *GOOD* in capital letters in the margin. I don't remember now whether this passage was a result of my own independent thinking or a quotation from other books without reference to the source. In it I presented a summary of the existential dialectic in Kierkegaard's philosophy, describing individual existence as one threatened by contradictions and disputed by situations of "uncertainty, risk, passion, anguish, longing." I ended the text in the following manner:

To the individual existing thus, finality, in whatever form it comes—historical, natural, scientific, speculative—breaks down at the fact of the fluttering moment of decision. Passionately striving, infinitely longing, and inwardly isolated, the existing individual is grounded in a situation which the existential dialectic reflects and accentuates; it is one permeated with opposites, constantly surging with becoming, everlastingly changing according to the unique situation: Illusiveness, uncertainty, risk, passion, anguish and longing formulate true grounds of this existential situation. The existential dialectic strives to capture and represent the situation thus.

During Wahl's residence in Chicago, a tragic event took place that shook us all but which he faced with tremendous courage. His wife, a young woman who had been a student of his in Paris, gave birth to a baby boy a short while after their arrival in Chicago. One morning, Wahl woke up to find the baby lying motionless on its back. He touched it and discovered it was dead. The baby's covers had become twisted around its neck somehow during the night so that it could not breathe and he died of strangulation. Wahl did not excuse himself from class the following day, but gave his lecture as if nothing had happened.

-4-

I don't remember how or why I chose to take Charles Morris's course on pragmatic philosophy. There were more students taking his course than those taking McKeon's and Wahl's courses. The atmosphere of his class was very lighthearted, and a spirit of familiarity and geniality prevailed. As soon as I entered his class, I felt I was entering a café, not a philosophy lecture: the students were telling jokes, laughing, eating sandwiches, drinking Coca Cola and smoking. When Morris entered the room the students didn't change their postures but continued talking as animatedly as before. Morris sat at his table on the platform, then turned to one of the students and said: "What kind of sandwich are you eating? I've never seen a sandwich that big before!"

Morris' method differed completely from that of McKeon or Wahl. He avoided the lecture format and gave ample opportunity for dialogue and discussion. It was his custom to leave his chair on the platform and sit down among the students, and the students talked to him as if he were one of them. Sometimes the discussions even became quite heated, but without any tension, and they always ended in good humor, Morris himself participating with natural spontaneity.

At that time, Morris was in his middle forties and his

name had begun to be known in academic circles after the publication of his book on the philosopher, George Mead. During this time, he subscribed to Sheldon's theory that posited that the basis of personality was the actual physical constitution of the body. A short, fat individual belonged to the *endomorph* group; a tall, thin one, to the *ectomorph* group; and a person of moderate height and strong muscles belonged to the *mesomorph group*. The first was good—tempered, happy and carefree; the second was high-strung and easily overcome by anxiety; and the third was inclined to deep thought, seriousness and hard work. Each of these groups had a specific pattern of behavior. The first group, the endomorph, was characterized by contentment and satisfaction, its aim in life being to secure an easy living. The second group, the ectomorph, did not accept life as it was and had difficulty dealing with others, its members being inclined to isolation and solitude. The third group, the mesomorph, differed from both of the others by being practical in its methods and aiming at high achievement in work and behavior.

Since my knowledge in the social sciences was limited at the time, I didn't realize how superficial this theory was, and its narrow parameters escaped me. For more than twenty-five years, this subject remained without a satisfactory solution for me until the early 1970s, when I dedicated a lot of effort to study it. My book, *Muqaddimat li-Dirasat al-Mujtama al-`Arabi* (Prologues to the Study of Arab Society), published in 1975, was a partial outcome of that effort.

In my research paper for Morris's course, I chose to compare existentialist philosophy with the philosophy of William James. When I presented it to Morris, he liked it very much. Returning it to me, he said: "Nobody has ever dealt with this topic, and your treatment of it is excellent. I suggest that you publish it in one of the philosophical journals." His compliment pleased me and restored in me a great deal of self-confidence, which I had almost lost during my first icy months in Chicago. From that day on I began taking part in class discussions, since I had spent most of my time in class sitting in silence. A strong friendship arose between Morris and me, and we began to meet each other outside the classroom over a cup of coffee, or for a stroll on the Midway after the weather warmed up, talking about whatever came up. These conversations had a strong effect on me, for Morris gave me—through his clear empirical insights—what I was greatly in need of at that time, namely, a new intellectual direction that would extract me from the metaphysical and idealistic intellectual world I was in. Yet, although pragmatic philosophy did not save me completely from my idealistic tendencies, a new intellectual horizon opened up in front of me, outlining new ways and methods to pursue.

In the Spring of 1949, a few months after I returned to Beirut from the United States, I received a letter from Morris informing me that he was traveling to Japan to attend a scholarly conference, and that he could pass through Beirut on his way back, if that was convenient for me. I immediately wrote back and invited him to visit, and met him at the airport a few weeks later. Before his arrival, I had reserved a room for him at the Normandy Hotel which, in those days was rated to be of the same class as the Saint George. But he preferred to stay at a second or even third class hotel, not because he wanted to economize, but simply because he hated first-class hotels. So I took him to the New Royal Hotel, which was in the neighborhood of the Normandy, and opened directly onto the sea. It was a hotel where merchants from Aleppo and Damascus stayed, and where artists working at the Lido and the Kit Kat nightclubs lived. We left Morris's luggage in his room and headed for the university. In the evening, I took him to Faysal's Restaurant where a number of friends joined us, including Joseph Salama, Fadluh Khuli, and Nabih `Atiyya (who emigrated to South Africa at the end of the year). Nabih had a bottle of French cognac, which he opened, offering a glass to each of us, then put it under the table. Morris drank his glass down at one gulp, so Nabih poured him another. Morris drank the second glass the same way as he continued talking, so Nabih poured him a third, then a fourth and so on until Morris had drunk the whole bottle, talking all the while and showing no effect whatever of the liquor. When we reached the New Royal Hotel on foot, Morris remarked, as he said goodbye to us: "Please, thank your friend who brought the cognac. Tonight I will sleep soundly. Good night!" He climbed up the hotel stairs with firm steps, and I remembered what he had once told me in Chicago, that on one of his visits to certain islands in the Atlantic Ocean, he ate a dish of fried spiders and really liked it.

A few hours before his departure, I took Morris to meet Anton Sa`adeh. Morris sat in the reception hall and I entered the Leader's room to inform him of our arrival. I found him shaving as he dictated his weekly article for publication in *Kull Shay'* newspaper. After he finished shaving, he received Morris with his customary hospitality, and conducted the conversation in English—with some difficulty, but with precision and clarity. Morris was happy with the meeting and admired Sa`adeh immensely, which also pleased me a great deal.

-5-

The professor I became closest to during my time at the University of Chicago was Arnold Bergstraesser, professor of German history and chairman of the Committee on the History of Culture, which I joined during the studies for my doctoral thesis. Bergstraesser left his country in 1938 and took refuge in England. After that he moved to the United States and taught at several universities before ending up at the University of Chicago. During the Second World War, he wrote a book in English on modern German history. The Jews attacked him severely because he did not condemn the German people and their culture. They demanded his dismissal from the university, but Robert Hutchins, the president of the university at that time, stood by him, and Professor Bergstraesser retained his position.

During the period of his residence in the United States, from 1938 to 1951, Professor Bergstraesser continued to feel that he was in a foreign country. He never sought naturalization as an American citizen, as did his German (Jewish) colleagues at the university, such as Hans Morgenthau, and others. Whenever Morgenthau, with his thick German accent, used to refer to himself in his lectures, he would say, "We Americans." But I never heard Bergstraesser ever say anything that gave the impression that he was other than German. On the contrary, whenever he said, "We," it was clear that he meant, "We Germans."

In his politics Bergstraesser was a conservative liberal and a staunch enemy of Nazism. After the war ended, he looked forward to the moment when he could return to his homeland and start his life anew, although in 1949 he was fifty years old. He was married to a German woman with whom he had a daughter who, at the age of ten, spoke both English and German fluently. His greatest fear was that after the Nazi defeat and unconditional surrender, the Allies would deprive Germany of its heavy industry and impose an agricultural system on her, which is what Henry Morgenthau, the Jewish Secretary of the Treasury in President Roosevelt's administration, requested in a famous memorandum published at the time. Despite Bergstraesser's strong opposition to anti-Semitism, he was also against Zionism, and feared the consequences of the rapidly rising Jewish influence in the United States after the end of the war. He avoided expressing his anti-Zionist feelings publicly, and generally refrained from the subject altogether, but often discussed it with me when we were alone.

Bergstraesser returned to Germany in 1951 and was appointed professor at the University of Freiburg. We remained in touch with each other until he died in 1967. He invited me several times to visit him in Freiburg, and every time I accepted his invitation and began to prepare for the trip, something would happen at the last minute that prevented me from going.

I finally visited Freiburg after his death, and went to the institute named after him at the university, the Arnold Bergstraesser Institute for Political Studies, which today is one of the most important university institutes in Europe for the study of contemporary politics.

In the first semester, I chose Bergstraesser's course, "Nietzsche's Philosophy," and immediately after the first class I went to the bookstore and bought a single volume of Nietzsche's works, the Modern Library edition, which I still have and occasionally peruse, with all my handwritten marginalia. Bergstraesser used to wake up very early in the morning and always held his class at 8:00 a.m. During that first semester, I got up at 6:30 a.m. three times a week, took a bath, had my breakfast, and read a little to clear my mind. Then I would put on my heavy overcoat and earmuffs, go out into the bitter cold, and walk knee-deep in snow to the classroom in the Harbor Building. It wasn't that far from the International House, but the trip took me about twenty minutes because of the snow. Classrooms were always overheated to the point of suffocation, and we never really adjusted to the temperature—if we opened a window, icy cold would invade us; if we closed it, the heat would become unbearable. With the window open we would put on our overcoats, and when the window was closed we would take them off, as well as our multiple layers of sweaters. But Professor Bergstraesser ignored these matters entirely. Yet, for the first time I understood the Nietzsche's philosophy, which made all the hardships worthwhile.

In the first weeks of the winter of 1948, the bonds of friendship between Professor Bergstraesser and myself became strong. He often invited me to a cup of coffee at the drugstore, or to lunch at the faculty club, where I later worked briefly as a waiter when my financial resources ran out. We even occasionally ventured off campus to an Italian or Chinese restaurant on Fifty-fifth Street, but I used to dread these outings and attempted to avoid them, because they required the use of

Bergstraesser's old car. What aroused my fears wasn't the car itself, but rather Bergstraesser's driving style, especially on icy streets. He would turn the car on, step on the gas pedal and let the car jerk forward, usually skidding violently on the ice. Unfazed, he would turn to talk to me, while I sat frozen in my seat fearfully focusing my gaze forward. I would nod now and then to signal agreement with what he said, until we reached the restaurant. His parking style was no better. He would slam on the brakes and slide on the ice for a few feet before colliding with the rear end of the car in front of him. When we finally sat down to eat, my appetite was gone.

But Bergstraesser was like a psychological savior to me at the time. I don't think I would have been able to overcome the difficulties I faced those first few months as quickly as I did without his kindness, encouragement, and help. He was an elder brother, and a friend I could depend on, a characteristic of mine I have had all my life, and which I haven't freed myself from even now. But whatever the psychological causes were that nourished my relation with Bergstraesser, there were also intellectual factors that united us, and he had a deep influence on my intellectual transformation as well. In a letter I sent him on February 14, 1948, six weeks after the beginning of my studies with him, I commented on his method of teaching Nietzsche and surveyed the points by which we should be bound: "Your method of presenting Nietzsche's thought and of rationalizing him leads, in my view, to killing the unique side of him. Nietzsche writes in parables, not analytically. He writes in the language of magic. That is why the treatment of his writings should be in the spirit of Zarathustra, i.e., in a positively committed spirit." Then I went on to survey the conditions I felt one must follow, the most important being that the professor should be, in the words I used, "Nietzschean" in his thought and method:

I believe that it is impossible for a follower of

Nietzsche—and a professor lecturing on Nietzsche must be one of his followers—to discuss his thought in a classroom without allowing Nietzsche's spirit to dominate the discussion completely. This cannot be achieved unless one highlights the existential side of Nietzsche's life in the imagination of those studying him seriously and in depth, showing his suffering, his sickness, his difficult isolation, his permanent infatuation with the Alps, and his living in rented dark rooms in Italy....It is possible to kindle the fire of philosophy in the hearts of students when their professor himself understands Nietzsche's thought and when its light burns in his own heart. I believe that raising up this light that illuminates all Nietzsche's philosophy is the basic condition to understand Nietzsche as a philosopher, a poet, and a prophet....

And I ended my letter by saying:

My dear professor, I end these remarks by wishing you, as a professor teaching Nietzsche's philosophy, many intelligent students who are capable of sitting under 'the tree on the hill.'

Two days later I received Bergstraesser's response. Without exaggerating, I will say that I have never received a letter that had a greater intellectual impact on my soul, for it made me, for the first time, face the basic problem of methodology I had never faced before. Bergstraesser contradicted all I had learned at the American University of Beirut. In his letter he said:

In this age, the university cannot permit itself to depart from any position but that of unbiased criticism with regard to the way it poses intellectual issues and the methods it uses to deal with them. Dealing with

Nietzsche's philosophy in the committed manner you suggest in your letter utterly contradicts the aim and task of the university....Following such a method would inevitably lead to adopting a biased attitude toward every philosophy or intellectual trend, for it presupposes that the professor should be a believer in that philosophy or intellectual trend, and should teach it as a doctrine and faith. This in turn would lead to the undermining of the intellectual foundations on which the university stands as an independent cultural institution, the foremost of which is to preserve a common intellectual language and an ability for mutual understanding based on objective analysis and open dialogue.

Thus, Bergstraesser distinguished between two things: the cultured person's need for having specific intellectual and ideological positions, and the university's task of providing him with the intellectual and analytical tools to enable him to take those positions. He said:

The task of the university focuses on providing the scholarly opportunity for an educated person to be able to understand the issues discussed in our present age and analyze them with a sound and critical spirit.... Placing limitations on this educational task of the university raises some doubt in the minds of young people about the value of a university education. The university does not offer them the solution they seek, but only the method and the way. What you say in your letter expresses a general attitude, but the situation you are in may be an open and creative one if the people experiencing it have sufficient courage and determination to face it. It is a situation arising from an acute intellectual crisis that does not accept easy solutions, especially those offered by theories claiming to have the whole truth. The courageous and determined stance required in this instance is not only in admitting its surrounding difficulties and risks, but in seeking to bring them to light, to face them, and then to take them one step "forward" in order to overcome them and transcend them.

In time, the objective methodology which I began to grasp in the first months after joining the University enabled me to rid myself of the subjective habits of my former education, and I took big intellectual steps "forward." But I failed to arrive at a critical attitude toward it or discover its role in supporting the dominant way of thinking and the prevalent sociopolitical reality until many years later. The non-objective aspects of "scientific objectivity" escaped me at the time and concealed from me the intellectual truth of its so-called "neutrality," a "neutrality" that hides an *a priori* commitment to a specific viewpoint reflecting the dominant ideology and its abstract contemplative nature, which characterizes all bourgeois thought.

This also made me fail to see the reality of the conservative liberal stances taken by most of my professors. I accepted them without questioning. My thinking became saturated with the (Anglo-Saxon) American liberal outlook, adopting a position hostile to communism and the Soviet Union, accepting the theory of free enterprise and parliamentary democracy without any hesitation or questioning. But it was at this time that the antiquated psychological molds formed in me by the old social acculturation I brought with me were broken. And I must credit Bergstraesser as the direct cause of this liberation, as well as for my move from the study of philosophy to the study of the philosophy of history and European culture. This move was perhaps the most important step I ever took in my university education, thereby getting rid of the abstract philosophical outlook I grew up with and consequently being spared the fate of the professional philosopher. New horizons and ways

At home with Henry, 1997.

opened up in front of me and led me to discover the social sciences and the scientific principles usually concealed behind an idealistic existentialist philosophy that exalts itself above all that is scientific and perceptible.

-6-

In the 1960s, after having become a professor at Georgetown University, a strong friendship arose between a colleague of mine named Heinrich Roman and myself, which was similar to the one that had arisen between Bergstraesser and me. Like Bergstraesser, Roman was a non-Jewish German, and similarly had emigrated from Germany because of the Nazi regime. My friendship with him was like a continuation of my friendship with Bergstraesser. We used to sit at a café near the university frequented by students called Tahhan's because it was owned by a Lebanese man with that name. We drank beer there and talked. I often asked Roman about his life in Germany, about the First World War and about Nazism. We discussed many of the same subjects that I used to talk to Bergstraesser about. He was fond of smoking cigars, so whenever I got hold of Havana cigars (forbidden in the United States at the time), I gave them to Roman as a present. He smoked cigars continuously. One day he felt a pain in his chest, so he went to the hospital for tests. He was told he had lung cancer and was forbidden to smoke. His disease was so advanced there was no hope of recovery. But Professor Roman continued to teach until the last day of his life.

One day, before he entered the hospital for the last time in the Fall of 1966, we were walking together on the university campus. It was cold, and autumn leaves were falling all around us. I inquired about his health. He answered briefly, as though the matter no longer concerned him, saying simply that everything was all right. Then he turned to me and added: "I have made all the arrangements for my wife. My life insurance, my pension. And I've registered the house in her name." His wife was a small German woman who still spoke English with a thick German accent. Her mannerisms, speech and gestures gave the impression she didn't seem to know where she was or what she was doing. Roman spoke about her with a great deal of passion and anxiety, as if he felt that his separation from her was imminent.

He spoke to me about the past, about his student days, about how he met his wife and about their life together. This ailing old man appeared to me to be young and in the prime of life, full of strength and vitality. He talked about his wife as if she were still the beautiful young woman he had fallen in love with more than forty years ago. At that moment he saw himself as still a youth. How Time defeats us! We grow old, yet our hearts remain as they have always been. Time doesn't change hearts, and the love and pain we have experienced remain with them. The further we advance in years, the more the past

377

comes closer to us with its sorrows, joys and memories.

He told me, "Before our wedding, I said to her: 'I can't promise you a life full of happiness and joy, but I promise you solemnly it will be a life full of enjoyable adventures.' And I have fulfilled my promise to her!" I saw him for the last time at Georgetown Hospital, lying in bed in a state of semi-consciousness because of the drugs he was given to kill the pain in his chest. He looked up at me but didn't recognize me at first. Then he closed his eyes, and opened them slowly, as the shadow of a smile appeared on his face. "Do you want to know how many cigars per day I smoke these days?" he asked, since I always asked him, "How many cigars have you smoked today?" I smiled encouragingly, "Yes, tell me, how many cigars?" He turned his face away, trying to control himself because of the pain. I didn't know what to do. I felt that a dear friend was about to depart and I couldn't properly say goodbye to him. He was about to leave this life without a last word from me to remind him of the love that bound us together.

On the day Roman died, I saw his wife returning from the hospital. She walked quickly with little mincing steps. When I got close to her, I saw that her eyes were red from weeping. When she saw me she stopped, and I asked her: "Is there anything I can do for you?" She looked at me but said nothing. I don't think she recognized me. She said, "Thank you," and went on her way.

In the first few months of my studies at the University of Chicago, I suffered from intellectual indigestion. The courses I took in the first semester were more than I could possibly understand or grasp. While Bergstraesser dealt with materials from the historical cultural point of view, Morris dealt with them from the pragmatic point of view, and McKeon and Wahl from the analytical philosophical point of view. In the classroom, I often felt as though I was in a dream, especially the first few weeks, and I did not fully understand what was going on around me.   My loneliness added to my confusion. However, I had no choice but to patiently endure my loneliness and intellectual indigestion until the clouds began to disperse and things slowly began to become clear.

I don't ever remember a professor entering one of our classrooms empty-handed or giving his lecture while fingering his key chain as our professors in Beirut used to do, except for Morgenthau.  Morgenthau used to give his lectures impromptu without making a mistake in content, expression, or mental organization.  He lectured as if he were reading from a written text in front of him.  He cited figures, dates, and quotations by heart.  I regularly audited one of the courses he gave, though I hadn't officially registered for it. I also attended his public lectures, which he gave in the largest university halls available. He would enter the hall, his hand in his pocket, and stand in front of the audience as he did in the classroom, and deliver his lecture for a full hour without stopping, in a charming literary style. He used to write his articles in the same manner: he dictated them to his secretary as he paced his office, then she typed them and gave them to him ready for publication.

In spite of the fact that he was Jewish, he never said a word at the time that gave the impression he sympathized with Israel or supported Zionism.  Perhaps the reason he remained silent on this matter was because of his ambition to become an adviser in the State Department or the White House, as did his German Jewish colleague, Henry Kissinger.  But after he retired and abandoned any hope of obtaining a government post, he displayed his true colors as a committed Zionist.

-7-

I was constantly on the lookout for public lectures or special weekly seminars, and the seminar I regularly attended every week was the Committee on Social Thought.  It was held every Wednesday evening at 8:00 p.m. in a room on the second floor of Harbor Hall.  Those who attended this seminar were usually no more than twelve or thirteen people, mostly students. They all sat at a round table that filled the room, presided over by John Neef, Chairman of the Committee. Neef began the meeting by introducing a student whose task was to present the subject of the day's session. After the initial presentation, which took about an hour, people began discussions, and anyone wishing to participate was free to so. I used to sit silently and follow what was happening without daring to participate. The discussions were always very quiet, no emotional outbursts, and differences of opinion never became verbal battles. Instead of clashes, differing viewpoints would inspire people to offer additional details and to clarify their positions, and consequently a better and deeper understanding of the subject was obtained. My American peers were the same age as myself or slightly older, and they dealt with the issues under discussion with confidence and equanimity, talking to Professor Neef without fear or circumspection, as though he were simply another colleague of theirs. I measured my bashful and diffident behavior against their natural and confident behavior, and often tried to discover the reason for this difference, but without success.

A number of Arab students attended the Social Thought seminar from time to time. One of them would attend once or twice, then drop out. Their number in any one session never exceeded two or three, and they were mostly students of economics or political science. They used to sit next to each other, constantly whispering among themselves and laughing. When one of them took part in the discussion, he presented his opinion in such an emotional and rhetorical tone, and in such broken English, that I was horribly embarrassed and wished the earth would open up and swallow me. Professor Neef always gave them an opportunity to participate in the discussion, and listened to them very carefully, which only added fuel to their conceit and made them go to even greater extremes in their comments on the ideas he presented and the positions he took.

In that seminar, as well as outside it, I had the opportunity to observe the behavior of my Arab colleagues closely, and to compare it with that of my American colleagues. The first thing that drew my attention in the Americans' behavior was their spirit of commitment and their sense of responsibility. To an American student, study and reading and preparation were basic duties to which all other considerations were secondary. When an American student was alone in his room or in the library, nothing stopped him from studying and reading, and he did not permit himself any rest or entertainment until he finished his task. The Arab student's behavior was completely contrary to this. He was always ready to put his books aside if he had an opportunity to drink a cup of coffee with a girl. His sense of responsibility was related to something outside himself, to an authority above him, not to an internal motive that bound him autonomously. When this outside authority (his father or his professor) was absent, a chaotic tendency would take its place and it made him shirk responsibility and seek pleasure. If he ever had free time, he was unable to use his freedom. To this day, I feel there are two stern eyes observing everything I do and evaluating everything I turn out. I still experience the fear and anxiety I used to feel as a schoolboy. I always wonder: "Am I wrong? Have I said anything to anger anyone? Have I done what is proper and necessary?" I always expect to be judged and evaluated by others. My view of myself is constituted by how others see me.

-25-

In June of 1948, the first armistice in Palestine was declared. Several months passed by, during which I did not hear from my family. The last news I heard was that my mother and younger brother Khalid were in Acre at my grandfather's. When the Jews later attacked the city, all my relatives escaped to Beirut and stayed with a lady related to my grandmother, named Khayriyya Hanim, who lived in a small apartment in Ras Beirut

Akka (Acre), my grandfather's home.

near the Shawran Hill. They later moved to a small apartment
in the Basta Quarter, on the tramway line. A few months later,
my brother Khalid died, and soon after that my grandfather.
Only the women remained alive, my mother, my grandmother,
my great aunt (my grandfather's sister), and my two maternal
aunts. My father and elder brother Nizam were in Jaffa when
the Jews attacked it. They escaped to Nablus, my father's
birthplace, and they lived there a few months before moving to
Amman, where they stayed with my uncle Shakib who had
been living there before the war.

-26-

At first, I didn't realize that what happened to us in Palestine
was a blow that greatly differed from all our previous
afflictions. All our past had been a chain of misfortunes, but
misfortunes came and went, and our lives continued with little

382

change. Now, however, our very roots were torn out and we lost the land our lives were rooted in...

### -27-

Carol's mother arrived from California. She wanted to live near her daughter [my girl friend]. She was an attractive middle-aged woman. I was depressed at the time I saw her and could not be complaisant. I silently carried her bags to the apartment she had rented in the Midway, opposite the International House, then we went to a nearby drugstore to eat. I had no appetite, and was overwhelmed by a deep melancholy as I drank my coffee. I listened to the mother and daughter talking, but my mind was distracted by other thoughts in another world.

A few days later, Muhsin Mahdi arrived and my morale improved. As soon as he arrived, he rented a room in a house near the university. The next day, I took him to the university and introduced him to Professor Bergstraesser and my other professors. He quickly settled down and put his affairs in order. That helped me, for I now had a dear friend who shared my exile.

*(Translated by Issa J. Boullata)*

# FRAGRANCE
# FROM THE GARDEN:
Darwish
Al-Hakim
Al-Ashqar
Saudi
Taha Husain
Zajal Libnani

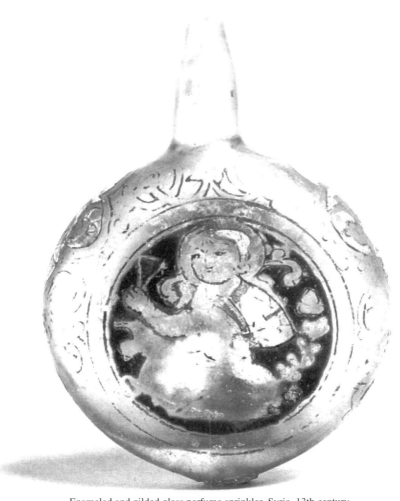

Enameled and gilded glass perfume sprinkler, Syria, 13th century.

# Mahmoud Darwish

# WE WILL CHOOSE SOPHOCLES

If this should be the final autumn, let us ask pardon
for the rise and ebb of the sea and memories
for what we made of our brothers before the age of brass:
We wounded many creatures with arms forged
from our brothers'bones, so that we become
their descendants by the water of the springs.
And let us ask pardon of the kin of the gazelle
for what we made of her
by the water of the springs
where crimson thread poured forth upon the water.
We did not see
it was our own blood
writing our history in the anemones of this beautiful place.

❏

And if this should be the final autumn, let us unite in clouds
to rain for this plant hung atop our hymns
to rain upon the stems of legend
and the mothers who devoted their youth
to retrieving our tales from storytellers
who prolong in them the season of migration.
Was it not in our power to amend, a bit, the season of migration

386

to calm in us the cry of the date palm
❏


We were born there on our horses
and we were burnt by the ancient sun of Jericho.
We raised the roofs of houses so shade would wear our bodies.
We celebrated the feast of the vine
and the feast of the barley
and the land adorned our names
with the lily of the valley and its name.
We burnished our stones so they would grow smooth...
grow smooth slowly in houses polished by light and oranges
and we hung our days on pegs of cyprus wood.
We lived slowly
and life had the taste of the seasons' faint shiftings.

❏


And if this should be the final autumn, let us leave behind
this sky of exile and the tree of others.
We grew older
and we did not detect the wrinkles in the cadence of the flute.
The path grew long and we did not admit
we were walking Caesar's road.
We did not see the poem that had drained its people
of passions to widen its shores
and we raised our tents where the wars between
Athens, Persia, Egypt and Iraq fell upon us.
We love plows more than swords
we love the breeze of autumn, we love the rain,
we love the earth adorned with tales
of gods born among us to protect us from winds of drought
and the horses of unknown foes.
Yet our gates between Egypt and Babylon
are open to wars and flight.


387

❑

And if this should be the final autumn
let us cut short our praises of ancient artifacts
upon which  we carved our psalms.
Others have carved other psalms upon them
and they have yet to break.
Wild mallow grows on their ancient armor
and its red flowers hide what the sword made of the name.
Green shadows will grow from our footprints
if we reach our mother
at the end of this long passage.

❑

We have what we have.
And all we have: words of farewell
which prepare us for the rite of their adornment.
Every word is a woman at the door
guarding the echo's return.
Every word is a tree beating with the wind
the lock of the far flung expanse.
Every word is a rampart
rising over patches of fog in the empty land
rising over the shadow of the dove's feather.

❑

We have what we have.
All that is there is ours... our past
which arranges our dreams, image by image
and refines our days and the days of our brothers of old
and the days of our enemies of old.
We who were burnt by the sun of faraway lands
we who came to the edge of the earth

to travel the roads of old
and to possess the rose of old
and to utter the language of old
we will choose Sophocles before Imru` al-Qays*
no matter that the shepherds' fig has changed
no matter that our brothers of old and our enemies of old
have together prayed to Caesar in the feast of darkness
no matter that the chanters of our creed have changed.

There must be a poet  who seeks
a bird in the crowd to scratch the dead face of marble
and open passageways above the mountainside
for gods who crossed from here
to unfold a land of sky upon the land.
There must be remembrance so we may forget and pardon
when peace resolves all that is between us
and the gazelle and the wolf.
There must be remembrance
so we may choose Sophocles, in the end
so he may break the circle.
There must be a horse
above the worlds of neighing.

❑

We have in the autumn a poem of love
a short poem of love.
We turn by the wind, love
we fall by the lake as captives.
We treat the ailing breeze.
We shake the boughs to hear the breeze's pulse.
We shorten the worship rites, we leave our gods
to the peoples on the two shores
and carry the smallest of them with our provisions.
We carry this road and we walk

At the springs we read our traces:
Did we pass this way?
Are we the owners of this colored glass?
Are we us?
We will know before long
what the sword made of the name.
Oh love
leave us what is ours...
of the breezes of the fields.

❑

We have a poem of love in autumn
a final poem of love.
We could not shorten the years of the road
but our lifetimes pursue us
to urge our steps toward the edge of love.
Oh love, we were the foxes of that hedge
the camomile of the plain.
We saw what we felt, and we cracked hazelnuts
on the bells of time.
In us lay a solitary road to the moon's court
and there was no night in night
but the fruit of the mulberry.
We had one moon in our speech
and we were the tellers of tales
before the conquerors arrived in our tomorrow.
If only we were a tree in our songs
to become a door of a hut, and the roof of a house
a table for a dinner of friends, or a chair for a midday rest.
And love, leave us a little
with which to weave
a beautiful cloak made of mirages.

❑

390

At night our shadows entertain us in the south
the female beasts howl at the red moon above.
We will touch the shepherds' bread and wear
the linen of their cloaks to surprise ourselves.
        Those days of ours
pass in front of us in a slow and ordered gait.
        Those days of ours
pass over soldiers' convoys and throw their greeting
        to the sparse mountainsides:
*Peace be upon the land of Canaan, crimson land of the gazelle.*
        And those days of ours
steal away, thread by thread, and we are the ones
who wove the cloak of our days.
The gods had no role but to talk with us at night
and pour upon us their wine.
        Those days of ours
tower over us so that we thirst more...

We did not recognize our wound
in the throng of ancient wounds
but this bleeding-land bears our names.
We were not mistaken
        because we were born here.
We are not mistaken
        because many conquerors rose against us here,
        and loved our panegyrics to wine
        and loved our legends and the silver of our olives.
We were not mistaken
        because the virgins of Canaan
        tied their underskirts to the heads of mountain goats
        so the prairie fig would ripen
        and the plum of the plain would swell.
And we were not mistaken...
        because many storytellers came to our alphabets

to describe our land, like us, like us.
Those voices of ours now intersect with theirs
above the hills
an echo of an echo.
The flute mingles with the flute
and the wind howls and howls in vain
as if our hymns in the autumn were their hymns  in the autumn
as if the land dictates what we say.
Yet we have the feast of barley
we have Jericho
we have our sayings in praise of our homes
and the raising of daisies and wheat.

*Peace be upon the land of Canaan*
*crimson land*
*of the gazelle.*
*(Translated by Patricia Khleif)*


**Mahmoud Darwish**,  a leadng Arab poet from the village of al-Barweh in
Galilee-Palestine. His symbolist poetry, which is of great subtlety and at
times unique purity, expresses at once his political and social as well as his
existential concerns, His life and his work have one theme: Exile. The
recipient of many world literary awards, his poetry has been translated in
over twelve languages.

* **IMRU' AL-QAYS** (d. c. 550), Arab poet, acknowledged as the most
distinguished poet of pre-Islamic times. He is author of one of the seven
odes in the famed collection of pre-Islamic poetry Al-Mu'allaqat.

# Tawfiq al-Hakim

# *THE SONG OF SONGS*
### Excerpts

ONE

Revive me with the kisses of your mouth
    For your love is sweeter than wine
    your ointments, more pleasant to the senses
    your name scents the sky with its fragrance
    No wonder you are adorned by the virgins

Sweep me with you
Let me run after you
    that we may come into the king's palace
There shall we rejoice and be glad
And there shall I be graced with your love
    sing its praises and extol it more than wine

Though of dark complexion, I am fair
    and as pleasing as Kedar's tents
    and Solomon's wing
So heed not my dark color, maids of Jerusalem
    For the sun has tanned me

My mother's children turned their anger on me

They made me a keeper of their vineyards
   and my own vineyard I have deserted.

Tell me where do you graze your flock, love
Where would you let them crawl
And why am I to stray blindly
   by the flocks of your companions?

Most beautiful of all women
follow the track of my sheep
And let your sheep graze by the shepherds' tents

You are like a mare in Pharaoh's chariots
Your cheeks are lovely
   extolling beads of gold
Your neck is comely among all necklaces of gems

We shall make for you a necklace of goldwork
   set in silver gilt

My love is a bundle of myrrh
   that I would let lie between my breasts
He is to me a bunch of grapes from  Ein-Gedi vineyards

Most beautiful you are and most charming
You have a dove's eyes

Most charming of all men, my love
Our couch is luxuriant

Our house is of cedar wood
   its ornaments are of the pines

I am the rose of Sharon
   the lily of the valley

You are among the maids
   like a lily among the thorns

My love among the men
   is like the apple tree in a jungle.
How much I yearn to sleep in his shade
   mingling my breath with his
   and filling my mouth with his luscious fruit

Bring me into the winery
Shroud me with the banner of your love

Revive me with raisins
Refresh me with apples
   for I am sick with love

Place your left hand under my head
   and embrace me with your right hand

I charge you, maids of Jerusalem
   by the hinds and does of the pastures
Do not stir nor wake my love
   until she please

TWO

It's His voice ...the voice of my love
There He is ... he comes along
He leaps upon the mountains
    skips upon the hills
He runs across the valleys
    like a roe of the pastures
Here He is ...He stands there, behind our wall
He says out loudly: Up my beloved
Up most fair of all women, come along
    For winter has gone
    the rains are over
    flowers have blossomed, beautified the earth
It's time to sing.
Doves pour forth their songs
The fig trees ripen their luscious fruit
The sky is heavy with the vines' fragrance
Up my love ...come along with quick steps

Who imprisoned you there in the cranny cliffs?
    Who hid you out, there above?
Show me your face, most fair of all women
    And let me hear the marvelous
        modulations of your voice

Come along, beloved
Let us hunt the foxes' cubs
    That spoil our blooming vineyards

My love is mine and I am his
He grazes his flock among the lilies

Come back to me, beloved

396

before the day vanishes
before the shadows creep away
Come up to the hills that separate us
Come up with the swiftness of fawns

All through the night I sought my love in bed
I sought the one whom my soul loves
But found him nowhere...

I woke up, I searched for my love
    strolled up in the streets of the city
    all through the marketplaces
    But did not found him ˙

I met the city's watchmen
I asked them if they have seen my love!
It was but a little that I passed them
    when I found him, whom my soul loves
I embraced him and did not release him
Until I brought him to my mother's house
    to the room where she bore me

I charge you maids of Jerusalem
    by the hinds and gazelles of the pastures
Do not stir nor wake my love
    until she please

Who is she who ascends from the wilds
    like a column of smoke
    redolent of myrrh and olibanum
    suffused with all ointments of
            the merchants
        [........]

397

♥

Most charming you are beloved
Your two eyes are peaceful like a doves 'eyes
    behind your veil
Your hair is a flood of darkness
    a herd of goats
    crawling on Gilead Mountain
Your teeth are a row of pearls
    a flock of shorn sheep
    coming up from the washing
None is barren among them
        and everyone a very twin to the other's twin
                Your two lips are a strand of scarlet
Your mouth is a rose-bud of ambrosial juice
Your cheeks are two halves of a pomegranate
    gleaming behind your veil [....]
Your two breasts are twin fawns
    of a female gazelle
    grazing among the lilies.
Before the day vanishes
Before the shadows flee
Come along my beloved
    Up to the hill of myrrh
    up to the mountain of frankincense

You are altogether fair, love
Your fair skin unblemished
Come along with me from Lebanon, beloved
    let your glances run from Amana's peak
    From the top of Shenir and Hermon
    From the lions' dens
    From the jungle of panthers
A thief you are, beloved
    gripping my passion with awful intensity
    and ravishing my heart

I am carried away
   with the flashes of your eyes
   with the one chain of your neck

How sweet is your tempting love, my sister, my spouse.
How much more delicious is your love than wine
And more pleasant is the fragrance of your breath
   than all apothecaries' shops

Your two lips drop liquid myrrh
   and under your tongue is honey and milk
Your garment suffuses fragrance
   a scent of Lebanon.

You are an enclosed paradise, my spouse
   a fountain shut up
   a sealed spring
   a fountain of living water
    flowing streams as is paradise
    with pomegranates in flower
      and vines in bloom
       with all sorts of roses and flowers
    of all myrrh and spikenard
    of all trees of aloe and frankincense

Blow up north wind blow
Come along south wind
   blow upon my garden your soft breeze
   that its fragrance fills the air with delight

Let my love come into his paradise
   to eat and be full of its luscious fruit

I am coming into my paradise, my
    sister and my spouse
  to gather the myrrh and spices
  eat honeycomb with its honey
  and drink my fill of milk and wine

Eat your fill and get drunken, friends
Be full  and get drunken of love.


THREE

I was asleep but my heart was awake
I heard his honey-voiced ring in my ears:
"Open to me, my sister, my love, my dove
My hair is drenched with dew
  my face wet with the night's damp"

I took off my shirt, rose up and put it on
I washed my feet, resoiled them.
My love extended his hand
  through a hole in the door
My heart stirred for him
I rose up to open for my beloved
  with my hands sticky, dripping with myrrh
  with my fingers sweaty with olibanum
    tinging the handle of the door.

I opened the door for my love
But did not find him
My love has gone
My senses have almost left me

I sought him but found him nowhere
I called him, but no answer was returned

At night while I strode down the streets
The watchmen saw me. They smote me
They stripped me of my robe

I charge you, maids of Jerusalem
If you find my love
Tell him I am sick of love

Most fair of women
What is your love more than others?
What is he distinguished by
   that you put us upon oath?

My love is beautiful beyond men
   in face and form
He stands out among ten thousand
His head is of pure gold
His locks hang in raven-black
His eyes like a dove's eyes
   washed with milk by the rim of the rill
His cheeks are fragrant thickets
His two lips are lilies dropping honey
His hands are two chains of gold
   studded with aquamarine
His stature is of polished ivory
   inlaid with lapis-lazuli
His two legs are two white limestone columns
   resting on two pedestals of pure gold.

My love is fair as Lebanon

majestic as its cedars
His mouth is a honeyed rose-bud
He is altogether charming, maids of Jerusalem.

❤

Most fair of women
Whereto has your love gone
   that we may seek him with you?

❤

My love has gone down into his paradise
   to the fragrant thickets
   to graze his flock
   and pluck lilies
I am his and my love is mine
He grazes his flock among the lilies

You are charming as Tirza
   beautiful as Jerusalem
   majestic as an army with banners

Turn your eyes away from me
   for they have disturbed my heart

Your dark hair is a storm of wind
   a herd of goats streaming on Gilead Mountain
Your teeth, a row of pearls, a herd of ewes
   coming up white from washing
   with none barren among them
   and every one becomes its twin

Your cheeks are two halves of a pomegranate
   gleaming behind your veil
My love is altogether perfect
She is most fair among sixty queens

and eighty concubines
She is her mother's favored child
   her mother's darling
   the chosen one of she who bore her
The virgins saw her and they praised her
   the queens and concubines blessed her

Who is she who flushes like the dawn's light
   fair as a new moon
   pure and clear as the sun
   overwhelming like a bannered army?

I went down into the almond grove   to enjoy the valley's verdure
   the vineyards' blossoms
   and the flowering and budding of pomegranates
Yet...before I was aware
   I was stirred by longing
   My soul's fancy seated me
   In a chariot of my people


FOUR

How graceful are your feet in sandals, princely daughter
The curves of your thighs are chains of gold
   fashioned by a craftsman
Your navel is a rounded goblet
   that wants no flavored wine
Your belly is a mound of wheat
   adorned and beautified with lilies
Your two breasts are twin fawns

403

of a female gazelle
Your neck is a tower of ivory...
Your nose tips high
   as Lebanon's tower
   looking down upon Damascus
Your lofty head is like the Carmel
Your tresses are purple
   that would captivate a king
How beautiful you are my love
How lovely is that which delights
Your heart knows naught but love
Your charms enmesh me in the magic of a trance
You are the palm tree
   And your two breasts are clusters of dates
Said I: Let me climb up this palm tree
   and hold its fronds
   and let your two breasts be the vine clusters
Your mouth is more delectable than the best of wines

That would drip down, smoothly and sweet
   for my love's sake
that would drop honey  over his lips
I am his and my love is mine.

Come along to the pastures, love
Let us lodge in the villages
Start at dawn to the vineyards
   to see if they blossomed
   if the petals opened
   if pomegranates flowered and budded
And there, I shall give you my love...

The mandrake sent forth its fragrance
I plucked from all seasons

mounds of luscious fruit
   laid them up for you, my love

If only you were my brother
   nursed at my mother's breasts
I would have kissed you unreservedly
   in full view of all people
   with no one of them to scorn me

And would have accompanied you
   to my mother's house
   that you would teach me there
   And would have made you drink wine
   mixed with a pomegranate liqueur of my own.

Place your left hand under my head
   and wind me with your right hand, my love

I charge you maids of Jerusalem
   do not wake or stir my beloved
      until she please

Who is she ascending from the wilderness
   leaning on her beloved's arm?

Under the quince tree I roused you
   Where you were brought forth by your mother
Where she made you to see the first beams of daylight
   She who bore you...

Set me a seal upon your heart

405

Jealousy is horrible as hell itself
And love is strong as death
   its blazing flames are the very flames of God
   that tempestuous floods cannot quench its passion
   nor raging rivers can drown it
And what treasures are offered for love
   they would be utterly scorned
We have a small sister
Whose two breasts are not yet swelled
So what shall we do for her
   at her wedding feast?
If she were a wall
   we would have set on it a silver tower
If she were a door
   we would have supported it
     with cedar boards [...]

O you who dwell in paradise
   The friends are listening to your voice
   Make me hear it too

Let us flee to the fragrant mountain, love
Let us flee as swift as the roes of the pastures
   As the gazelles of the forests

            *(Translated by Noel Abdulahad)*

**Tawfiq al-Hakim** (1899-1987) was one of the great formative figures of twentieth-century Egyptian literature, founder of contemporary Egyptian drama and a leading figure in modern Arabic literature. Al-Hakim won fame as a dramatist with *Ahl al-kahf* (1933; "The People of the Cave"). This introduced his series of "dramas of ideas," or of "symbolism." They include *Shahrazad* (1934), based on The Thousand and One Nights, as well as the plays *Al-Malik Udib* (1939; "King Oedipus"), *Pijmaliyun* (1942; "Pygmalion"), and *Sulayman al-Hakim* (1934; "Solomon the Wise"). His output of more than 50 plays also includes many on Egyptian social themes, such as *Sirr al-muntahirah* (1937; "The Secret of the Suicide Girl") and *Rusasah fi al-Qalb* (1944; "A Bullet in the Heart"). His boldest drama was the lengthy *Muhammad* (1936), which was not intended for performance.

# Yusuf Habashi al-Ashqar*

# THE SHADOW
# AND THE ECHO

Um Iskandar's body was laid out in the living room. Women all around her prayed quietly. Her youngest son received condolences on the lower floor. There was little conversation, and when there was, it was about the war.

Some asked about Iskandar. His brother said there was no way they could get hold of him. "What would be the purpose of his coming here?" said some. Others, "Does a son attend his mother's funeral for a purpose?" Others, "But, since he doesn't know..." And others answered, "There's always a way to find out such things. For his father's sake, at least, he should come. His father might live a couple more days, or might not. He might live just to see him one last time before he dies."

Iskandar's brother was quiet. He didn't join in the conversation. Deep inside he prayed for Iskandar not to come.

Out on the balcony across from the living room, Jurji al-Hammani sat on a high-backed chair, wearing a wide-brimmed hat to protect his head from the hot sun. He wasn't crying or grieving or paying any attention to what was going on around his wife's body. He looked into the distance, praying.

"A hundred years in my eyes are but one second in yours, Oh Lord, from the very start. And now they seem like one second to me, too. Have I begun to unite with you? Have I come to resemble you? A hundred years have passed over my body, and here it is now, searching for you; this body you brought into your world, where it has lived and thrived. Thank you. You preserved my sight and hearing and gave me the grace of memory, and long years of waiting. My soul never faltered in searching for you, seeking to find you and worship you."

Jurji al-Hammani sat on the bamboo rocking chair out on the narrow marble-tiled balcony, behind the wrought iron railing; there at his house at the foot of the mountain. He sat, and beside him sat his hundred years, peeping out from between his shoulders that never slouched, from his hands spotted brown with age, his sparse and immaculate white hair, and his blue eyes that sparkled with youth.

"Lord, you have given me so much, and I have taken care of your gifts. I know it's not for me to weigh the talents, but Lord, if I am counted among the righteous, I pray you, don't let Iskandar come. If I ever prayed to you not to close my eyes before filling them with the sight of his face, forget that prayer, God, and please don't let him come, don't let him die because of my selfishness.

"If I were able, Lord, I would kneel down; I would stand and raise my arms up to you for hours. I would. Begging you to answer my prayer: Don't let Iskandar come, Oh God. Don't let Iskandar come, Oh God. Oh God! Oh God!

"Oh God! No one—not I, not my father, not my father's father—no one ever remembered a time as evil as this one, when it was acceptable to spill another man's blood, to rob him of his money, his possessions and his pride.

"For hundreds of years, ever since our first migration for survival, no man has deprived another man of his humanity, his ideas, his dreams. What crime did we commit against you that caused the years to change in a matter of months, and the months to change in a matter of days? Save us from your anger, O Lord!

"Your anger was what caused people to kill out of greed and spite, as easily as taking a sip of water. Your anger made brothers turn against brothers and friends against friends, and people against people, the murderer not knowing why he murdered, or the victim why he was killed.

"Help us understand that in your house there are many mansions, and that whoever calls his brother a fool deserves the fires of hell.

"Help us believe again that there is hell and there is heaven.

"Forgive us, Lord, and let us be what we were before: man the way he was, his greatest luck to receive you, his greatest dream to satisfy you, his reward eternal life.

"Ever since you hid your face from us, everything has been ruined, everything has become permissible. So Lord, hide not your face from us, keep us from stealing, from killing, from bearing false witness, and calling our brothers fools.

"Protect the righteous among us. Other than you, who knows what's in the hearts of men? Don't let Iskandar come, and if he comes, protect him from the evil he does not want and does not deserve, and forgive me, Lord, for I have tested the limits of your will."

Jurji Al-Hammani gazed out into the distance. His eyes found comfort. He felt that God had answered his prayer and that he would not see any evil touch his son.

The relationship between Jurji al-Hammani and God was as deep as the sea, as wide.

His eyes wandered over the houses in the village whose red tiled roofs gave them their special beauty. He was sitting there in perfect harmony with life. Not judging, not predicting, not regretting or crying out. He saw things from the past as though he were reading a book, or watching water flow along in a river.

He felt that the burden of being had been lifted from him. And doesn't man have to be freed of this burden in order to transcend being? The burden of being is exile. Every confrontation with the world is exile, and every confrontation with the world is a confrontation with God. Only the burden of being confronts the world. To be in harmony with the world is to meet God, just as the tree is in harmony with the seasons.

Jurji al-Hammani saw everything that had been a part of his life flow from the extreme of peace and serenity to the other extreme of anxiety and fear, the way water gushes forth from the rock fresh and sweet, collects mud and debris along the way and eventually flows into the salty sea.

As if seen through the eyes of a child, the village appeared sky blue--the adobe roofs, the terraced orchards, the bright stone benches on the patios. The village was silk, pottery, weaving, silk fabric, and church bells.

And the village was also mule caravans, children, men and women, young and old, a swarm of bees droning in a hive.

The people worked in the summer and sang in the winter. Death was God's will; the quality of life was up to man. They prayed for hours without tiring. They hoped and rested and worked joyfully for hours on end, never complaining. One for all, all for one, and one and all lived in harmony with all of creation, with the donkeys and the mules and the cows and the goats and the chickens, with the grapevines, with the olives, the figs, the carob trees, and the plants, all in a procession towards a place they knew well, to die in it, naturally, like a grain of wheat.

Jurji al-Hammani lifted his eyes to the sky and prayed Iskandar would not come from Beirut. Then he focused on a little attic-house in the middle of the village that was still standing. Some of its red roof-tiles were missing, like a child's teeth.

In that attic-house, he was born. By the nearby spring, he had played. And down in the four terraces below, he had picked olives and spread out mulberry leaves for the silk worms.

"Butros and Maria are grinding the bulgur[1] and storing

provisions for the winter—lentils, chickpeas, wheat, beans, olive oil, raisins, and cured lamb. My mother and sisters are preparing kishk [2] and fermenting our grapes. We sit around the still in the vineyard, waiting for the drops of arak[3] to fall, one by one.

"Our little house is white, all white, the chair covers, the tablecloths. The walls are like white silk. My mother is embroidering the edges of the curtain that hangs between the living area and the storage bins, copying geometric designs and various flower patterns out of the yellowed, musty pages of an old book written in French.

"Hundreds work in the mills making silk fabric—flocking, dying, threading, weaving. Hundreds more work in silk production—cocoons and silk threads. Hundreds more run the caravans. Dozens make pottery, still others melt steel and pour it into molds for scales and bells. Others are buying and selling.

"The village is a beehive, people working, singing and praying.

"Once a year, the town crier calls out from Ras al-Sannad high in the hills, reminding people it's time to pay their taxes.

"Kfarmellat, stretching from the mountains to the seacoast, is two open arms. It is the capital of all the villages in the lower elevations, all the way down to where the river joins the sea. Kfarmellat is a storehouse for merchants, a center for artisans, the starting point for caravans, a place of refuge. Its people came from Yanouh, Turtuj, Jaj, Bajja and Cordoba, in wave after wave of migration, searching for new frontiers. They cultivated the land, carving out of its mountainsides terraces embedded in the famous Kfarmellat black stone.

"Each wave brought a new family searching for a place to live beside a spring. Kfarmellat was blessed with an abundance of water that gushed from its rocks and hillsides. Each family would plant a little garden next to the spring and look for a bigger piece of land some distance away that needed little irrigation and was suitable for olive trees, grapevines and fig

411

trees. Then the family would build a small church with a roof just like the roofs of the houses around it except for the steeple with the bell inside it that would sway back and forth. Near the church they would build the school and clear out a spot for a cemetery. Then they would live close to God and the dead, honoring both.

"All of Kfarmellat was a daily mass. The monks followed the families, staying up in the hills away from people. With their own hands and their own sweat they built their churches and their monasteries and tilled the land and made it green and fruitful. They taught and learned, casting a mantle of holiness upon the earth. At work and during prayer no one could tell which were the farmers or the builders or the church servants.

"Times were better under the Ottomans. The sectarian wars ended. One policeman in Bhannis was enough to keep order all the way from Antelias to Duhoor al-Shwayr. People could afford to be happy, to have peace of mind. Worshipping God came from the heart and the mantle of the Lord shaded the earth.

"My beard has started to grow. Every three months I come back from my school at Qurnat Shahwan to spend a few days in the village. My father says, 'Learn, learn. Good for you. Make sure your handwriting is good. Make sure your pronunciation is good. Open your mind. Learn your language. And don't forget —pay attention to your French. That is where the wind is blowing from.'

"My brother and my sisters are studying in the village—my brother with Master Gabriel and my sisters with the nuns.

"My father scans lines of poetry, writes math problems, or plays cards in the evenings.

"My mother is like a bee in and around the house, always coming and going like a shuttle in a loom.

"My grandmother tells us her stories without looking up from the stockings she is knitting with four knitting needles and coarse honey-colored wool.

412

"My father puts some money away in the cabinet after the harvest. It is called 'land money.' He buys up the land that surrounds our house."

His great-grandfather, and his grandfather and his father all did the same when they came to Kfarmellat. Each one kept land money in the cabinet and bought what he could to increase the property.

"My father said, 'Property grows just like people do. When you can't extend it out any further, increase it. Buy some land away from the house. That's all right. Every tree is special and gives its reward. The olive tree, the pine tree, the fig tree, the cactus, the carob, and the walnut all offer their rewards. And the mulberry, too. And the grapevine is a fountain of comfort and peace of mind... Don't forget."

His father's voice rang in his ears, as though he were sitting next to him. "Your land is your house's pillar, my son."

"My aunt came back from Egypt and brought me a dog the size of a rat. That's as big as it will get. It's brown, with a cute mouth and ears, large eyes. I keep it in my pocket.

"It jumps out of my pocket and runs around our little house. The black cat is jealous. I chase the cat to the roof.

"The cat jumps off the roof and kills the dog.

"I take my father's cane and smash her head. I cry over both of them.

"Why is there evil? I ask my father. Why is there revenge?

"My father says, 'Evil is the work of the devil. Revenge is the work of the fool. Stay away from both of them, and let your heart know nothing but love.'

"My grandmother tells the story of Abu Zayd al-Hilali[4] and Al-Zeer Bu Layla al-Muhalhal[5] and the story of Antar[6]. She ends with the story of Yusuf Bay Karam[7]. 'Your father knew him,' she says. 'What a loss.'

"My mother recites poetry and sings the praises of heroic and glorious deeds—self denial, sacrifice and generosity. She saves them up for me in the hope that they become my virtues.

These, in the end, are what govern life.

"The world is an organized system, governed by a God who judges. Chaos is only a temporary condition, or a punishment.

"In the morning we pray. And in the evening we pray, for those we know, and those we don't know. We pray for travelers and sinners and the sick and the poor.

"The whole village prays in the morning and in the evening. For everyone and everything it prays and sings.

"The village is a true believer. It fights the devil, fears him, wards him off with incantations and incense and the name of the Father and the Son and the Holy Spirit.

"The whole village is a melody, rising up to Heaven."

Bits of memories wafted from Jurji al-Hammani's clear blue eyes, from his white hair and the old aba that had taken on the smell of his own body, and from his long tapered fingers - the story of a century in which he watched the world spiral downward from one of peace to one of crime, ever since the shooting star.

"The shooting star!

"The churches are packed with people kneeling and praying.

"My father says, 'This is the phase of the Devil. Satan has vanquished the angels. The shooting star will take peace of mind with it, and happiness, tranquility and the worship of God. The shooting star is gold. Gold is coveted. And everything that is coveted and is not alive is evil.'

"Emigration began. It was on everyone's mind, in everyone's eyes. After gold. After gold that doesn't satisfy because it cannot be drunk, cannot be eaten, is not alive. Everything that doesn't satisfy is evil.

"The mountain's main concern is silk. Production is down, income is down, and the workers are few. The mountain lives off of the silk worm, and the looms and the silk factories. The mountain trembles in fear. The population grows. Farming the

414

mountain will not provide enough for everyone. Too many rocks and too little water.

"The fear of hunger is like the fear of war. Fear is not a ghost. It has a body and a face even if it looks ridiculous.

"Emigrate. Emigrate. For food. For food."

During those anxious times their dark days came back to haunt them. Days of war, of forced emigration, memories that came to them through their grandparents, their great grandparents and their great great grandparents. Each generation retained their history. They were like an inexhaustible fuel for an everlasting fire that blazed around them. Fuel that never runs out, does not turn to ash, because the life within them was strong.

During those anxious times they would recall the days of fear, without yielding to them; the days of terror and the ultimate question: Why are we here? Why are we what we are? And they would answer: we are here because we are here, and we are what we are because we are what we are. No one can change the color of his eyes or the length of his ears. We are in what we are in and we will never change it. This is our destiny, they would say.

In Kfarmellat, Tawfiq Khrayru and Ibrahim Qamar and others like them fluttered about befriending the village people. They would eat their food and fill their minds with dreams of emigrating. The country is poor. The world is wide open, no need even to knock at the door. The world is free for everyone. Go to it. Eat. Satisfy your hunger. Eat like gluttons. The hungry don't dream of satisfying their hunger. They dream of gluttony. The shooting star has done its job—has instilled fear and sparked hope.

"Oh God," Jurji wondered sadly. "Why has everything changed?"

The money-lenders opened their bags wide. Khillu smacked his lips and rubbed his hands together greedily. Emigration started. The people were poor. Khillu sat at his doorstep laughing and waiting.

On his way to the river Tobia the baker slipped under his load of kindling wood. A piece scraped his back. He threw the bundle down and swore never to carry anything ever again. For the first time in his life he followed the road to the river without carrying anything. He did not stop at his house but went straight to Khillu's. "It's hard work, here or there. It's degradation, here or there. But there it's degradation plus gold. I'll never carry anything again. I'm not a donkey. Never. Never again."

Tobia mortgaged his house and possessions to Khillu for ten gold pounds. In a year he would owe him twenty or lose the house.

Early the next morning Tobia went to Beirut and got on the first ship. "To America," he said.

Along with Tobia went many people from Bkfayya, Ayn Aar, Zikreet and Shawiyyeh.

The boat anchored in Marseilles and from there they were all taken to Africa. America is very far, they whispered to them. Africa is better. They herded them like sheep.

A year later Tobia sent Khillu twenty gold pounds. His wife retrieved the deed. Tobia didn't know how to read or write.

"'Emigration is the future,' people said. 'The shooting star swept by,' my father said. 'Travel does not fill your stomach.'

"Watching the people of the village and the neighboring villages was painful to my eyes," al-Hammani said. "The Bukihlis, the Sabbaghs, the Buzakharrias, the Khourys all left. Khillu's bag was spilling over. His properties were eating up the whole village. The emigrants were dying by the dozens.

"My brother wants to go. My father says, 'Emigration is not in our cards.'

" 'Don't you see how much money they're sending back?' my brother says.

"'Money? Making money is hard work. Our clothes are

always clean, our beds always smell of lavender. We eat our fill and we rest after we eat. You won't be able to make money there. You'll see that it's better to work at your own pace than to get rich. Money for money's sake is evil. A rich man cannot enter the kingdom of Heaven.'

"The emigrants to Africa and America load their vending carts with goods and sell them in remote areas. They don't care if they sleep on a board or a hay mattress, in a hut or out in the open. They'll eat anything they can get, whether they like the food or not.

" 'And what do you want me to do here? Be a baker?' my brother asks.

" 'A baker? No. Not a baker. That's hard work.'

" 'A carpenter then?'

" 'Why not? Jesus was a carpenter.'

"It's been ten years since the emigration began. Ibrahim Qamar and Tawfiq Khrayru travel from village to village. The people of Kfarmellat are leaving and dying by the dozens. My father says, 'Now do you see the price they pay for money? Anxiety, then fear, then greed, then crime. The emigrants will give you half a pound and charge you for one. They'll give you a yard for the price of a meter, and they'll sell you a mirror claiming it has magic powers. Cheating is a crime,' my father says. 'Money for money's sake is evil. And when this becomes the way of the world, the world will be destroyed.'

"My oldest sister got married. Her husband is a businessman in Beirut. 'Go and work with him,' my father says.

" 'No,' I say. 'I want to publish a newspaper when I grow up.' My father is quiet. My grandmother says, ' He wants to be a writer like you. He's the lion's cub, after all.'

" 'I enjoy writing,' my father says. 'But you can't live on it.'

" 'My brothers Father Hanna and Father Mubarak live by their pens,' my mother says.

" 'Not by their pens, Rifqa. By being priests. By being priests.'

417

"In my lifetime they all emigrated, searching for food. They fell in love with the new life in the Americas and in Africa. And soon they forgot all about food and panted after the power of money and the prestige it gave them, gobbling it up like animals chomping down hay."

"Gold is evil," Jurji said, just as his father said before him. "Anything you can't have a dialogue with is evil. It begins with anxiety and ends in crime. Emigration has become the passageway to the new man with the lustful eye for a mirage of power, for a meaningless gluttony of money. All they are really doing is dowsing time with kerosene and setting it ablaze in an instant without enjoying it, communing with it, or enter into it. Time—which has become for them a way to kill fear with illusions and power, and kill anxiety with anxiety."

His clear blue eyes compared his decision to stay with theirs to go, focusing first on his life, which passed slowly, full of bliss, tranquility and rest, and then on their eyes, which remained closed to all of that.

" 'The doorway of our house is low. Whoever enters must bow down,' my grandfather used to say. 'I built it that way on purpose, so whoever enters, no matter who he is, will have to bow down.' My grandmother Barbara would laugh and say, 'No. You built it that way so the cavalry men couldn't enter on their horses. They used to do that, son, come right into our houses on their horses.'

"My father is lying on his soft mat inside our little house. He has his pillows all around him. He's wearing his white aba and his face is radiant. His eyes are blue, his moustache is speckled with white. His long white fingers twirl the cane he is holding. On the little table next to him are an ink well and papers. My father reads the letters that come from the emigrants to their relatives and writes back to them. Yusuf Makhoul's letter was the talk of the neighborhood.

"The Khoury boys died. Shawul's son has blood in his urine. There was no news from the Saqr boys. Mass graves of emigrants from our mountains and villages have sprung up along the byways and remote areas of the strange lands they found themselves in.

"My father gives me the letter and says, 'Read Yusuf Makhoul's letter and mark my words: This land will never be the same. There will be more rocks and fewer people. The shooting star took along with it peace of mind and the tranquility of faith.' I read the letter.

"Yusuf Makhoul had been gone for five years. No one had heard anything from him. Jurji Eid of Bkfayya came back for good. He brought with him Yusuf Makhoul's letter and along with it a large number of gold pounds. Jurji had soon realized that he wouldn't be able to work in Africa. He reopened his cobbler shop and started working again. Yusuf Makhoul's letter was important, very important. Everyone understood it. And all those who left afterwards left having been forewarned that they were placing themselves in danger. Yusuf Makhoul did not write the letter himself. He didn't know how to write. Elias Jabr wrote it for him. Elias Jabr studied at Qurnat Shahwan. He knew how to read and write French. He didn't write the letter to Yusuf Makhoul's wife and children only, he wrote it for the whole village to read, for all of Lebanon, and he made it clear that he wrote the letter.

*To my dear wife, children, brothers and sisters,*

*I am indebted to Khawaja[8] Elias Jabr for writing this letter to you for me after such a long absence. If I have been guilty of not sending news about myself to the village sooner it is not because I have not been thinking of you or missed seeing you, but rather because of the hard days I have lived through and the difficult times I have endured. If it hadn't been for God's*

*help, glory to His name, and for the brothers Elias Jabr and
Yusuf Naja, we would have all been dead and totally
humiliated. Khawaja Elias told me he had written many letters
for people from our village. One of them was our relative
Tobia, and I am sure you have heard all about what happened
to us after we got on the ship. The weather was very bad. It was
terrifying. We were all in bad shape, because we were like a
herd of sheep. On clear days we slept out on the deck, and on
rainy days in the engine rooms. Anyway, thank God, we made
it to Marseilles without losing anyone. In Marseilles they said
it would be at least another month before there would be a ship
to America. We were very scared because we had little money.
But they told us there was a new place that had opened up, full
of opportunities and riches like America, and even more so.
And it belongs to France, our dear mother, and over there we'd
live the easy life, and it's not as far as America. It's called
Conakry, in Africa. The people there are black and very nice.
We put our lives in God's hands and we said this must be
God's will. The next day we left for Conakry on a ship bigger
than the one we took to Marseilles. And thank God, the
weather was nice. We spent the time on the deck and didn't
have to sleep in the engine room.*

 *To make a long story short, we arrived in Conakry, those of
us who went with Khrayru and the others who left with Ibrahim
Qamar. The weather there was so hot, and the place was, Oh
my God, you can't imagine. Each tree was as high as a
mountain, and monkeys. From the very moment we arrived we
didn't know what to do. Sign language was of no use, and the
French people there couldn't speak our language. But with
God's help we managed. They told us to wait and an hour later
our brothers Yusuf Naja and Elias Jabr came by to help us.
They showed us where the French settlements were and taught
us how to start work. We each bought a knapsack, filled it with
beads and mirrors and combs and things like that and each
went off in a different direction. It was a huge place—too far to*

420

*cross on foot, but in this place, men carry men. The black people carried us in big baskets from one place to another. We slept under trees or in the black people's houses, rooms made of mud and hay. Thank God it was a safe place. No one stole from anyone or tried to beat up anyone. That is the only good thing, because there are many diseases. And the weather? In the winter you have floods, and in the summer you suffocate. The black people's language was easy. We learned it and started our business.*

*I went to a place way out of the way. Khawaja Elias gave me the address of a settlement there where I could stay and buy goods on credit and then pay after selling them. It took me a year to get there because I managed to do some good business on the way and learn all about the tricks of the trade.*

*In that place I met Rasheed Budagher. He had gotten there two years ahead of us. He helped me and let me stay at his house. Two slabs of adobe and two sheets of tin on top. In that God-forsaken place there was no one I could send you a letter with. I said I was going to make it, that God would help me out and I would find a way to get back to Conakry and figure out how to send you a letter.*

*The where I am is called L'Abbe'. The weather is just like back home. They say it's the only place in New Guinea with good weather. Maybe that's why I survived, because when I went back to Conakry, Khawaja Elias told me that half of the people who had come died of mosquito bites and malaria and blood in their urine, sunstroke, exhaustion and diseases. You have to be made of steel to get out of here alive. I found out a few weeks ago when I was in Conakry that Yusuf Shawul, Elias Dabbis, Ibrahim Saqr, Khalil Shaya and Milhem Yammeen all died. My condolences. When this letter reaches you I will have gone back to L'Abbe' where business is very good, and I have a roof over my head and a little store and I'm on good terms with the settlements and business is really good. Anyway, if you survive and you know how to make it, you'll get rich here. But*

421

*if you die, it's all over for you, or if you take things easy, you'll stay exactly how you were, or even worse. God willing, in a year's time I'll come visit you.*

"Tawfiq Khrayru and Ibrahim Qamar prowl the area looking for prospective emigrants. My father says the French consulate pays them to bring customers—the French need workers to build their settlements.

"The Lebanese people are leaving their villages in droves. The houses are emptying of their men.

"Elias Jabr's letter didn't do its job. The villagers heard the syllables but didn't listen to a single word. Each new emigrant says, "Yes, some people will die, just like those others who died, but not me. I'm going to live and get rich like the ones who got rich. Leave the goat pens for the goats. Leave 'our daily bread' to prayers. Prayers are one thing, but in every one of us there's a Caesar." Times have changed. People don't just dream of getting rich. It has become their life's goal—a value for which they will risk anything, even their lives. Money has become a homeland. A son. A home. Roots.

*(Translated by Paula and Adnan Haydar)*

\* **Yusuf Habshi al-Ashqar** was born in 1922 in Bayt Shabab, a Lebanese mountain village famous for its breathtaking views, church bells, and literary giants. Ashqar died in 1992, some four years after completing his manuscript for *Al-Zill Wa al-Sada*, ("The Shadow and the Echo") published by the Beirut press Daar Al-Nahaar in 1989.

The *"Shadow and the Echo"* is the last novel in an epic trilogy that tracks the life of protagonist Iskandar Al-Hammani as he moves in and out of relationships with other characters -- Unsi, Asmar, Mona, Mira, Marthe, Yusuf -- over a thirty-year period. The history of previous generations, especially of Iskandar's parents' generation, also figures prominently throughout the trilogy.

In the first book, *Arbᶜat Afraas Humr* ("Four Red Horses"; Daar Al-Kutub, 1964), Iskandar is a young man in his mid-twenties, full of idealistic dreams and an insatiable appetite for material possessions. He is a writer and a loner who is greatly disliked and considered a traitor by all of his friends, not only for his unwillingness to participate unselfishly in personal relationships, but also for his skeptic views on political life (which foreshadowed the events leading to the Lebanese civil war (1975-1990)). In the trilogy, the civil war begins between the second book, *La Tanbut Judhoor Fi al-Samaa'* ("Roots Don't Grow in the Sky"; Daar Al-Nahaar, 1971) and "The Shadow and the Echo," though hints about civil strife begin in the second.

In the wide space of the 1,395 pages that compose the trilogy, which was published over a span of thirty years, Iskandar Al-Hammani ages and develops. We meet him first as a young, self-centered, idealistic twenty-year-old in "Four Red Horses." He then returns in "Roots Don't Grow in the Sky" as a thirty-eight-year-old who tries, unsuccessfully, to find his roots within the estrangement of an inherited fortune and its accompanying material riches and luxuries, and who tries to control his destiny by pursuing a long series of sexual relationships while remaining unwilling to love and incapable of giving. In 'The Shadow and the Echo," we see Iskandar as a fifty-year-old recluse whose inability to establish any "dialogue" with anyone or any belief system has led him finally to a self-imposed hermitage within the confines of his "palace," which is now crumbling like his dreams. His nearly-mad solitary existence is nevertheless under constant threat from the many enemies he has acquired throughout his life who, having entered into the civil war from various ideological standpoints, all see him as a traitor for not having chosen sides and for not having used his wealth to support their struggle.

When "Four Red Horses" first appeared in 1964, the literary community was pleasantly surprised by this new genre in Arabic fiction termed, "the psychological novel." The term underscores Ashqar's exceptional ability to delve into his characters' minds while employing many of the novelistic techniques we associate with the modern novel in the West, such as stream of consciousness, flashback, and multiple points of view. Ashqar's literary style is also characterized by language which vacillates between dense directness and complex exposition, making his scenes striking and his narrative both pleasurable and demanding as it draws upon Ashqar's sophisticated familiarity with world literature, philosophy, mythology, religion, politics, and history.

Ashqar's trilogy is an important witness to the factors leading up to the Lebanese war and to how Lebanese identity changed during the last century. The hundred years preceding the recent civil war are seen through Iskandar's father's eyes in "The Shadow and the Echo," as a long, downward spiral from a world of harmony, faith, community, and traditional values, to one of selfishness, social rebellion, faithlessness and eventually complete chaos. Fortunately for the Lebanese, not very long after the publication of "The Shadow and the Echo," which was written during perhaps the most hopeless period in Lebanese history, the war did come to an end and though Lebanese identity has suffered irrevocable changes, a spirit of pride and a stubborn, creative drive remain its essential characteristics, and have propelled the Lebanese people forward and upward in one of the quickest and most remarkable reconstruction efforts in history.

Yusuf Habshi al-Ashqar is also the author of several short story collections in Arabic, and a long play called *Mubarak* ("Blessed One"). While he is perhaps one of the greatest modern Arab novelists, little of his work has been translated into English.

1. Cooked, parched and crushed wheat.
2. A dough made of bulgur and sour milk, cut into small pieces, dried and used for the preparation of other dishes.
3. Strong, colorless liquor made of grapes; milky white when diluted with water.
4. Heroic figure in the stories of the Arab tribes of sand Hilal, 11th Century.
5. Pre-Islamic poet (531) famous for his elegiac verse in honor of his brother, Kulayb, whose murder was pan of a series of events that resulted in the 40 year Basus War.
6. Antara Bin Shaddad (525-615), legendary Pre-Islamic poet and knight and devoted lover of his unattainable cousin, Abla His heroic deeds are recorded in a multi-volume Arabic collection entitled *Seerat Antara* (the Biography of Antara).
7. Lebanese hero (1822-1889) famous for his brave opposition to Ottoman Rule.
8. "Mr." -- title and form of address, especially for Christians and Westerns.

# Adnan Haydar

# MKHAMMAS MARDÛD IN LEBANESE *ZAJAL*
## *an analysis*

In a previous study of Lebanese *zajal* زجل metrics[1], I argued that the poets of *zajal* render their lines in two musical styles, one characterized by a free rhythm, the other by a regularly rhythmed underlay. In other words, the various genres of Lebanese *zajal* divide along the two traditional styles of Arabic music: *nathr al-naghamāt* نثر النغمات, and *nazm al-naghamāt* نظم النغمات. The former (literally, "musical prose") refers to "a vocal or instrumental performance without regularly recurring rhythmic patterns."[2] The latter, or "ordering of tones," defines a musical style based on a "traditional melody" and characterized by regular beats.[3] In general, formal long poems in long meters used in verbal duels and concerned with various degrees of *iṣabat al-maᶜnā* إصابة المعنى are closely associated with the *nathr* style. Informal, lighter, and shorter poems, such as jokes, popular songs, counting rhymes (*ᶜaddiyyat* عــديات), and verbal tricks, abound in the *nazm* style.

The main meter in the *nazm* style is the *qarrādi* قــرادي meter, which has a strict rhythmic pattern imposed by a musical meter, producing a neutral realization of the following trochaic pattern $-\acute{} \, - \, - \, \acute{} \, - \, -\acute{} \, - \, - \, \acute{}$ with a wide variety of internal and external rhyme schemes and strophic divisions.

The purpose of this study is to introduce *al-mukhammas al-mardûd* المخمّس المردود (or *mkhammas mardûd* مْخمّس مــردود), a

425

very popular *qarrādi* composition used in verbal duels and other *zajal* occasions, primarily for psychological and sometimes comic relief and as a means of establishing the poets' credentials with their audiences. While its rhyming phrases along with the repetition and reversal of word order allow for audience participation, its simple but ornate musical rendition facilitates this participation and establishes a psychological space, a relief from the heated verbal arguments preceding and succeeding it. A typical *mukhammas mardûd* consists of a four hemistich *maṭ laᶜ* مطلع (or proem-refrain) rhyming a b, a b or a a, b a and a nine-hemistich *dawr* دور (or *simṭ* سمط):

## Example A

| *maṭlaᶜ* | _____ a | _____ a |
|---|---|---|
| | _____ b | _____ a |
| *dawr* | _____ c | _____ d |
| | _____ c | _____ d |
| | _____ c | _____ d |
| | _____ c | _____ e |
| | _____ a | |

## Example B

| *maṭlaᶜ* | _____ a | _____ b |
|---|---|---|
| | _____ a | _____ b |
| *dawr* | _____ c | _____ d |
| | _____ c | _____ d |
| | _____ c | _____ d |
| | _____ c | _____ e |
| | _____ b | |

## Example A, Arabic

مـين قَللو عَ السّاحة نْزال     العـامـل حالو مْن الأبـطـال
نشيـلِ القَيمِة المـاتنشال     بَدنا بالزِّنــــدِ المفتـول

بْزَقفة كَفّ بنينا أسـاس     وعَ المتـراس الشّمِل التفّ
بْنَينـا أساس بْزقَفَة كفّ     التَفّ الشّمِل ع المتـراس
قْبـال النّـاس وقِفنا صفّ     بْدَفّ وموّالــــين وكاس

426

صَفَّ وقِفنا قْبال الناس  بْمـــوّال وكاس ودفّين
ودَفّ وكاسَين ومـوال

## English Transliteration and Translation

*maṭla*[c]

| | | |
|---|---|---|
| Il <sup>c</sup>āmil ḥalu-m-nil abṭāl | // | min 'allu <sup>c</sup>as-sāḥa-n-zāl |
| He who considers himself a hero | // | who asked him to descend on the arena? |
| | | |
| Bad-nā biz-zin-dil-maftūl | // | Nshīl-lil-'aymi-l-mab-tinshāl |
| We want [s.o.] with muscles to | // | lift the weight that cannot be lifted |

*dawr*

| | | |
|---|---|---|
| Bza'fit kaff-ib-nay-na'-sās | // | W<sup>c</sup>al-mitrā-sish-sham-l-il-taff |
| With a [mere] clap we laid the foundation | // | and on the battle front the friends met |
| | | |
| Iltaff-ishamli-<sup>c</sup>-lal-mitrās | // | Bnay-na-'-sā-sib-za'fit kaff |
| The friends met on the battle front | // | We laid the foundation with a [mere] clap |
| | | |
| Bdaff-iw-miw-wālay-niw-kās | // | 'Bā-lin-nā-siw-'if-nā ṣaff |
| with one tambourine, two *mawwāls* and one drink // | | in front of the crowds we stood in a line |
| | | |
| Ṣaff-iw-'if-nā'-bā-lin-nā s | // | Bmiwwāl-iw kā s-iw-daffayn |
| In a line we stood in front of the crowds | // | with one *mawwāl*, one cup and two tambourines |

Wdaff-iw kāsayn-iw-miwwāl
And one tambourine, two cups and one *mawwāl*

## Example B, Arabic

وجُوْقتنـا قَلعة أشـــعار        ســاحتنا مَلعَب للخيْـل
بِكلمة نـــور وكلمـة نـار        مِبنيّةً عَ جْنـــــاح الليل

شَعرو شاب وخاف الدّهر        لما النّهر زْرَعتـــو دْياب
لما دْياب زْرَعـــــت النّهر        خاف الدهر وشَعرو شاب
سَبْع الغَاب حبَستو شهر        بْلوح وْ مِسـمارينْ وْ باب
بمسـمار وْ بابَين ولَـوْح        حْبَستو شهر السَّبع الغاب
ولَوْحين وْ باب ومِسمار

427

## English Transliteration and Translation

*maṭlaᶜ*

| | | |
|---|---|---|
| Sāḥit-nā malᶜab lil-khayl | // | Wjaw'itnā 'lᶜit-ashᶜār |
| Our arena is a playground for horses | // | And our troupe is a citadel for poetry |

| | | |
|---|---|---|
| Mibniyyï ᶜajnāḥ-il-layl | // | Bkilmit nūr-iw-kilmit nār |
| Erected on night's wings | // | with words of light and words of fire |

*dawr*

| | | |
|---|---|---|
| Lamma-n-nahr-izraᶜtu-d-yāb | // | Shaᶜrū shāb-iw-khaāf-id-dahr |
| When in the river I planted wolves | // | Its hair grew white and fate was scared |

| | | |
|---|---|---|
| Khāf-id-dahr-iw-shaᶜrū shāb | // | Lamma dyab-izraᶜti-n-nahr |
| Fate was scared and its hair grew white | // | when wolves I planted in the river |

| | | |
|---|---|---|
| Blawḥ-iw-mismārayn-iw bāb | // | Sabᶜ-il-ghāb-iḥ-bastū shahr |
| With one board, two nails and one door | // | the lion of the jungle I imprisoned one whole month |

| | | |
|---|---|---|
| Ḥbastū shahr-il-sabᶜ-il ghāb | // | Bmismār-iw bābayn-iw-lawḥ |
| I imprisoned for a whole month the lion of the jungle | // | with one nail, two doors, and one board |

Wbāb-iw-lawḥay-niw-mismār
And one door, two boards and one nail

Several features are apparent in the two examples above. With specific reference to Example A, the nine-hemistich *dawr* consists of two major divisions. The first four hemistichs break into phrases or clauses, two per hemistich, with the following internal rhyme:

a' b' // b' a'
c' b' // b' a'

Example A

{Bza'fit kaff}- {bnay-na'-sās} // {W ᶜal-mitrās}- {ish-sham-l-il-taff}
 a'         b'              b'            a'

{Iltaff-ishmli}- {ᶜ-lal-mitrās   //   {Bnay-na'-sā-s} - {b-za'fit kaff}
 c'         b'                       b'              a'

Each phrase or clause if further divided into two words: a': 1) *za'fit* and 2) *kaff*; b': 1) *bnay-na* and 2) *'sās*; b ' : 1) *ᶜlā* and 2) *mitrās*; a': 1) *shaml* and 2) *il-taff*; c': 1) *il-taff* and 2) *shaml*; b': 1) *ᶜlā* and 2) *mitrās* ; b': 1) *bnay-na* and 2) *'sās*; and a': 1) *za'fit* and

428

2) *kaff*, altogether adding up to 16. When the words are numbered in order from 1 to 16, the following internal rhymes obtain: 1/15, 2/8/9/16, 3/13, 4/6/12/14, 5/11.

Example A

{Bza'fit} {kaff} {bnay-na } {'sās}   //   {W <sup>c</sup>al} {mitrās} {ishshaml} {iltaff}
  1        2          3         4             5        6        7        8

{Iltaff} {ishshaml} {<sup>c</sup>-lal} {mitrās}   //   {Bnay-na} {'sās} {bza'fit} {kaff}
  9     10     11     12         13        14      15     16

In addition to this mosaic of rhyming words, phrases, and clauses, there is a clear transposition of the words in clauses a' and c', *shaml* and *iltaff* versus *iltaff* and *shaml,* the rest of the clauses being repeated without transposition.

Involved as these divisions and subdivisions are, they are predictable and thus enable the educated *zajal* audiences to become actual participants in the song.

The second major division consists of the last   five hemistichs in the *dawr* .

{Bdaff -iw - miwwāly - niw - kās}   //   {'Bā- lin- nā- siw - 'if - na ṣāff}
              1                                 2

{Ṣaff - iw - 'if - na' - bā lin - nās }   //   {Bmiwwāl- iw- kās- iw- daffayn}
             3                               4

{Wdaff- iw kāsayn- iw- miwwāl}
               5

(Within the whole *dawr,* these are hemistichs 5,6,7,8,9.)

This time around audience . participation is further encouraged by predictable strategies of a slightly different kind. Three words are introduced in hemistich number 5, two in the singular and one in dual form: one *daff,* two *miwwāls,* and one *kās.* These words then go through a different sort of transposition in hemistichs 8 and 9, with *daff* in 5 appearing in dual form at the end of 8 and with *kās* in 5 becoming *kāsayn* in dual form in 9. It is important for one of the words in 5 to rhyme in its singular form with rhyme a of the *matla<sup>c</sup>* . Thus *miwwālyn* (dual, two *miwwāls* ) or *miwwāl* (in singular form) rhymes perfectly with "a" of the *matla*ᶜ . Hemistichs 6 and 7 repeat the internal rhymes of the previous four hemistichs (but not the actual words) and the transpositions that take place in hemistichs 2 and 3 of the first major division of the *dawr*.

While such complicated features suggest a great deal of deliberateness and artificiality on the part of the oral poet, they nevertheless enable the accomplished poet to improvise, precisely because the genre has a clearly delineated structure and a relatively small number of rhyming words, phrases, and clauses.

The etymology of the name *mukhammas mardûd* presents a problem. *Mukhammas* suggests that we are dealing with quintuples, arrangements of lines or metrical units in fives, but nothing on the level of structure or metrical feet allows for the nomenclature of this genre. The *matla*ᶜ consists of four hemistichs, not five, each of which is rendered with four distinct musical beats and four stressed poetic syllables. The *dawr* follows the same poetic stress pattern as the *matla*ᶜ, and the rhyme schemes of both the *matla*ᶜ and the *dawr* cannot be grouped into quinary systems or arrangements. Antoine Akkari claims that:

> *Al-mukhammas almaraûd,* refers to any *zajal* composition whose *matla*ᶜ is comprised of four hemistichs and whose *dawr* has been quintupled by responding to [or returning to] the third hemistich. This is the derivation of the terms *mukhammas* and *mardûd.* It [this method] can be found in the various genres of colloquial poetry such as the maᶜanna[مْعَنَّ], the *qarradi,* the *qaṣîd* [قصيد] - both short and long varieties-and other [genres].

This bewildering statement does not accord with the huge number of *mukhammas mardûd* compositions available in print and on tape throughout Lebanon and clearly identified by poets as *mukhammas mardûd* . How the *dawr is* "quintupled" by returning to the third hemistich (of the *dawr,* one would suppose) is not made clear. Nor does Akkari offer a specific example. The two examples above bear no such claim. As to Akkari's statement that *mukhammas mardûd* may be "found" in *ma$^c$nna* and *qaṣid* compositions, I have yet to see one such example, except perhaps that some ma$^c$nna and *qaṣid* compositions, and there is ample proof to such a claim, may employ the kind of repetition and transpositions discussed above as formal features of *mukhammas mardûd* . It seems to me that Akkari, like other Lebanese writers on *zajal,* confuses genre with rhyme schemes and other poetic features.

Still, where does the name come from? Since *mukhammas mardûd is* sung to a strict musical tune, part of the answer, at least, should be sought in music. As the musical transcription below makes clear, it is highly probable that the early singers of *mukhammas mardûd* were speaking in musical terms of the musical return (Da Capo) of the last hemistich (#9) in the *dawr,* to the *matla$^c$* . This explains the term *mardûd* (literally "that which is returned to"). As for the word *mukhammas, it* is equally probable that the "quintupling" sense of the word refers to the 5th hemistich of the second major division of the *dawr* (hemistichs 5, 6, 7, 8 and 9) which initiates the play on the three words *"daff,"* *"miwwālayn ,"* and *"kās ."* In this second division hemistich #5 (or #9 in the *dawr )* ends the play on words begun in hemistich #5 of the whole *dawr* or hemistich #1 of the second major division. In other words, the fifth hemistich of the second division returns to the fifth hemistich of the whole *dawr.* When I presented this explanation to Tawfiq Abdo, a well-known *zajal* poet, he admitted that he composed his *mukhammas mardud* pieces with precisely this explanation in the back of his mind, but that he could not express it in words.

When the *mukhammas mardûd* is introduced in a verbal duel or a less formal occasion, a poet sings the *matla$^c$* and follows it with his *dawr* . The chorus and the audience take their cue from

431

the last hemistich in the *dawr* and sing the *matla^c* again. Another poet then introduces his own *dawr,* ending it with a rhyme that "returns" to that of the *matla^c*, and so on. While the various *dawrs* vary their rhyme schemes, the transpositions in the second division are executed in the same manner and the last word in the *dawr* is made to rhyme with the last word of the *matla^c*.

Clearly such artificial word-transposition is not conducive to verbal duelling in the strict sense of the phrase, the emphasis being on word-play in *mukhammas mardûd* rather than on theme and topic. However, since the poet's strategy in a verbal duel is to prevail in an argument, it is important for the poet to establish rapport with the audience by demonstrating his or her knowledge of rhyme and word-play. Moreover, if the poet has a good voice in singing, this can only earn him or her points in the context of the whole duel.

The musical transcription below is of a popular song by Fayrouz, Lebanon's most famous female singer, and her male counterpart Nasri Shamsiddin. As part of a longer operetta entitled "A Love Poem," it is intended, in my opinion, as a musical ornamentation to highlight the theme of love in the operetta. It is chosen here because the sophisticated music accompanying it represents clearly the beats, accents and ornaments in live *zajal* performances and because the *dawr*s that follow exhibit slight variations in form and length, typical of musical adaptations of *zajal* genres.

## Mkhammas Mardûd[5]

The *matla^c,* or choral refrain, resembles the standard *matla^c* of the previous two examples. The *dawr*, however, is rendered in five hemistichs, the first and third of which introduce two different sets of three-word phrases. Hemistich #3 initiates the word-transposition-play familiar in *mukhammas maraûd* compositions. The *dawr*s that follow consist of five hemistichs

each and repeat the form of the first *dawr*, except for the second *dawr* which initiates the three-word transposition in hemistich #3 only:

**Fayrouz**
**Arabic:**

قفولة ومْفاتيــــح جْـداد     باب البوابة ببــابين

إلليْلِ وْ عَنتَر بنْ شــدّاد     عَ البَوّابة في عَبــدَين

العاشـق غطّ العَاشـق طار     حلــوة وْشــبّاكَين وْ دار

عوّادَين وْ نَغمــــة وْ نار     نغمة وْنــار وعوّادَيـن

وْ نارَين ونغمة وْ عوّاد

| matla<sup>c</sup>: | Bab-il-biwāb-bib-bābayn | // | 'Fūli-wim-fātiḥ-ij-dā d |
|---|---|---|---|
| | The gate consists of two doors | // | locks and new keys |
| | <sup>c</sup>Al biwābi fi <sup>c</sup>abdayn | // | il-lay-liw-<sup>c</sup>Antar Bin Shidā d |
| | At the gate there are two black [men, things] | // | The night and <sup>c</sup>Antar Bin Shaddad |

433

Ḥilwi-w-shibbākayn-iw-dár // L‘āshi' ghaṭ-ṭil-‘āshi' ṭār
One pretty girl, two windows and one house // The lover alights, the lover flies off

Nagh-miw-nār-iw-‘iw-wā-dayn // ‘Iw-wā-dayn-iw-nagh-miw-nār
One tune, one fire, and two ‘oud players // two ‘oud players, one tune and one fire

Wnárayn-iw-nagh-miw-‘iw-wád
Two fires, a tune and an ‘oud player
(maṭla‘ repeated)

# English Transliteration and translation:
## Nasri
## Arabic:

ياحلـــوة اللّي ريفـك رَفّ  بتـمشي وْ خَلفك يـمشي الصَّفّ
دَفّ وكَفّ وْ رِدّادَيـــــن  رِدّادَيــــن وْ دَفّ وْ كَــــفّ

وْكَفَّيْـــــن وْ دَفّ وْ رِدّاد

# English Transliteration and Translation:

Ya ḥilwi-l-li rífik raff // Btimshi-w-khalfik yimshiṣ-ṣaf
O, pretty one with fluttering eyelashes // You walk and people que up behind you

Daff-iw-kaff-iw-riddā dayn // Riddā dayn-iw daff-iw-kaff
One tambourine, one palm [of a hand] and // Two chorus members, one tambourine,
two chorus members // one palm

Wkaffayn-iw-daff-iw-riddā d
Two palms, one tambourine and a chorus member

(maṭla‘ repeated)

## Fayrouz
## Arabic:

صحــرا وْ قافلتَـيـن وْ خَيْل  العَتمة مَيْل النِّجمة مَيل
فحــم وْ ليْـلِ وحِدّادَيـــن  حدّادَيـــن وفَحـمِ وْ ليْـــل

وْ لَيْلَيْـن وْ فَحـمِ وْ حِدّاد

434

## English Transliteration and Translation:

Ṣaḥ ra-w-'āfiltayn-iw khayl     //   Lᶜatmi mayl-in-nijmi mayl
One desert, two caravans and horses     //   Darkness on one side, the star on the other

Faḥm-iw-layl-iw ḥiddā dayn     //   Hiddā dayn-iw-faḥm-iw layl
Charcoal, a night, and two blacksmiths     //   Two blacksmiths, charcoal and night

Wlaylayn-iw-faḥm-iw-ḥiddā d
Two nights, charcoal and one blacksmith
(maṭlaᶜ repeated)

## Nasri
## Arabic

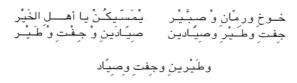

## English Transliteration and Translation:

Khawkh-iw-rimmān-iw ṣibbayr     //   Ymassikun yā ah-lil khayr
Plums, pommegranate and cactus     //   I bid you good evening, good people.

Jift-iw-ṭayr-iw ṣiyyā dayn     //   Ṣiyyā dayn-iw-jift-iw ṭayr
One shotgun, one bird and two hunters     //   Two hunters, one shotgun and one bird

Wṭayrayn-iw jift-iw-ṣiyyā d
Two birds, one shotgun and one hunter
(maṭlaᶜ repeated)

The unifying theme of these vignettes is love. The power of suggestion is managed here in words resembling ideograms, that allow the audience to write out, as it were, the various love scenes, without the intervention of logical connections and narrative sequence. The same power of suggestion is evident in

435

Examples A and B above, except that in those examples the theme is that of boasting and vainglory. In all cases, *mukhammas* *mardûd* compositions invite audience participation, by enabling the audience to partake in the creative act of composition.

In terms of the overall musical structure, this is a professional rendition of a folk melody and text, which shows sophisticated adaptation of folk material for modern performance. The song consists of a refrain and *dawr*s, sung by Fayrouz and Nasri as alternating soloists followed by choral rendition of the refrain preceding and succeeding each *dawr*. Variations and melodic excursions are introduced for each new *dawr* to avoid literal repetition. However, the melodic material remains basically the same throughout the song even though some of the variants add extra measures or modify key structural pitches.

The rhythmic activity of each *dawr* increases toward its end. Each phrase ends with a brief downward flurry of motion that mirrors the same idea in miniature, imparting a sense of structural cohesiveness to the whole.

Structurally the refrain consists of two phrases (transcribed above as full 4/4 measures) combined in a question-answer (antecedent-consequent) format into a two-measure phrase which is then repeated. The pulse is regular and strongly marked. The structure of the verse, on the other hand, is extended in its fifth measure, corresponding to the fifth poetic phrase. This may account for the allusion to "five" (*mukhammas* ) in the name of the genre. Moreover, there is the sense that the last line of the music "returns" without stopping, or breathing; it "falls into" the refrain without pause.

The musical accents coincide with the beats, heavy accents fall on the poetic syllables 1, 3, 5, 7 and produce a typical *qarradi* meter. This coincidence characterizes all poetry in the *nazm* style, where the music writes the poetry. The musical formula is ready made, and the poet's function is to fill the formula with words, observing the strict trochaic pattern imposed by the musical meter. Finally, because the musical meter is essential to the composition, writing the poetry as it does and dislocating poetic and natural stress patterns, it ceases to be language-specific. This is why the so-called *qarradi* meter exists in all languages, especially in children songs and counting rhymes. Two familiar examples, one from French, one from English, may suffice:

FRENCH:                    ENGLISH:

Úne póule súr un múr       Éeny, méeny, míny, mó
Qui picóte dú pain dúr     Cátch a tíger by the tóe
Pícotí picótá              If he hóllers, lét him gó,
Lá voilá quí s'en vá       Éeny, méeny, míny, mó

The singing of these tunes, as with the typical Arabic *qarradi*, superimposes a musical trochaic accentual pattern into which words are made to fit, sometimes even against the natural stress patterns of the particular language.

*Taha Hussein* by Zareh

# George Tarabishi

# TAHA HUSSEIN'S FAILURE
## To distinguish Modernization from Westernization

When he made the famous proclamation in "*The Future of Culture in Egypt*" that "we should become European in every respect...," Taha Hussein appeared as if he wanted to release an evil genie from its bottle.

Yet the devil, in our judgement, is not to be found in this controversial statement as much as in the title of the book itself. For the first time in the history of Arab culture, as well as the history of the Arab-Islamic culture, the future has become an established concept.

Thus, the concept of the future becomes an indicator of the state of the future. Were we to relate Hussein's controversial statement to the title of his book, one could even go further and affirm that since the onset of European modernization, the future has become a single institutionalized concept for all different human cultures.

Europe's pioneering achievement of modernization has defined the path of the future throughout the world. The future then ceased to be a hidden screen and part of the metaphysical world to be discovered only through speculation and prophetic gnosticism; instead it became the arrival station which every train would unavoidably reach over the rails of modernization, what we might call the railway of development and underdevelopment.

The presence of the developed became the future of the underdeveloped. If the image of the railroad suggests inevitability, we can alleviate this effect by talking about historical necessity.

The necessity of arrival is not synonymous with the inevitability of arrival, especially considering that the railroad connecting the station of underdevelopment with that of development is not already built. Thus, each train would have to make its own way, relying on the intelligence of its operator, the power of its fuel, and the speed it travels as decided by its passengers. Although the location of both stations—departure and arrival—is determined by historical necessity, the distance separating them is not clearly defined. The path is then not pre-determined but open for creation, or at least for re-creation. Following European modernization, we, as well as other peoples, have lost the option of not developing. That is the inevitability. It is effective at the level of teleology. As for freedom, its scope is confined by method. Thus, the question: "How do we develop?" This question will remain as controversial as it has been since the onset of the enlightenment in the last century, and could remain so throughout the twenty-first century.

Our difference with the author of *"The Future of Culture in Egypt"* centers on his formulation of the problem at the level of identity by mixing teleology and method together. "To become Europeans in every respect" means that we should develop as they did; we should converse with them, closely imitate their path of development, setting aside the task of creation and re-creation in favor of simple replication. While calling for unconditional identification, Hussein says: "Believe me, Mr. Reader, that our correct patriotic duty following our independence and the implementation of democracy in Egypt, is that we exert what we have of resources and effort, including time and money, to enable Egyptians to feel, as individuals and groups, that God has created them for glory not shame, for strength not weakness, for sovereignty not submission, for intelligence not apathy. We need also to erase from the hearts of the Egyptians—individuals and groups—the evil and offensive illusion that portrays them to be made from a clay different from which Europeans are made, created according to a temperament unlike that used in creating Europeans, granted brains different than those given to Europeans...We have to become Europeans in every respect...We have to follow the course of the Europeans, travel their path to become their equals, partners in culture, including its good and evil, its sweetness and bitterness, lovable and hateful aspects, and what is praised as well what is blamed."

One need not expose the confusion and difficulties posed by the courageous text of Hussein. The author of "The Future of Culture" merges the teleological and the methodical in the call for progress. The latter is interpreted as mere "quibbling," ruling out every margin of freedom while establishing a deplorable fatalism, confusing two courses which contemporary psychologists and sociologists warn against--identity and identification. Thus, Hussein calls upon the Egyptians, and also Arabs, Muslims and Third World peoples, to relinquish their identity so they could become "Europeans in every respect." Rather than demanding partial identification with certain European accomplishments, Hussein goes to extremes in urging total imitation, to the extent of adopting what is evil, painful, hateful, and dishonorable in European culture, and not only what is good, sweet, beloved, and commendable.

It is quite clear that the call for total identification presents a severe criticism of the concept of identity: instead of having identity as an organic synthesis of all partial identifications, the total and unconditional identification tends to be mere mechanical substitution of identity by another that is different or contradictory. Instead of partial identification which constitutes an element in identity formation as well as an enrichment of personality, total identification, on the contrary, produces only the identity of caricature. The mechanism of total identification depends on tradition and emulation as opposed to originality, environment, renewal, reproduction and re-creation. Thus, total identification ceases to be an element of identity formation, and on the contrary, it becomes a factor of deprivation and dissociation of identity, an impoverishment and superficialization of personality. Rather than making identification, as its etymology suggests, as a way of gaining identification, the mechanisms of imitation reduces it to a dull, parroting act, that demeans the dignity of the identity and reduces it to the level of dependence and inferiority. In a word, partial and conditional identification can be an exercise in the freedom of identity, yet imitation is inherently enslaving.

Without erecting a Chinese Wall between the principle of identity and the mechanism of identification, we could re-emphasize the distinction we have shown between teleology and method in the course of development. Teleology defines an enriching and creative level of identification while that of method defines an impoverishing, classical level of enslaving identity. Reproduction of progress, and not imitation or cloning, is needed first and last. Achieving progress becomes possible if we reformulate the problem so to distinguish between occidentalization and modernization. Occidentalization is a movement at the level of identity which means displacement, extraction and negation. Modernization, however, is a movement at the level of conditional, partial and gradual identification. Occidentalization negates identity, replaces it, and impoverishes it to the point of deprivation; modernization develops identity, enriches it, and allows the personality infinite opportunities. As much as the accomplishments of modernization are susceptible to psychological manifestations, occidentalization is a metabolism rejected by the psychological system.

It is not then a mere coincidence to find the etymology of "occidentalization" indicating an alienation from the self in

442

addition to the meaning of "Europeanized," that is, Westernized. Taha Hussein's mistake—forgiven by his courage—lies in his implicit confusion between occidentalization and modernization, especially when the latter is broader, richer, deeper, more dialectical and acceptable by the psychological metabolism, individually and collectively. Occidentalization is unilaterally authoritative and compulsorily in model, yet, modernization is an open commitment to a diversity of models, alternatives and creative solutions. It is a light burden on the narcisstic wound because modernization does not reduce the cultural process, as in the case of occidentalization, to a one-sided relationship between two groups, one active the other reactive. Instead, it is supposed to be a mutual partnership based on give and take, fertilization and reproduction. Contrary to occidentalization, which results in cultural process experiencing a rupture with identity, modernization leads to continuity and communication in which identification with the other becomes possible without a loss of identity. In much as occidentalization responds to its predecessors and others, recognizing practically the existence of the other only to seize it and eliminate it. Modernization, which understands identification with the other to be an evolution and enrichment of self-identity neither breaks with the past nor with the tradition of the self. Rather, it employs it as a wonderful process in the cultural transformation of the self.

This last point is extremely significant, particularly for the Arab nation to which *turath* [henceforth, tradition] so important. Besides the fact that occidentalization breaks with the tradition of the self, it also goes against the traditionalization [tatreeth] that breaks away from modern culture described as the culture of the other. Employing tradition as an ideological weapon in the war against modern culture, modernization creates a rare historical opportunity to revive tradition. Modernization would enable tradition to regain what it loses through evolution and renew itself with the assistance offered by modern culture of unparalleled scientific methods in investigative research, excavation, criticism, re-reading and interpretation. Contact with modern culture, rather than a break from it, could add something new to tradition, a surplus to its value, injecting life in its death, and uncovering with the aid of modern knowledge and its architecture, the site of a treasure whose existence was not suspected before. In a word, opening up to modernization could present traditions with new questions, extract new answers, and reformulate them, in parts and wholes, into new problematics.

Based on what was said, poetry, an art deeply-rooted in tradition, underwent an astounding development as a result of modernization. Our treasure of modern poetry almost matches today, and will inevitably in the future, our wealth of classical poetry. The same can be said about the art of narration and the story, which evolved in our modern literature into novels and theatrical productions worthy of consideration and full of promise. In this modernist context, we can always talk about wealth and revolution together in contemporary Arab fine arts, though we still note, comparably speaking, failure in musical modernization. Throughout the twentieth century, literary modernization has achieved unquestionable success. By the end of this century, the active forces in contemporary Arab culture are moving toward modernizing the intellectual tradition, in the fields of jurisprudence (Fiqh), theology, philosophy, linguistics and history in the same manner as literary modernization. It is well known that the modernization of this tradition—from Taha Hussein to Nasr Hamed Abu Zeid—has met more stiff resistance than that faced by literary modernization. Despite this, there is no alternative but to continue the battle—or rather war—for modernizing tradition since it is the main item on the present moment's historical agenda. Modernizing tradition paves the way for the stipulated conditions of a higher and consecutive phase of modernization: the theological and philosophical.

If we allow ourselves an exercise in reading the future, we can expect the process of modernizing tradition to continue throughout the first half of the next century. As for philosophical and theological modernization, this process is expected to last through the second half of the twenty-first century.

Theological modernization emancipates the text from the text. Philosophical modernization emancipates reason from the text.

These possibilities are contingent on the failure of regressive and reactionary forces which might prevent the birth of a Muslim Luther and Arab Voltaire.

Scientific modernization remains absent from this picture of the future. This part of the picture remains lost in the shadows, shadows gathering into darkness. Nothing indicates today that the Arab world will move or will change in the twenty-first century from the position of consumerism to that of scientific production.

*(Translated and edited by Elie Chalala)*

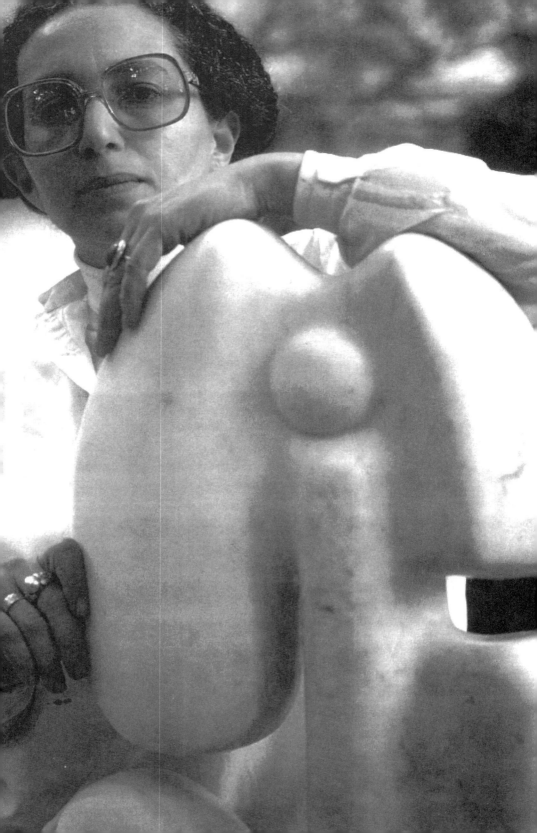

# Sarah Rogers

# IN MONA'S GARDEN

The smooth, precise lines of the stone beckon to be touched and traced with the fingers, with the mind. Outline becomes form. A two-dimensional line gives three dimensional shape to the stone and its surrounding space, a complexity of shapes made from a simplicity of cuts. Essence of concept is abstracted and visualized. The forms of the marble and granite are ones natural to the earth, yet the Arab artist Mona Saudi has given these pieces of earth their form.

Mona Saudi chose to hold her recent exhibition in her home, secluded from the chaos of downtown Beirut. In her small garden, rest several of Mona's sculptures. During the Civil War, the sculptures were damaged and Mona has decided not to repair them. The damaged sculptures stand witness to the reality outside the melodious paradise of Mona's garden. The harmony of the sculptures, disrupted for a moment, live on in new forms. Passing through the garden, Mona's statuesque figure and mild voice greets each visitor as he/she enters the house. As Beirut reconstructs itself outside the gates of Mona's house, the exhibition space inside the gates stands testimony to the endurance of the creative spirit.

Non-confrontational to the viewer, Mona Saudi's sculptures envelop him/her in the works' balance. Upon closer examination, however, the complexity of Mona's work subtly

447

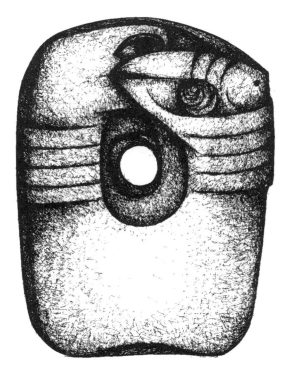

Mona Saudi, *White Fullness*, ink, 1980

reveals itself. Encompassed within the forms are layers of dichotomies: the two-dimensional and the three-dimensional, the traditional and the modern, the particular and the universal. Although the physical identity of the stone is rooted in specific locations of the Arab World, the geometric forms convey a universal quality by exploring themes such as love, nature and maternity. The art critic Paul Richards proposes that Mona Saudi "an admirer of Brancusi" similarly uses her stone pieces to suggest both "the ageless and the modern." Mona acknowledges Brancusi as an extremely significant influence in her work. The simplicity in her work exemplifies Mona's

448

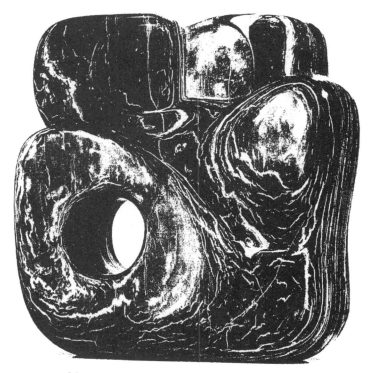

Mona Saudi, *Mother Earth*, marble of Jordan, 1981

constant reference to the essentials of form, recalling the old civilization of the Arab World. In Mona's recent *Petra Series*, the ancient Arab culture inspires a modern work.

In her series on Petra, Mona mates the forms of shape with the forms of writing. When I spoke with her, she expressed the historical importance of poetry in Arab thinking and life, describing Arabs as 'living in poetry." Mona's work is inspired both by the poetry, which she writes and the poetry, which she reads, especially the work of Darwish and Adonis. Mona also explores the ability of words to take on an abstract nature. Just as a few words have the ability to spark a trail of ideas in the

449

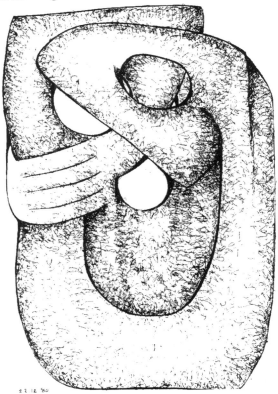

Mona Saudi, *Hymn*, ink, 1980

mind, so the simple forms of Mona's work have the ability to express conceptual intricacy.

Mona Saudi, who presently resides in Beirut, knew at a young age that she wanted, "to make forms." After graduating from high school, Mona left Jordan and came to Beirut against the will of her family. In Beirut, Mona held her first exhibition. With the money she earned from the exhibition, she bought a plane ticket to Paris and enrolled in *L'Ecole Nationale Superieur des Beaux Arts*. In 1965, Mona sold her first stone sculpture, *Mother Earth*, from which much of her work stems. As Mona recounts her difficult and rebellious beginning as a female sculptor, her work surrounds us, bathing us in color.

Since graduating from *L'Ecole Nationale Superieur des Beaux Arts* in 1972, Mona has gone on to exhibit extensively, both group and solo shows, in Beirut, Paris, London, Oslo, Washington, D.C. and Canada. Mona also has been commissioned for several public works, including her 1983 sculpture *The River* at the Petra Bank in Amrnan her 1986 work *The Circle of Seven Days* at the University of Technology in Jordan, and her 1987 work *Spiritual Geometry* at the Institute du Monde Arabe in Paris. In 1993, the Jordanian government honored Mona with the National Award for the Arts. Mona views public sculpture as an important component to her career as an artist and she is currently working on a public sculpture for downtown Beirut. Large sculptures for public spaces serve as focal points for contemplation and give meaning to space. Locating art in a public space, which is accessible to everyone, helps to transcend the ideologies of elitism surrounding the contemporary art world. Through her public sculptures, Mona Saudi gives back to the culture, which fosters her art.

Her present exhibition includes Mona's most recent work of watercolors on paper. Mona sees this work as closely connected to her sculptural work, despite the difference in mediums and the use of colors. She views her body of work as "a chain." The internal relation within her body of work is both visually and conceptually apparent. The forms in the two dimensional works, for example, are very sculptural in their line. With only a touch of coffee as paint and a few black lines, Mona gives the two dimensional paper a three dimensional quality. Using a material integral to the Arab culture, coffee, Mona continues to bridge the traditional Arab culture with the international world of contemporary art. Mona also pointed out to me that the artistic process is very similar between a watercolor on paper and a large-scale stone sculpture. Interestingly, while giving careful attention to geometric composition, Mona also leaves plenty of space for spontaneity both in sculpture and drawing.

451

In her works on paper, the visual relationship between colors, whether it be between different tones of blue or the contrasting nature of orange and blue, burst with character. In some works, the relationship between colors and tones contrasts with the compositional equilibrium. In other works the relationship between colors mates peacefully with the geometric rhythm. Mona's art is an exercise in visual feeling and thought.

Although Mona claims not to consider an audience when working on a piece, even one for a public commission, she continues to please her audience. Unsure about the future, Mona assured me that "she has many dreams," and views her body of work as a journey. As an Arab American Art Historian, I am pleased that Mona Saudi has chosen to visualize her journey and share it with both her present and future audience. The serenity of her work defies stereotypes concerning the Arab World and visualizes the vitality of the Arab culture.

Mona Saudi,
*Woman-Rose*,
marble, 1974.

453

# Contributors' Notes

**Noel Abdulahad** is a Palestinian American critic and translator. His most recent work is a revised version of Gibran's *Prophet* in modern English. His Arabic translation of *The Prophet* was published in Amman, Jordan. Noel lives in Phoenix, Arizona.

**Kathryn K. Abdul-Baki** was born in Washington D.C. to a Palestinian father and American mother. Her published works include a collection of short stories, *Fields of Fig and Olive: Ameera and Other Stories of the Middle East*, and *Tower of Dreams*, a novel, both published by Three Continents Press. She received the Mary Roberts Rinehart award for short fiction in 1984. Currently she resides in McLean, Virginia with her husband and three children.

**Elmaz Abinader** is an Arab American author, poet and performer. Her book, *Children of the Roojme: A Family's Journey from Lebanon* is based on family diaries. Her poetry *In the Country of My Dreams...* is being released May 1999. Her performance piece *Country of Origin* has toured throughout the United States and the Middle East. Elmaz has recently been a Fulbright Scholar in Egypt and now teaches at Mills College in Oakland, California.

**Diana Abu-Jaber,** currently Writer-in-Residence at Portland State University, attended schools in New York and Amman, and received her doctorate from the State University of New York. Her first novel, *Arabian Jazz,* won the Oregon Book Award and was a finalist for the national PEN/Hemingway award. Her forthcoming novel, *Memories of Birth,* won an NEA grant.

**Evelyne Accad,** born and raised in Beirut, Lebanon (Oct. 1943), is Professor at the University of Illinois, Champaign-Urbana at the French Department. Her works include: *Wounding Words: A Woman's Journal in Tunisia,* (Heinemann, 1996); *Sexuality and War: Literary Masks of the Middle East.* (New York: N.Y.U. Press, 1990); *Contemporary Arab Women Writers and Poets* (Beirut: IWSAW, 1986); and *The Excised* Colorado: Three Continents Press, 1989 and 1995)

**Etel Adnan** is a poet, novelist and painter. Among her works are *Sitt Mary Rose* (a novel), *Beirut Express, The Arab Apocalypse, The Indian Never had a Horse* and *Five Senses for One Death* (collections of Poetry). Her paintings have been exhibited in Paris, San Francisco, London, New York, Beirut and many Arab and European capitals. Etel lives between San Francisco and Paris, writes in English and French.

**Saladin Ahmed** has performed his poetry with artists such as The Last Poets and as a member of Detroit's 1997 and 1998 National Poetry Slam teams. His poetry is featured in forthcoming anthologies from Wayne State University Press and Henry Holt & Co. He is a Libra.

**Munir Akash**, Editor and founder of *Jusoor*, is critic and science writer. His literary books include *Questions in Poetry, The World from Above* and *On*

*Poetry, Love and Revolution* (co-authored with Nizar Kabbani). The 1983 recipient of *Targa Euoropa* (decoration of Europe), his recent published work, *The Talmud According to Uncle Sam*, has focused on comparative religion and cultural genocide of indigenous Arabs and Native Americans.

**Nuar Alsadir** was born in New Haven, CT to Iraqi parents. She grew up in Chicago, received her B.A. from Amherst College and an M.A. in Creative writing from New York University, where she is currently working toward a Ph.D. in English Literature. She has received writing fellowships from The Fine Arts Work Center in Provincetown, Yaddo, The MacDowell Colony, and Ledig House International Writers' Colony. Recent poems of hers have appeared in *Grand Street*, *The Women's Review of Books*, *Agni*, *Callaloo*, *Gulf Coast*, and *Ribot* among other journals. She lives in New York City.

**Hakim Archuletta**: Childhood in Manhattan Beach Calif. Weaned in Berkeley in the sixties. Painter, sculptor, film maker, musician, recently writing poetry although hung out with beat poets in the fifties as a teen. Accepted Islam in 69 traveled for ten years and studied traditional Islamic medicine and homeopathy practice and teach it around the world.

**Halim Barakat**, novelist, sociologist, and Research Professor of Society and Culture at the Center for Contemporary Arab Studies, has been with Georgetown University since 1976. Barakat's sociological works include *The Arab World: Society, Culture and State* (University of California Press, 1993), and *Lebanon in Strife* (University of Texas Press, 1977). He has also published six novels and a collection of short stories.

**Nadia Benabid** was born in Rabat, Morocco in 1955. In 1972, she made what she thought was a temporary move to the United States (where she still resides) to attend Princeton University. Her translation of Driss Chraïbi's *Muhammad (l'Homme du Livre)* was published by Lynne Rienner Publishers in 1998.

**Walid Bitar** was born in Beirut in 1961. His collection of poems, *2 Guys on Holy Land*, was published by Wesleyan in 1993.

**Issa J. Boullata** was born in Jerusalem, Palestine. He taught at Hartford Seminary in Connecticut, then joined McGill University, where he is currently professor of Arabic literature and language. His publications include *Outlines of Romanticism in Modern Arabic Poetry* (1960) and *Badr Shakir al-Sayyab: His Life and Poetry* (1971), both in arabic; *Modern Arab Poets*, 1950-1975 (1976), an anthology in English translation; he is editor of *Critical Perspectives on Modern Arabic Literature* (1980), and translator of Ahmed Amin's *My Life* (1978) and Emily Nasrallah's *Flight Against Time* (1987).

**Elie Chalala** teaches political science at Santa Monica College and edits Al Jadid, a review and record of Arab culture and arts. Chalala's research has focused on the international relations of the Middle East and contemporary

Arab political thought. His articles and commentaries appeared in professional journals, books, and national newspapers and magazines.

**Hayan Charara** was born in Detroit, Michigan, in 1972. His poems have appeared in many publications, including *The Cream City Review, The Literary Review, Press,* and *Hanging Loose.* He received his M.A. from New York University's Draper Program in Humanities & Social Thought. He lives in New York City, where he edits *Graffiti Rag.*

**Sharif Elmusa**, Coeditor with Greg Orfalea of *Grape Leaves; A Century of Arab American Poetry* (Utah University Press). His poetry appeared in several anthologies and numerous literary journals.

**Amira El-Zein** is professor of Arabic and Comparative Literature at Georgetown University. She published two books of poetry, *The Book of Palm Trees* and *Bedouin of Hell,* translated many French books into Arabic: Le Clézio's *La Guerre,* Gaetan Picon's *André Malraux par lui-même* and others. Her book *The Seen and Unseen: Jinn Among Mankind* will be published by Fons Vitae.

**Bassam Frangieh** is professor of Arabic at Yale University. He is the author of *Alienation in the Palestinian Novel* and the translator of leading Arab poets and novelists including Abdul Wahab Al Bayati, Nizar Kabbani, Hanna Mina and Halim Barakat.

**Joseph Geha** is the author of *Through and Through: Toledo Stories* (Graywolf, 1990). He has been awarded a Pushcart Prize as well as a National Endowment for the Arts Fellowship. His short stories, reviews and essays have appeared widely in anthologies and literary journals. He teaches at Iowa State University.

**Suheir Hammad** is the author of *Born Palestinian, Born Black* and *Drops of This Story,* both by Harlem River Press. Her work has appeared in several anthologies and journals.

**Nathalie Handal** has lived in the United States, Europe, the Caribbean, and traveled extensively in the Middle East and Eastern Europe. Poet, writer, and literary researcher her work has appeared in numerous literary journals worldwide. Her poetic sequence, *the never field,* is forthcoming from The Post-Apollo Press, California.

**Adnan Haydar** is Director of the King Fahd Middle East Studies Program at the University of Arkansas, and Professor of Arabic and Comparative Literature. He has co-authored and co-edited several books and translations, and critical interpretations of poetry and fiction. His articles on modern literary theory and oral poetry have appeared in premiere literary journals in the U.S. and in the Middle East. He is the recipient of outstanding teaching awards from the University of Pennsylvania and the University of Massachusetts, and in 1991-92 was awarded a Fulbright Senior Research fellowship in Jordan and the West Bank.

457

**Paula Haydar** completes a Master of Fine Arts degree in literary translation at the University of Arkansas this spring, where she also teaches Arabic language. She has published translations of three novels by the Lebanese writer Elias Khoury: *The Gates of the City*, *The Journey of Little Gandhi*, and *The Kingdom of Strangers*. She has also been the recipient of a National Endowment for the Arts grant

**Samuel Hazo**, The author of books of poetry, fiction, essays and plays, is the Director of the International Poetry Forum in Pittsburgh, Pennsylvania, where he is also McAnulty Distinguished Professor at Duquesne University. His latest books are *The Holy Surprise of Right Now* (poetry), *The Rest is Prose* (essays), *Stills* (fiction), and *Feather* (play). He has been a National Book Award finalist and was chosen the first State Poet of the Commonwealth of Pennsylvania by Governor Robert Casey in 1993, a position he still holds.

**Penny Johnson** is the Assistant Director of the Women's Studies Center at Birzeit University and a member of the University's human rights committee since 1982. Her published work has focused on gender issues in Palestinian society, social policy, Palestinian higher education, and human rights. She is an Associate Editor of *Middle East Report*. Her stories in *Jusoor* are her first published fiction.

**Mohja Kahf** is professor in the Department of English and the Middle East Studies Program at the University of Arkansas, Fayetteville. She has published poetry in *Exquisite Corpse* and *Visions International*.

**Pauline Kaldas** was born in Egypt and immigrated to the Unnited States in 1969 at the age of eight. Her work has appeared in *Food for Our Grandmothers*, *The Space Between Our Footsteps*, and *Cultural Activisms*. She received her Ph.D. from SUNY Binghamton and is currently living in Roanoke, Virginia.

**Lisa Suhair Majaj** is a Palestinian-American writer and critic. Her poetry and prose have appeared in various journals and anthologies, including *International Quarterly*, *Visions International*, *Forkroads*, and *Food for our Grandmothers*. Her co-edited collection *The Politics of Reception: Third World Women in a Transnational Frame* is forthcoming from Garland Publishing. She is completing a dissertation on Arab-American literature for the University of Michigan, and is currently a Visiting Scholar in Women's Studies at Northeastern University.

**Khaled Mattawa** is the author of a book of poems, *Ismailia Eclipse* (The Sheep Meadow Press, 1995) and the translator of two books of Arabic poetry, Hatif Janabi's *Questions and their Retinue* (U. of Arkansas Press, 1996), and Fadhil Al-Azzawi's *In Every Well A Joseph is Weeping* (Quarterly Review of Literature. 1997). Recently awarded a Guggenheim fellowship and an NFA translation grant, his poems and essays have appeared in numerous journals and anthologies.

**Dunya Mikhail** was born in Baghdad in 1965. She studied English Literature at Baghdad University and has published four collections of poetry. She has lived in Michigan since 1996 and is studding for an MA degree in Oriental Studies at Wayne State University.

**Salah el Moncef** is associate professor of English at the University of Nantes, France, and was a Fulbright doctoral fellow at Indiana University at Bloomington. He has written highly acclaimed essays on Modernist poetey and postmodern fiction. At present, he is completing *Atopian Limits*, a study on postmodern American narrative, and *Diamond Point*, a novel.

**Daniel Abdal-Hayy Moore**: Born in California, 1940, became Muslim, 1970. First published book, *Dawn Visions*, 1964, City Lights Books, most recently *The Ramadan Sonnets*, 1996. Active as poet and mentor, presently lives in Philadelphia.

**Naomi Shihab Nye** lives in San Antonio. Her books include *Fuel* (poems), *Habibi* (a novel for teens), and *Lullaby Raft* (a picture book). Her most recent anthology is *The Space Between our Footsteps: Poems & Paintings from the Middle East*.

**Sara Nadia Rashad** is a writer, actress and film-maker who lives in Los Angeles. She is the child of an Egyptian father and an Irish mother. Sara is a graduate of Cornish College of the Arts and is currently studying film at the University of Southern California.

**Sarah Rogers** graduated from Bates College with a degree in Art History. There, she wrote her thesis, *Utilization and Definition of the Self in Contemporary Arab-Islamic Art*. She is presently finishing her Masters degree in Art History at Tufts University, where she continues researching Contemporary Arab art. She is planning on moving to Beirut next year before entering a doctoral program.

**Sekeena Shaben** is a poet and fictlon writer. She studied writing at the Jack Kerouac School of Disembodied Poetics in Boulder, Colorado and has published in journals in the US and Canada. She is the author of *Regular Joe*, a book of poetry, and is currently working on a novel.

**Evelyn Shakir**, daughter of Lebanese immigrants, is author of *Bint Arab: Arab And Arab American Women in the United States* (Praeger, 1997). An associate professor of English at Bentley College (Waltham, MA), she has published a number of essays on Arab American literature and on Arab American women. This is her first published work of fiction.

**Hisham Sharabi** is Professor Emeritus of European Intellectual History at Georgetown University, and the author of many books on Palestinian and Arab issues. In particular, his book *Neopatriarchy: A Theory of Distorted Change in Arab Society*, is considered a landmark in field of sociological studies of the Arab World. Professor Sharabi is the Chairman of The Jerusalem Fund for Education and Community Development, which he co-founded in 1977, and the Chairman of the Center of Policy Analysis on Palestine, both are in Washington DC.

**Patricia Sarrafian Ward** was born in Beirut, Lebanon and is of Armenian-Danish-American heritage. She moved to the U.S. when she was eighteen and received her BA from Sarah Lawrence and MFA from University of Michigan. Her writing has appeared in *Ararat Quarterly, The Literary Review*, and *Hanging Loose*. She lives in Charlottesville, Virginia. *The Bullet Collection* won an Avery Hopwood Award in Fiction, University of Michigan, 1996.

**David Williams** is the author of *Traveling Mercies* (Alice James Books), a poetry collection, and has recently completed a novel. His poems have appeared in a number of magazines, among them *The Atlantic, Kenyon Review, Hayden's Ferry Review, Many Mountains Moving*, and *Sierra*. He has been awarded a fellowship from the Massachusetts Cultural Commission. All his grandparents came from Lebanon; the family name Melhem was changed to Williams at Ellis Island.

**Mechelle Zarou** is a Palestinian-American, born and raised in Northville, Michigan. She is currently a second-year law student at Duke University School of Law. In addition to her legal studies, she is pursuing a Masters of Arts Degree in English at Duke University. She holds a Bachelor of Arts degree with Honors in Creative Writing from the University of Michigan.